Hey Gunther! Why Are You Here?

Walt Fluegel

Walt Fluegel

DEDICATION

To all (older) writers who know they have had an interesting life and think that story worth telling. Write it down as best as you can and join a writers club. Chances are someone will help you in several ways and you in turn will make your life more interesting for yourself and them.

INTRODUCTION

Three months after he was born in Germany, Walter Gunther's father died thus making his mother a single parent during the Great Depression in 1928. She was "encouraged" to immigrate with Walter to America to live with her sister's family. However, that led to placing Walter in the Wartburg orphanage in Mount Vernon, New York until he was 14 years old. For most of that time mother and son lived separate lives except on visiting Sunday and special rare times.

In those years Nazi Germany was rising to power, which influenced their lives before and during the WW2. Less than ten years after being molded in the orphanage, Walt decided to go to the University of Alaska. The reader may now wonder about, "Hey Gunther! Why are you here?" at that one particular time. The different "here" at different short times in the Territory of Alaska tells us that Gunther had quite a few life experiences, challenges, and adventures as he was maturing into a young man in that far off place.

What did he do in high school that made it possible for him to pay his way to Alaska when few other students ever went to college in the late 40's? Once in the Territory he needed money to continue college so campus jobs and summer employment were necessary. "Here" jobs gave Walt more insights into real life with its few adherents to civil restrictions. The Yukon River freighter job was the start in some of life lessons off campus. McKinley Hotel, and the ALCAN highway jobs followed. The Territory of Alaska was growing at that time after WW2 ended so various short-term summer construction jobs were good college money sources too.

Hey Gunther! Why Are You Here?

But why go to college? What was college life like in the Territory? These are simple questions to ask but Walt had to answer these himself. He observed and he adapted. He loved learning and also wanted to know about himself and the society around him. He also had to know more about his origins and his mother's life so he could understand his own life better. After his mother joined him in Alaska and he built a house for her, they began to know more of each other. However, while pursuing a higher degree in Fargo, North Dakota, Walt met Maxine Lott.

WALT FLUEGEL

Walt Fluegel
PROLOGUE FOR MY READERS.

Sometimes some folks get philosophical and ask one main question of themselves, 'Why am I here?' meaning being alive, being on the earth. For me, the question has a very simple biological reason. We are "here" because moms and dads conceive babies. Thenceforth, genetics, parental and cultural influences determine much of the future life that was just born. Over the centuries, wars, natural disasters, and economic conditions too influence what people do for themselves and their children. Some of that will unfold in this narrative. Some people can relate why they are "here" in this town or that town, in this country or the place of their birth. At other times folks can relate the details or reasons that dictated the final "here." You will find several "here's" in the life of Mrs. Gunther's son, as both had to live their lives mostly apart and far from their place of birth.

How much of a memory can anyone retain or reveal about what a mother tells about herself while her child was a boy and a bit later when that boy becomes a young man? That is roughly what you, the reader, can expect from this writing. If someone made a different decision to stay rather than go elsewhere, what would that "stay" decision have led to? It will unfold in this story that decisions made by a mother for her child and herself to leave one "here" for a less familiar "here" turned out to be a reasonable decision acceptable at that time. That time being in late 1920s, a time of the Great Depression and the rise of the Nazi in Germany. Any life of parents and child certainly diverge since birth so how much is made up and how much was the truth as a mother told it? Should there be a disclaimer now or just let it go and say this is a memoir where absolute truth is really unknown? This is a collection of stories or events based upon a life remembered so we can answer the question of 'Why am I here?'

Hey Gunther! Why Are You Here?

Walt Fluegel

HEY GUNTHER! WHY ARE YOU HERE?

Dedication

Prologue

TABLE OF CONTENTS

Hey Gunther! Why Are You Here?

- Exploring A Garden

- Speak German?

- Army In Town
- Feather Bed
- A Neighbor's Heil Hitler
- Milking Goats
- Richard Sees Hitler

- Canaries
- Talk German Politics?
- Another Dog Named Tell

- Not A Perfect Aryan
- Homesickness Fades Away

- Mister Cohen Is A Jew

- Doctor's Office
- Saying Goodbye To The Cohens
- Something For The Boys At Half-B

- Officially Readmitted

Walt Fluegel

Hey Gunther! Why Are You Here?

Hey Gunther! Why Are You Here?

- The Magic Secret
- What To See In The Park
- Food Rebellion
- Excursion
- The Camera Snaps More Than Scenery
- Caribou Migration
- Other Animals & Animal Love-Making
- Artist & A Camera
- Gossip?

- Draino
- Bull Sessions
- Flavors

- Sourdough Club
- Latin Dancing
- The Chorus
- Snow & Ice
- Basketball
- The 22 Rifle
- Poker & Other Games

- Third Summer Job On The ALCAN Highway
- Citizenship Paper
- Midnight Sun
- Paperwork
- Super Carlson

- What You Don't Write Home About
- Mother Carlson

- The Green Chevy
- Jobs Through The Union
- Meeting Up With Woody
- Sheetrock Gets Heavy
- Teenage Artist
- Keeping Carpenters Happy
- Hammer
- Off Angle
- Ditch-Work, Greyhound, & The Jewish Boy
- Homework Assignment
- Ribbons Of Gravel

- Election Time
- Mother Comes To Alaska
- Building A Basement
- Searching For Something Higher
- Learning About Mother

- Pea-Sized Gravel
- Erik Lassen & Jack B

- Cafeteria Food

Hey Gunther! Why Are You Here?

- Studies
- What Was Important?
- About Girls
- Bring Your Laundry
- Introductions
- Passing Grades & Letters

- Ten Hours Not Eight
- Planting Time
- Greenhouse
- Utilidores
- Meeting Roger Again
- Mother Tells Son More Of Early Life

- *Why Are Sciences Not Part Of The Humanities?*
- Reacquainting
- The New Secretary
- A Cornucopia
- The Pharmacy Boyfriend
- Snow On A Christmas Tree
- That Would Be Fine
- I Don't Kiss & Tell
-

Walt Fluegel

HEY GUNTHER! WHY ARE YOU HERE?

Hey Gunther! Why Are You Here?

Hey Gunther! Why Are You Here?
Walt Fluegel

CHAPTER ONE: A MOTHER'S START IN LIFE

In 1903 in a small German, Bavarian village called Sparneck, a 13th child was born into a blended family. A blended family means there are two sets of siblings. The 13th child, Emelie, had 6 other siblings and six half siblings. With all these siblings what would this girl remember about her life to tell to a future child or children? Did the future Mrs. Gunther have the same basic family life as previous generations or did the times change so much that there were no similar comparisons? The answer can be summarized—as there were no comparisons—because the outside world then did change in drastic ways. This new sibling would become important indirectly when her sisters had children of their own and much later after Emelie bore her own child, Walter. But in the meantime Emelie was taken care of by her mother who was the wife of the village baker. Emelie never told Walter anything about the village of her birth. Did her early years in the village mold her in any way? There was no way of knowing. But it was the immediate family interactions that drove this story to be told.

As with many families with lots of children, the sooner the child could be given tasks to keep the family functioning Emelie became one part of the bakery commerce. How old was she at the time? We do not know but she remembered enough times to tell son Walter about one particular customer. This regular costumer wanted some freshly baked rolls at special times. The woman made it a habit to

1

Hey Gunther! Why Are You Here?

help Emelie get her delivery basket over her shoulders. In the process, a theft of rolls occurred. Because of this theft, Emelie could not understand how the last customer on her route did not get the full amount of rolls assigned. Walter does not remember his mother telling how she found out when or how the thefts occurred. Nor how important this was to the shop or between her and the bakery accounts? It was just one of the stories she told more than once. Did she learn any lessons about people and was it useful in her later life? She never indicated the consequences of this theft to the family business. Was it a lesson to Walter from his mother, or was it just information conveyed to someone?

But we can ask some questions about Emelie's early life, for example; when did Emelie deliver the rolls? Before school or after school? If before school did it interfere with her lessons for the day? Did she have to get up early to deliver the freshly baked rolls? How many customers and how far did she have to carry the basket? How old was she at the time? These questions popped into Walter's mind from time to time as he became older. But not when he was with his mother, and that was not very often.

Emelie's childhood duties increased because of her sisters' children. While her sisters helped in the bakery, Emelie helped in watching their babies. Aside from herding geese now and then and delivery of rolls to neighbors and helping her sisters, Emelie related very little to her son Walter about her own childhood. She did say that other children would shy away when they saw her coming with one of her younger cousins. Walter never knew what schooling his mother had because she never told him about that part of her life. His mother's childhood existence was largely a blank to Walter. He often wondered if that was the case of the boys he knew and with other people of his mothers age.

Somewhere he remembers his mother often saying "another mouth to feed" when she talked about her sisters new babies. With this frame of mind we can speculate on the attitude of Emelie growing up with her sisters or perhaps of the hard times in Germany during or after WW1. But those years were never recounted except the one time when Emelie told Walter of the time when she slept in the attic (or was it above the horse stables or above the hog pens?) On clear nights she could see stars through the cracks of the roof and wonder at the beauty of those stars.

Almost at the same time as seeing the stars she told of how her dancing shoes were nibbled on by mice. Her dancing shoes were not so special but were rubbed with lard to keep them supple. Dancing at times in any small village was a special event perhaps for school occasions, holidays, or weddings or other special times. How old was Emelie at this time? Walter never knew. His mother never gave any details only that she used to attend the events and the mice would be known to nibble on her dancing shoes. And she never told him how she learned how to dance or who was at the dances. Or who played the music. Or where the dances were held.

There was no conversation about religion, church or church activities in the village, but by default the Lutheran religion was accepted as the dominant faith. A future brother-in-law, Hans however, was Roman-Catholic. He became one of the reasons for the "here" in the question of why am I here?

There is no indication of childhood friendships with other village girls or boys as we find in our culture today. There is a big information blank between the time of being a young woman in the town and the apprenticeship of becoming a butcher. A butcher from a baker family? This decision proved in time to be the beginning of a traumatic turn of events (or another "here") for Emelie. But Emelie was not aware of any traumatic situation except perhaps going against the wishes of her parents. And as said in the beginning, one of the "here" from the philosophical point of view.

EMELIE BECOMING AN APPRENTICE.

Traditionally in Europe, to become successful in life or a trade, young people had to apprentice themselves and this meant travel to different shops in towns, villages, or cities to learn the trade. Apprentices always had a Guild book of a particular trade with them. Each guild regulated the rules and working conditions. At the end of an assignment the owner of the shop would sign and stamp an

Hey Gunther! Why Are You Here?

apprentice's book and write notes. Emelie did not tell Walter how she traveled, how long she had to stay with one shop or any details of the apprenticeship except for two main and important stories she told him when he was much older.

A few of the girls and women at Emelie's first butcher shop had some experience at being behind the counter. A new girl (or young woman) was supposed to learn the basic kinds of meat and study how to cater to customers, mostly local homemakers. Apprentices had to wait in the background until called upon by their mentor. At one time when the journey woman Emelie was assigned to was temporarily absent an elderly woman came to the counter and waited to be served. She beckoned Emelie. As Emelie approached the counter she realized she was not as tall as the other girls behind the counter. "Excuse me a moment," Emelie said then turned around. There was a small wooden box leaning against the back wall. Emelie dragged the box toward the counter, stood on it and began to converse with the customer.

After a few moments, Emelie got the meat the customer wanted; they talked some more and just when she was about to wrap the meat in butcher paper her mentor came behind her. She heard the stern; "Stop, I will finish the sale! I want to talk to you later." Emelie got off the box and was about to return to her post when the customer was heard to say.

"No, let her finish with me." Thereafter when that same woman came for some meat she waited or insisted that Emelie serve her. Other women began to ask for Emelie. Her mentor never asked those customers why they wanted to have Emelie serve them, and Emelie was reluctant to volunteer for fear of being reprimanded again. Her "secret" seemed natural to Emelie. Her conversations with the customers included the exchange of recipes and spice choices she learned from her mother in Bavaria. Almost all of her customers were from northern or eastern Germany near Poland and a good source to learn about variety in tastes. That story stayed with Walter as a time when he saw his mother relating something with glee. (But that glee soon faded into a serious new but same story when it related to his father.)

Walt Fluegel

After several weeks Emelie was assigned to a different butcher shop. At this new larger shop in a larger city, the owner, a Mister Martin Wieland read in Emelie's Guild book that at first Emelie was insubordinate but soon learned to obey the rules. One note mentioned about her initiative, and another note said she was good with customers. There wasn't room on the page to tell why.

At Wieland's shop Emelie began to learn how to make sausages, the curing, spicing, and salting of meats and different specialty cuts of meat. But most of the heavy lifting kinds of procedures were left to the young men and their mentors. Emelie began to explore the city after hours. About a month or two in this new shop it was announced that there would be an annual competition with other shops in the city. Easter was coming and whoever could make the best Easter display deserved some prize.

The two or three men in the shop got busy thinking about slicing and displaying meats in a certain way, or getting advice from their wives on how to decorate a ham or smoked bacon, or other meats with ribbon or lace and the things not ordinarily seen in any butcher shop. Emelie too thought of what she could do. In the meantime she consulted no one but managed to get a large tray and to put folded wet cloths into it. She did all her preparation at her lodging quarters a half a block from the shop. It was thought the apprentices were to observe and learn, not participate.

In a large city in the 1920s there may have been a place to get garden supplies but Emelie never told Walter how she obtained grass seeds, but she found a supply. Her tray with wet cloths was placed next to the window. Grass seed was sprinkled on the cloth and allowed to sprout. Time of germination and quantity of seed could be an anxious problem. The sprouting grass could not be too tall yet it had to be lush to get an effect. Also, how she was allowed to take some small sausages from the shop was never explained either.

The night before the competition the sprouted grass had grown just right. That evening, Emelie cut the sausage into long halves or strips and placed them on the grass to spell out 'Happy Easter' on the first line and the line beneath in the center it said 'Everyone.' But when she placed the sausage on the seedlings the grass spread out or

5

flattened because of the weight of the sausage. That did not matter to Emelie even though she pressed the sausage down until it touched the sprouts roots. Somehow she realized or knew that by overnight the grass would bend itself upright and around the sausage. Along the edge of the pan additional sausage stripes or slices added to the overall decor of the display.

Two days before the competition the lodge owner, Mrs. Schneider, knew about Emelie's project but gave her an enjoyable approval. But a small problem occurred on the final day. How to bring the display to the shop? Putting another cloth over the grass would disturb the grass and spoil the effect. Mrs. Schneider went into her kitchen and came back and asked, "How about we put this shallow wicker basket upside down over the tray?" It resembled a basket used in Emelie's home bakery where rolls were displayed on the counter. After a pause and smile Emelie said she could manage if she could hold the basket and tray without an accident on the way. After thanking Mrs. Schneider and having her open the door, Emelie walked slowly down the block toward the shop. A customer opened the door for her and she found a place to put her display in the front window.

It was a total surprise for everyone including Emelie's mentor because Emelie pretended to have no interest in what the other competitors in her shop were doing. She was new to the shop and didn't want to interfere with their plans. This was the final day. But Emelie also learned that the rules required all apprentices who entered the competition had to be supervised by a mentor as a way of learning from a master butcher. Her mentor was as surprised at her display and had to consult with Mister Wieland. After examining the display Mister Wieland quietly moved Emelie's creation to the center of the other displays. He also admonished her about following the rules.

To avoid the shop from being disqualified because of Emelie's display, Mister Wieland whispered something to Emelie's mentor. He then secured a bit of the same type of sausage Emelie used and made a small rosette. This he gingerly placed right between the words Happy * Easter. It was the shop's proof that the mentor was guiding Emelie in her project. It was also a strong non-verbal signal that no mention was to be made to the judges by the other competitors in the shop.

Before the day was over word spread by messenger and telephone that the Wieland shop got one of the top honors in the citywide competition. The other displays that flanked Emelie's display added to the overall appearance and honor award of the shop window. Other interested customers visited the shop after business hours but because the next day, being Easter Sunday the shop was closed for the day. However, all those who passed by viewed the shop window.

Years later when Emelie told Walter about her Easter display, there was a certain glee in her voice. She never mentioned the prize; whether it was money or an award? It seemed more important to mention that in her Guild book Mister Wieland wrote that she made a favorable impression on the reputation of his shop and he did not mention breaking rules.

Hey Gunther! Why Are You Here?

CHAPTER TWO: JOHAN AND EMELIE

All this time as an apprentice we only know that Emelie traveled to several industrial towns and cities in the northern part of Germany in the late 1920s. She learned a lot from her mentors and from her women customers who willingly exchanged recipes. We don't know her age or if she was following some male friend from one place to the other. That was customary at the time. But eventually she must have had a romantic relationship with Johan Gunther.

This detail of romantic life was never mentioned to Walter in all his boyhood and early manhood years when he knew his mother, except that his father was named Johan and that they did not have to get married like some of Walter's Aunts in Germany. Johan's brothers "had alcohol problems" except Johan himself. There was only one photograph of Johan with one of his brothers but which one was Johan? There are no photographs in any albums of Emelie and Johan together, no wedding photos either, no photos of friends, but there is a wedding certificate. Why the paucity of photos?

Their marriage is akin to two families who ancestrally were at odds with each other but not lethal, only at odds by tradition. A baker marrying a butcher or a butcher marrying a baker was discouraged and if ignored it was at the couple's detriment of future events. Those events were to come in a very short time. There was no discussion or talk that the marriage was possibly an elopement or sanctified in a church or at the local magistrates office. Details of the marriage were never revealed. Years later Walter wondered, but never asked why this phase of life was a void. He could only guess.

Hey Gunther! Why Are You Here?

A little over a month of being married, Johan offhandedly said, "Now, don't get pregnant." But Emelie knew vaguely her first child would be a honeymoon child. In this way Emelie was different from her sisters who had to get married "with a belly full" to give the coming child a name. It was commonly assumed in the 1920s that how babies came into the world was common knowledge accumulated from all sources as one slowly approached adulthood. However, the son to be born learned the basic baby biology long before he was 14 years old. But Walter did not learn this from his mother; he learned this thru the books he read from the bookmobile that visited the orphanage every two weeks.

After marriage Johan and Emelie set up a small butcher shop in Mulheim on the Rhur River in an industrial part of the city. It was not clear what the business arrangements were. Did they rent the butcher shop with the eventual buying of it or did they just manage the shop for someone else? But within a year all that did not matter because Johan died three months after baby Walter was born.

The baby was christened Walter much to the objections of Johan's Uncle. He was wealthier than the rest of the family and remained a bachelor because he could not find a woman wanting to marry him. Therefore, he was childless and willing to pay Johan as much as an average full year's income expected from their business if of course it were a boy and if they named their expected child after him. Emelie and Johan refused the money. It would pay off a big debt of getting started, but Johan first of all did not like this relative and second, Walter was their choice. In German one could not alter the name in any negative way. And all the time his mother called to him in the future it was 'Walter' but years later Walter unofficially wanted to be called 'Walt.'

HOW DID JOHAN DIE?

There are two versions of Johan's death, depending on who told about it and when. When Emelie and Johan got married Johan had a German shepherd dog named, 'Tell.' When Walter was born Tell always stayed near the baby crib or carriage if he was not with Johan

10

or Emelie. Tell let no one come close except well-known customers and neighbors. But one day there were rumors that a rabid dog was seen in town and for people to be careful. It so happened that the rabid dog did come close to where the baby was lying in an outside crib and Tell began to bark and growl. Johan rushed outside and tried to disengage both dogs. Johan did not know anything about this strange dog. A neighbor saw the commotion too and came out of his house with a heavy shovel. Both dogs and Johan received bite marks but the neighbor who knew about the rabid dog clubbed the rabid dog to death. Johan just washed and bandaged his wounds, and took care of Tell. He decided to see the doctor as soon as possible just in case there was an infection.

Word spread. The dead dog was indeed rabid. Also, Tell was beginning to act strange in a day or two so he was destroyed. This put fear into Johan. He heard stories of people getting rabies treatment and the treatments were painful and seemed drawn out. He was not rational for days and finally went to see a doctor. The doctor confirmed that Johan could be infected and made immediate plans to give him the Pasteur treatment. Johan did not come home that evening, but said earlier to Emelie he was going to the slaughter-house to make arrangements for a new meat supply. Early in the morning several men came to the shop and told Emelie, Johan was dead from an accident at the slaughterhouse. They brought Johan to the local morgue. Emelie was brought to the morgue to make identification but only Johan's face was made visible. Someone told her that Johan was carrying a side of beef on his shoulder and as he was turning around he slipped, fell and broke his neck. All official documents say that Johan died as a result of an accident.

The butcher guild made all funeral arrangements and did what they could to help Emelie adjust. Insurance was a lingering problem but as to a butcher business, that was over with and having to take care of the baby too left Emelie to think of other alternatives. The family sin of marrying outside the baker guild became a problem for Emelie. Her husband's family side knowing about the name refusal knew nothing of Emelie and none of Johan's brothers or one sister wanted to help her and the baby. "After all we are having hard times ourselves. Go back to your own baker family. Johan should never have married you." Her only other choice was to return to be with her mother in Bavaria.

The day before she was to leave by train for Bavaria, two men from the slaughterhouse came to visit her. They said they had serious business to discuss about Johan's death. They said Johan was a good friend. They knew Johan thought he might be infected with rabies. They needed confirmation. Emelie agreed. They also suggested that Johan was making mistakes in the past few days because he was troubled about his possible illness. Another confirmation. The two men then whispered to each other and approached Emelie. "We think he was not himself when he decided to take his own life. We found him hanging in the tree when we came that morning. We were one of the first ones at work and when we saw him..." Emelie fainted and did not hear the rest of the explanation. Evidently they were the ones who made it look like an accident after they took Johan's body down from the tree, then fabricated the story. Walter never knew this version of the story until he was 14 years old when he began to live once again with his mother.

CHAPTER THREE: GOING HOME WITH BABY

On the train heading for Bavaria to see her mother, Emelie began to think of many things, some of which could be alternative reasons why Johan took his own life. Because of just getting started in the business it wasn't the best time for them to have a baby now. She remembered Johan saying something about her not getting pregnant but it was too late. Did he not want the baby?

Also there were misunderstandings from time to time as to how to handle fussy customers. Every now and then Johan tried to convince a customer that a certain slice of meat was just what the customer wanted but they would hesitated; at one time in a fit of impatience he tossed the meat on to the back counter and called to Emelie. By this time she knew he was in one of his moods. Emelie would apologize to the customer and ask what she wanted. Emelie listened and in a surprised voice announced that she would go in the cooler and cut off just the right amount from a fresh side of (pork or beef.) Unbeknownst to the customer as Emelie went around the corner she quietly removed the same tossed meat from the counter and brought it to the cooler, a few moments later she came back, put a knife down and went to the customer. She showed the customer the meat and remembered well the techniques she practiced as an apprentice. She gingerly or carefully placed her hands under the meat but was still able to manipulate it now and then. She talked in whispering tones explaining that if the meat were treated this way or that way and if this spice and this amount of cooking time and every thing else needed to make the meat tasty her family would be pleased. Every

13

customer that rejected a piece of meat from Johan, Emelie was able to sell that same piece and perhaps another morsel too. There were other events that could be thought of as adding up to a somewhat turbulent series of events as Emelie was coming due.

Could Johan not be ready for fatherhood? She kept these thoughts to herself for many years but did not know if there would be a future time to reveal her thought. In the meantime Emelie was anxious to see her mother. Emelie never spoke of her father in any positive or negative way, almost as if he were never present in her life. She did however imply he was the absolute manager of the bakery. She and her siblings and perhaps an apprentice took orders from him alone while her mother took charge of household chores and maintenance and young children. As she also watched the baby sleeping she also wondered of his future. She did not realize it at the time but in about eight years from now he would be old enough to be traveling on a similar train to see his grandmother for the first time. He would be 9 years old in 1937 or two years before WW2 started. But this was 1928.

When she arrived home she reacquainted herself with her nieces and nephews and tried to justify marrying Johan to her full sisters and brothers who remained in the town. The other half-siblings were scattered into different towns in southern Germany and two of them immigrated to Chicago in America. One full sister Trina (Catherine) immigrated to America on Long Island, several years before Emelie left for her apprenticeship. The sisters now made contact with each other by mail.

There were no open hostilities with Emelie's siblings but it took some time for them to adjust to her again being with their mother. But within the six months after Johan's death and baby Walter being nine months old there was another event that would change Emelie's and Walter's lives once more. Trina was several years older than Emelie and she too married a butcher and they had a son named Herbert. The son was born in America on Long Island, New York. Hans took a chance to come to America because he saw an advertisement that a certain German-American company needed skilled butchers to work in a meat processing plant located on Long Island. Even though he

14

was newly married and a child was on the way the company accepted him because there were other German workers willing to go to America. Germany was having hard economic times in the 1920s and the prospects of working in America with other Germans seemed a natural thing to do.

Hey Gunther! Why Are You Here?

Walt Fluegel

CHAPTER FOUR: IMMIGRATION TO AMERICA (1929)

Trina suggested that Emelie could also come to America and stay with her and Hans and their son Herbert. She also wrote a "To whom it may concern" letter that Emelie should show to officials that Trina and Hans would make sure Emelie would not be burden to the new country. That letter vouched that Emelie had skills in the baking and meat business.

Much later in America, Emelie showed Walter one amateur photo found in an old photo album. The photo showed people lining up to go on the gangplank in Bremen. It shows an Uncle holding Walter while Emelie was rummaging in her purse for the boarding document. Her one-week trip by boat with nine month Walter was uneventful except for a day during a rainstorm.

But what should or could Emelie do in America? She would have to learn English or work with other Germans in enclaves where German speaking was acceptable. Hans managed with other Germans in the processing plant but employing women to do what men usually do was not practiced. Emelie's background was with retail in both the butchering and baking business. Could she find a place in America for use of these trades?

However there seemed to be a need in the New York City area for part time and full time domestic help with the more affluent people in the city. Through Trina's efforts Emelie began to learn some English, enough to familiarize herself of train, bus, and trolley schedules. Sometimes they worked together at the same house or other half-day jobs. Fortunately, one of Trina's neighbors could look after Herbert and Walter for those few hours. Gradually, through the Agency, Emelie began to find full day domestic jobs where the pay was better and that she could pay Hans some rent. That also allowed Trina more time at home with Herbert while she looked after Walter too.

Emelie was given one small bedroom in the modest three-bedroom house of Hans and Trina. Hans and Trina thought they would be in the house for the rest of their lives and Trina hoped for more children. Trina had a difficult delivery of Herbert. More births were not possible so the extra bedroom was given to Emelie for the present. Eventually Emelie worked full days coming home at night to be with her son and visiting with Trina. Trina liked to be with her nephew because she always wanted another child and little Walter was a good substitute during the day while Herbert was in the morning Kindergarten. Unfortunately, Emelie had to turn down potentially better paying jobs that would allow her to be a live-in domestic-nanny employee. Reason; she would not be allowed to have infant Walter with her and with their own children.

One of her recent daily employers was a Japanese businessman— Mister Haruko. He knew rudimentary German, enough to get along with international business employees in New York City. That is why the Agency placed her with Mister Haruko who needed someone who could cook and take care of two girl children after school hours while his wife went to Japan to see her mother. Her mother was ill and Mrs. Haruko was homesick and would be gone for one month. The children were of school age and at school most of the day and very Americanized. Their father was very used to American ways. But he had a noticeable accent. The children were old enough to almost forget their own language. They wanted to learn a bit of German because their father might be transferred to Germany soon after their mother came back from Japan. The children had a playful agreement with Emelie to help her learn English if she would teach them German. Everybody was happy with the arrangement, even if the housework was ignored occasionally. Emelie sometimes tried to show Mister Haruko how to cook something in a German style, but he preferred to eat it, not cook it. Emelie liked this Japanese family and wanted to tell Trina her latest progress in learning English from the two girls. She felt very happy that day on the way home.

Walt Fluegel

Emelie's workday schedules allowed her to spend evenings in her room with Walter while painting flowers or other ornamental designs on neckties, small handkerchiefs and some scarves. This was a brief time where Emelie tried doing some painting that she never did before. Emelie never again expressed herself as artistic in any way perhaps because of certain events that occurred a few months after she began to live with her sister Trina and Hans. She never told Walter about the kinds or quality of the neckties or how or when she sold them to make a few extra dollars. Also she never told him where she learned how to paint. All the time he knew her better after the age of 14 he never saw artist supplies of any kind in the house. It was only in a clearing out chore that Emelie mentioned her art experience. Emelie's memory was regenerated when she opened a small bag of odd pieces of silken material she found in one of her very old suitcases. The suitcase she brought from Germany years ago. "I forgot about this," she said as she riffled through the odd pieces. Then added, "Well what do you know!" as she looked deeply and fondly at one piece of green cloth with three painted pansies. It was years later when Emelie told Walter only part of the painting story, because by this time he knew some of the beginning.

Hey Gunther! Why Are You Here?

CHAPTER FIVE: UNCLE HANS AND EMELIE'S NEW PLANS

The beginning occurred one day after working at Mister Haruko apartment. As Emelie came close to Trina's house she could hear Walter crying and Hans's booming voice. He was scolding Trina in German to keep the baby quiet. Emelie opened the door to see Trina rocking Walter in her arms and he had a bandage on his left chin. There was some blood oozing from the edges. Trina was behind Hans as he boomed out again in German facing Emelie that the baby fell down the basement stairs in his attempt to walk. The door to the basement was in the kitchen and opened. As Emelie reached for crying Walter to calm him, she saw Trina put her index finger to her lips as a signal not to talk to Hans, a signal that also let him finish his booming. Trina seemed a bit frightened at Hans's booming voice. Emelie took Walter up stairs to her room and finally got him to sleep after being nursed.

The next day evening, in the kitchen when the dishes were being washed, Hans was in the small living room reading the papers while listening to the radio. He could not see the sisters at the kitchen sink but Trina put her finger to her lips and then thumbed over her shoulder toward the living room. She then leaned over and whispered into Emelie's ear, "Hans slapped Walter real hard." At the same time Trina grabbed Emelie's arm to prevent her from confronting Hans. Trina was older, taller and more muscular than Emelie and thus did overpower Emelie's urge to face Hans. At that same moment Hans called out that the sisters should come into the living room.

Hey Gunther! Why Are You Here?
NO MORE PAINTING

They dried their hands and came to his call. Emelie stood and faced Hans while Trina sat in a nearby chair. She reached over to turn off the radio. "I do not like the paint smell. When are you going to finish your painting?" Hans said in German with a demanding tone to his voice. At the same time he raised his hand toward Trina as if to say 'hush'. Emelie answered in English; "All paints smell and I work near an open window, but it takes quite a while for the paint to dry."

"I want you to stop. You are smelling up the whole house. I think that is why Herbert has a cold now," and with his last comment he raised his hand just a bit to let Trina know he had the last word and she should not defend her sister. He then reached for the radio to turn it back on. "No more painting!" came a louder voice as the sisters left the room. One louder demand followed in a booming tone, "Trina, no more!" The sisters looked at each other as they entered the kitchen and quietly finished the dishes. After dishes, Emelie went upstairs to be with baby Walter. Trina checked on Herbert and then joined Hans in listening to a radio program.

The next day with the Japanese family, Emelie could hardly wait for the businessman to return from work and to ask him for advice. He listened carefully, asked very few questions but then said "I think you should leave that house as soon as possible and I might be able to help." He then asked Emelie if she knew where she was going to work after his wife's return from seeing her mother. "I will go the Agency, that helped me find you." Mister Haruko then told Emelie he will be going to meetings this weekend. Saturday and Sunday the children have no school and if Emelie could stay with the children during the days he would appreciate that. Emelie was conflicted, she mentioned that Hans would be home too that weekend and did not know how much her sister could manage little Walter and Hans and her own Herbert at the same time. "Your child needs you more, me and the girls will manage."

The next Monday when Emelie came to work, it seemed like a usual day. The girls were already at school and Mister Haruko was getting ready to go to work. He asked Emelie if she knew how to read and understand English because half of what he had for her to read was in English and German. "Read this first and think about it during the day as you take care of what you do. Also, I might have a new job for you when Mrs. Haruko comes back. I will know more by tonight when I come back from work."

WARTBURG

As Mister Haruko closed the door behind him, Emelie speculated on the words—new job—but she also glanced at the pamphlets. One word, WARTBURG caught her eye. It was a vaguely familiar name she associated with knowing something about Germany's history. It was related to the Lutheran church in Germany. She read the German pamphlet first and hesitated now and then to think of the words orphanage, school, baby home, kindergarten, and church. She continued to read that in an orphanage there were about 200 other children who lost one or both parents and someone was taking care of them. What about Uncles and Aunts or grandparents? She thought about some of her classmates from her early school time who lost a father from the First World War or the Influenza epidemic. There were no orphanages that she knew about but there was always someone, a relative, maybe a grandmother or Aunt and Uncle to raise an orphaned child. But an institution just for orphans was a new thought for her. She thought about Walter not yet 18 moths old and in a brief moment also thought of Hans giving her child a hard slap. That thought brought her back to reality. She was alone in a foreign place where she needed a refuge for herself and her child as Mister Haruko words come to her; "You should leave that house!"

Before Mister Haruko came home, Emelie was busy in the kitchen preparing the evening meal. The girls were busy at the kitchen table practicing their spelling homework. At the same time they were teasing Emelie on her attempt to understand English spelling and she teasing back on their pronouncing the German word. They finally heard their father come into the apartment and then came immediately into the kitchen and greet his daughters and Emelie. He lifted the lid from one of the pots, gave a sniff and was about to ask his usual question of what was cooking when Emelie managed to say ahead of him, "I will teach you how to cook it so Mrs. Haruko can make it for you often," His usual response was "Not this time," then added, "I have information and maybe good news for you. Did you read what I gave you this morning?"

She nodded and said, "Yes."

"It is a big decision, but I think you have to leave your brother-in-law's house for the sake of the child," Mister Haruko said as he went to his nearest daughter and gave her a hug. Then he touched the other child on the shoulders.

Emelie asked in a low hesitating voice, "Can I visit that place—the Wartburg?" It was the first time that day she was hearing her thoughts about what could happen. Mister Haruko smiled and assured Emelie that he knew of the Wartburg indirectly. He would have to make a phone call after supper. He would make arrangements for Emelie and in a day or so and meet her possible new employer soon. He also asked Emelie not to tell her sister anything just in case things do not work out. The events of this day and her thoughts swam around and around but she had understood that this total Japanese stranger was trying to help her and she did not know why. When he gave his daughter a hug a few minutes ago that somehow triggered a complete trust in him. She needed to accept that things could be for the better for herself and for her child.

MEETING MISTER COHEN

In the remaining time before Mrs. Haruko would be home from Japan, Emelie met Mister Robert Cohen an executive for a large insurance company in New York City. He and his wife had three adult children, one in real estate in Florida and two in California in some business with radio. Mrs. Cohen also had a brother in California. If Emelie could be employed by Mister Cohn she would be a live-in domestic servant-cook with numerous small duties if she wanted the job. She would however have to place Walter at the Wartburg but could visit him on Visiting Sunday. She would also have one day on Wednesdays or Thursday as a personal day off. Her pay would be

24

modest in comparison to what she earned now but she would not have to pay rent. However, she was on call all day.

A day or two later after Mister Haruko told Emelie about the Cohens, Mister Cohen drove to the apartment of Mister Haruko to pick up Emelie at her usual time of arrival and introduced himself. He told Emelie they would drive to Mount Vernon and visit the Wartburg. They could talk on the way and get to know each other. At first it was awkward because Emelie never met someone in high business circles, only tradesmen, store clerks, lowly government officials, but no one in or from high business places. She had been in America for only a few months now and expressed the differences she noticed. She tried to express herself in English and often reverted to asking forgiveness if she got the wrong word. Mister Cohen listened for a while then said, "Mrs. Emelie Gunther, if you want to work for me you have to learn more English. There is a school where we live that gives evening classes where you can learn our language. There is a small fee to pay the teacher and the class is usually full but I will find out if you can enter. I believe a new class starts next month."

Suddenly he changed the topic and mentioned that Mister Haruko said that she was a good cook and it would be a big relief to Mrs. Cohen if she did not have to cook so much. "Where did you learn to cook?" Emelie answered in broken English that she learned from her mother and exchanged recipes with customers while serving them during her guild training. During her explanation she began to trail off and remembered a time in her own store with Johan. She got her handkerchief from her purse and began to wipe her tears. Mister Cohen thought Emelie was thinking about her mother. But the thought was about an unpleasant incident that occurred between one of Johan's customers concerning a piece of meat he tried to sell to her. Emelie solved it with a sale of that same piece of meat. This one memory and others close to it would be recalled occasionally during the years and many years later when Walter was a young man.

A GOOD EDUCATION

As they kept traveling Mister Cohen thought he would change the subject and stayed away from asking why she immigrated to America. He knew Emelie's situation from the conversations he had with Mister Haruko. It was years later during WW2 that he talked about his association with Mister Haruko while Emelie was in his employ. It all had to do with the insurance company and insurance with different foreign companies doing business in America. Mister Cohen stayed with conversing about the Wartburg and how good it would be for Walter. He tried to tell her that at the orphanage all the children there had lost one or both parents and there was a good chance all the children would receive a good education. The Wartburg always had a high reputation with the State Board Of Regents. Emelie did not understand what this meant other than she understood the words 'good education.' Good education could also mean that Walter would be there for many years. Somehow that did not seem right to her but Mister Cohen also told her she was not alone because the Wartburg was there for parents who lost a spouse and this was their best choice for the child or children until times got better. He said something about the whole world was in a business depression. Emelie did not know what that meant other than everyone she knew in Germany and now in America was having a hard time making enough money to live comfortably.

During a lull in the conversation, Emelie must have fallen asleep while sorting all the Wartburg information and wondering about her baby. Mister Cohen could have afforded to hire a chauffeur to drive them but he loved to drive himself. At one time while they were driving, Emelie remarked that she had never been in such a fancy car. He remarked that the car was three years old and he was going to get a new one next year. He let Emelie take her nap. He eventually called out, "We are almost there," which awakened her.

The car was going slowly up a gentle hill. They passed a light colored large stucco house with lots of windows and across the road she noticed a church. Up ahead there was a large flagpole inside a circular garden and outside the circle she saw this impressive large stone

26

building with lots of stairs leading up to massive doors. "Here we are; this is the Administration Building."

Hey Gunther! Why Are You Here?

Walt Fluegel

CHAPTER SIX: EMPLOYED BY THE COHENS

Years later Walter could describe in detail the entire campus of the Wartburg from the baby home, the Big Boys' house, the school, and from the entrance to the outlying farm and the other houses that encircled the central plaza of grass. All this and more because Emelie did agree to be employed by Mister Cohen and have Walter admitted. Because of his administrative experience Mister Cohen on his second visit within that week to the Wartburg made sure all the paper work was in order. The paper work included blanks to be filled in such as birth time, both parents name, mothers maiden name, and places for short notes. After each parents name there was a space to check for (alive) or (dead) with an additional space to give reason: died in accident was written in the blank for father. Walter was 18 months old when his name was finally written in the large ledger book kept in the office. When the medical exam was done it noted that he had a scar on the left side of his chin. Walter resided at the Wartburg until he was 14 years old. His story was now being recorded in official ledgers with other names, dates, and short notes of other "inmates" at the Wartburg. "Inmate" was the common or official word for orphans admitted to any institution.

After the first visit to the orphanage Emelie told Trina all the facts of committing Walter and her new employment. She asked Trina not to tell Hans until she was finally out of the house. Hans was becoming more abrupt with Emelie and more so when Trina and she were visiting upstairs. Mister Cohen was coming to pick her up in two days in the morning. The nights before she was to leave she filled her

29

suitcase (the same one from Germany) as full as possible with her things and baby clothes. She could not find a place for her painting supplies and other small items and asked Trina to save them for her when they visited each other on one of her day off. Trina was given the address and the phone number of the Cohen's house in Saint Albans—a suburb town of New York City. But Trina was asked not to phone until Emelie could know more about her situation. About 15 minutes after Hans drove off to work, a fancy car stopped at the house. Mister Cohen met Trina. Within fifteen minute both sisters hugged each other and wiped tears. Emelie and Walter entered the car. One big suitcase was loaded into the trunk of the car. Emelie and Trina did not see each other for several months after Hans stopped asking Trina if she and her sister saw each other.

In late afternoon when Trina heard Hans's car approaching she told Herbert who was at the kitchen table with crayons and a coloring book to go upstairs for a while until she called him down. Hans arrived home at his usual time in late afternoon and parked his car in the garage. He opened the side door entry into the kitchen as usual. And as usual Hans noticed Trina at the stove preparing supper but also noticed that the high chair next to the table was missing. A booming, "Where is that baby?" came from the doorway.

Hans was taking off his jacket at the same time while Trina said in German, "My sister got a new job and took the baby with her."

Upstairs, Herbert heard his parents talking in loud voices to words he could not understand. Words like orphanage, Wartburg, Lutheran, Jew, and things like visiting days. Eventually the voices calmed down and soon Herbert was called from the base of the stairs to come down and meet his father before supper but to wash up first. Herbert knew from his mother earlier that baby Walter would not be home for a long time and she hoped to have another playmate for him. She explained that 'Tanta' (German for Aunt) Emelie could visit on her days off from work. But in the argument between Hans and Trina, Hans forbade Trina to allow Emelie to see her except on the special Christian holidays of Christmas and Easter. Later after supper Hans asked if Emelie left anything that had to be sent to Saint Albans. When he saw the painting supplies he cursed out loud and boomed out, "Why can't you paint like her so you can make some money like she does." Trina could not answer but it became clear that the painting supplies were missing the next day. A few days later Hans revealed that all those supplies were taken away in the trash.

Because of their age difference the sisters hardly knew each other as adults in Germany. Now in America friendship flourished between them in the nine months they lived in the same house with each of their children. Two weeks after leaving, Emelie called Trina by phone. Emelie did not like to hear how Trina was being treated by Hans. New painting supplies could be bought again but for some unknown reason Emelie never pursued that interest, but if she had thoughts of reviving her painting, she always thought of her sister and Hans's booming voice.

A LIVE IN SERVANT

On the phone now and then, Trina heard a good amount of details of being a live-in domestic for Mrs. Jane Cohen. The Cohens lived in a large four-bedroom house. The bedrooms and a large bathroom were on the second floor. There was a powder room, kitchen, "sun room" facing north, living room with alcove, and formal dining room on the first floor. There was also a half basement with laundry facilities.

Mrs. Cohen recently began to work for the Life insurance company after their last grown child left home. But she worked in a different office. The Cohens often ate at restaurants for lunch and supper. They were now happy to have Emelie do the cooking for them in the evening. Emelie was also expected to prepare breakfast and when the Cohens left for work Emelie was expected to put "more than a face on the house." She was amazed to see the latest type of stove and refrigerator in the big kitchen, an almost new vacuum, a good iron and ironing board, faucets that did not drip, and an almost new washing machine in the basement laundry room. Things she did not see in Germany or at Hans's house.

Emelie was expected to wear a uniform all day except on her days off. The uniform was selected by Mrs. Cohen. It was a simple dress garment of dark magenta with small white buttons down the front, a white collar and cuffs and white pocket margins but with long sleeves when company was expected. As the Cohens began to know Emelie better their occasional dinner guest lists grew. Mrs. Cohen had no difficulty in teaching Emelie how to serve guests.

Mrs. Cohen had previously introduced Emelie to the grocery store owners where she shopped regularly. This allowed Emelie to walk to the grocery store or sometimes phone for what she needed. She always shopped in the morning when most boxed produce were delivered to the store. In the beginning when she was improving her English she would examine the meat herself and got to know the butchers in the store. It helped because one of the men knew a little German. When employees began to talk about meat or recognize her (in her uniform) the choices of meat were always the best. The groceries were delivered to the Cohen's house the first delivery round of late morning or early afternoon. She never paid but learned to read the bills carefully and signed for the Cohens only after examining the delivery. At the end of the month Mrs. Cohen checked over the lists, asked a few questions and made sure the bills added up correctly.

Emelie also began to know the trolley stops and bus schedules to save on walking. Emelie was thus allowed to go into the other shopping area of town and order items or pay for them herself for the house but at times Mrs. Cohen checked the bills against the items. Mrs. Cohen always reimbursed Emelie but had a tight grip on the household finances. Emelie did not know why, but she was delighted that she was trusted almost from the beginning of her employment and in turn her loyalty toward the Cohens grew.

Emelie's room was on the first floor and had two entries. One door led directly from her room into the kitchen. The other door opened to one side of the screened porch-like entry on the garden or south side of the house. The porch also had another door into the front or formal entry to the house. Guests used the main entry facing the street, not the 'side door' to the porch. The Cohens used the side door to get to the garage that could be seen from the kitchen sink window. The door from the porch into Emelie room used to be the entry for trades people but an alternate flagstone path led around to the garage and back door, which opened directly into the kitchen. The only natural

32

light into her room was from the glass top half of the porch door. However since she spent most of her days in the main part of the house with many windows she never suffered from light deprivation.

It was a mark of pride that Emelie could keep all those windows clean, inside and out. She learned in the beginning how to sit on the sill and clean the outside of the window without worry of falling. She also managed to find a system for cleaning the outside of the upper sash with a long handled brush wrapped with rags. Later Mister Cohen thought she should get help from a professional window cleaner for the second floor windows.

BECOMING AMERICANIZED

As promised, Mister Cohen managed to get Emelie enrolled into the night school to learn English. She kept studying and writing in English until she could read the Sunday New York Times without difficulty. She looked forward to Mondays when she straightened up the living room where the paper was in a casual array on the floor next to the large console radio by Mister Cohen's favorite chair. During her luncheon hour and whenever she could manage the time she read what she could from the day old Sunday paper.

Occasionally a salesman knocked on the back door in mid morning, trying to sell brushes, books, trinkets, cleaning supplies and other small items. They would open the conversation and when Emelie was able to respond most of them smiled and then began to change the conversation to German because of her accent. Without hesitation Emelie looked them in the eye and said, "In this country I want to speak like an American, don't insult me, goodbye!" She slammed the door in their face. Others who kept talking in English were listened to politely but refused. She was more inclined to talk with Mister Cohen than Mrs. Cohen about these incidents and to ask him questions about being an American and telling him her progress in reading and understanding what was in the papers. Emelie was also learning a bit about America in her English classes.

Whenever there was company Emelie was always available at Mrs. Cohen's requests and when guests spoke to her she gradually responded in good English but with her German accent. Sometimes someone asked her where she learned to cook and her answer was always the same; "My mother was a good teacher." That was usually followed by Mrs. Cohen's general response that she felt lucky to have found Emelie. Emelie knew not to talk to guests unless they started the conversation and to keep it short. It was the Great Depression time but Emelie intuitively did not talk about the national situation to the Cohens either. She pretended not have an interest in the greater world, only her duties. Thus she also learned different viewpoints by just listening to guests. The Cohens appeared to be quiet Republicans and began to talk negatively sometimes about a new man named Roosevelt. But the Sunday NY Times seemed to give a more inclusive account of him. Later when Walter was in high school he remembered how his mother admired "that good man."

Walt Fluegel

CHAPTER SEVEN: VISITING SUNDAY AT THE WARTBURG

There was always the first Sunday of the month, Visiting Sunday at the Wartburg. The Cohens respected this day for Emelie by never having company at home that required Emelie to be present. On Visiting Sunday she would arrive around one o'clock in the afternoon by bus that stopped on a street corner a block away from the Wartburg entrance. This entrance had two eight foot tall and wide columns on each side of the road at the base of a gentle hill. These columns were made of large rectangular stones and capped with a lantern.

About every half hour during that Sunday afternoon a bus filled with people disembarked and walked toward the Wartburg entry. These people came from as far away as Long Island or Connecticut. Some of the people knew each other from previous visits and continued conversations engendered on the bus. Emelie too began to recognize and then know several others as the months turned into years. Their mixed conversations were of the children, and at other times their own problems, or the national financial situation, political thoughts, and general conversation of every day happenings. One wide sidewalk on the left side of the entry road guided small clusters of two and three people up the hill.

When the visits became a type of routine, Emelie was well aware she was not alone in her situation. There were other single parents due to loss of a spouse in accidents, illness, divorce, abandonment, or neglect. Some folks told of being an uncle or aunt and in a few cases grandparents unable to care for a child at their home. Occupations of the visitors varied from being a milk delivery man, carpenter, nurse, teacher, secretary, live-in domestic like her, factory worker, telephone operator, salesman or sales woman, car mechanic, and others fortunate to be earning a living. Each had different thoughts or dreams of doing what they thought were best for their child.

When the hill became gentler, the first house they saw on their left was the Half-B house (for half orphan boys) a large stucco building. Across from Half-B on the right a sidewalk led from the road to the brick parsonage where the director and his wife and two sons lived. At first quite a few people went to the left toward the Half-B house but directly in front of Half-B the sidewalk turned toward Half-G (half orphan girls) the sidewalk continued toward the Half-G house and then to the 2-B house while Emelie and a handful of folks continued up the hill toward the Administration building then to the Baby Home where Walter was being taken care of by "Tanta" Anna and older girls from the Big Girls home.

BABYHOOD TO BOYHOOD

From the day Walter was given into Tanta Anna's care two sets of lives, one for Emelie and the other for her son diverged. Separation was a way of life for all the orphans and half orphans and their kin. It was a "normal" thing to do in those days. It was normal for decades going back into the late 1880's and now into the Great Depression. Taking care of unfortunate children was institutionalized for many years and in some cases for the better and in other cases with negative results. (Readers will have to decide for themselves where the Wartburg fit on the approval scale. An accounting of life for Walter at Half-B from age 6 o 14 can be found in the book "You Don't Belong Here Anymore.)

Walter had typical early childhood amnesia not remembering anything about the Baby Home and sometime later at about 3 years old the Kindergarten house. There was however one vague memory about getting his head caught between the upright bars of the white iron bed. Was this incident from the Baby Home or the Kindergarten house? He does remember a big burly man who came to the bed and pulled on the bars to make the space wide enough for someone to move Walter's head up and out from the confining bars. (It was an interesting puzzle for him during his maturity to wonder how anyone who got his head caught between bars could not wiggle back out.) But when he entered the Half-B house at age 6 years his mother had many visiting Sundays to become adjusted to her visiting routines and Walter his adventures at Half-B.

Hey Gunther! Why Are You Here?

CHAPTER EIGHT: WASHING MACHINE ACCIDENT

At one time when Walter was about 9 years old his mother visited but her left hand was wrapped in a large bandage. All of the people she knew on the bus that day had to know what happened, but her main concern was how to explain it to a young child. It appears that while she was doing laundry at the Cohens she got her hand caught in the washing machine wringer. The safety spring was supposed to disengage if there was too much pressure between the wringer rolls, it didn't work. Her hand was severely damaged and her pinky finger had to be amputated. Walter could not understand at the time because he never saw a washing machine or knew what a washing machine did. All laundry at the Wartburg was done on the lower floor basement of the 2-G house. So when the bandages were finally removed he had to get used to seeing his mother without a pinky. But losing that pinky also led to a rejoining with his mother in the summer of 1937 and visiting his grandmother in Germany.

Emelie became very homesick to see her mother during her convalescence and the Cohens too made sure Emelie had the best of care at that time. Knowing of her homesickness, the insurance money from the accident was set aside for her passage. Also from time to time Mister Cohen would inquire about Johan's death insurance from Germany. From what Mister Cohen could learn, there was a problem especially now with the German government under Hitler. It seems that anyone who no longer resided in Germany could not transfer the money to another country. The money had to be spent inside

Germany. Mister Cohen's insurance company did what they could on the quiet but no solution was found.

In the meantime letters between Mister Cohen and the Wartburg were being exchanged. Mister Cohen wrote letters requesting that Walter could leave with his mother for a trip to Germany to see her mother. Also Walter would be well taken care of to and from Germany and he also assured the Wartburg a through medical exam would be given to make sure the boy brought back no communicable diseases. When all the proper letters were exchanged, approval for taking Walter out of the orphanage was given. He would return in 6 or 7 weeks during the summer months.

A SHORT TIME AT THE COHEN'S HOUSE

Getting ready for a trip to Germany also meant mother and son would get to know each other for more than a few hours on Visiting Sunday. They traveled the same Visiting Sunday homeward bound route back to Saint Albans established over all these years. Everything Walter saw along the way was new or strange to him, including the Cohen's house. As soon as he entered the house he asked where the bathroom was; it was important and he just had to go! He had never before been in a bathroom with one toilet and one sink. And a door to be closed. He heard his mother call that to make sure he washed his hands and he could use the towel. The Cohens were not at home this evening but would be home sometime after he went to bed. He had his first supper with his mother alone in an unfamiliar place. There were no other boys around, only his mother and himself at a kitchen table. There is no remembrance of conversation or what was eaten at supper. But he did remember the protective glove his mother wore on her left hand.

After supper Walter felt a tightening in his lower throat or upper chest and tried to explain what it felt like. He told his mother it sometimes happened when he and some of the boys would deliberately swallow air and let it go to make a loud noise. This time he could not "make it go" and he dared not swallow air in front of his mother because that noise was not a polite thing to do. A bit later Emelie showed Walter around the first floor but it was getting late. He would be sleeping for

40

the night in his mother's bed in her room. He was not used to a bed with a table lamp he could control himself. His throat pain persisted. Emelie tried to rub his back to relax him and urged him to try to sleep. It took a while after his mother said 'good night' that Walter decided to 'make it go'. When he thought his mother was asleep on a made up bed on the porch and her door to the porch was open, he swallowed a bunch of air and let out a big belch. His mother quickly got up and looked in after him asking if he was all right. Had he known the word belch or a stuck burp his initial problem would have been solved with a Bromo-Selzer. Having a burp was normal and one should say 'excuse me' when making it, she told him. But having a very loud belch was a mark of disgust and should be avoided. He then went to the bathroom and after that they both slept soundly.

Walter woke up to noises in the kitchen. The kitchen door was open slightly but the porch door was closed. He finally realized where he was and got out of bed and headed for the kitchen door. He readjusted his pajamas. As he slowly opened the door and saw his mother he said, "I have to make urine." At that same time his mother saw him and said, "Good morning." She ushered him around the corner in the living room and showed him the bathroom door. Memories of last night's experience were being relived with the wonderment of this new place. Emelie told Walter that the Cohens were already off to work and she had made breakfast for them and that she made extra pancakes. This was a new experience; pancakes with butter and syrup. He had to be shown how to eat this kind of food. His usual breakfast was some kind of porridge of oatmeal and milk or maybe farina or some other cereal with no name. Often there were stewed prunes or pears or sliced canned peaches mixed into the cereal. Maybe he had a hard boiled egg twice a week.

EXPLORING A GARDEN

After breakfast and washing dishes they both went outside by the porch door toward the garden on the south side of the house. The property grounds including the house and garden took over one forth of a city block. Knee high hedge bushes followed the sidewalk until they met their southern neighbors hedge. The neighbor's bushes were

41

two feet taller and continued to follow the sidewalk. Where the properties met the higher bushes continued and acted as a container for the Cohen's garden. It made a U-shaped display of tall flowers in the back graduating to smaller flowers until they met the edge of the lawn. Inside the bush made U there was a smaller rose garden with a bright-mirrored sphere on a short pedestal. All Walter could do was to look, and look and be overwhelmed. He did not know what to say and hardly heard his mother trying to tell him the names of the flowers. He did know lilies and daisies and poppies.

They walked back toward the house on the lawn following the garden when Emelie suddenly stopped and bent down to pick off a leaf from a larger plant. She rubbed and crushed the leaf between her fingers and gave it a sniff. She then directed the crushed leaf towards Walter's nose and asked him to sniff too. She said something that sounded like 'basil' a word never before heard by Walter. There were little or no flowers in this part of the garden. Emelie tried to explain to him that this garden section was dedicated to herbs used as spices in cooking. It was all new. He knew nothing about cooking and the only green leaves he knew to eat were lettuce, spinach and of course kale. Emelie realized she would have to be patient in teaching Walter a lot of new things. Later in the day Walter found out that an Italian man with his two grown sons always took care of the garden and lawn under the supervision of Mrs. Cohen.

In the meantime Emelie made contact with Sophia, one of her half sisters from Chicago. In a day or two they would meet. So many new things were happening in Walter's life at this time very little was absorbed. He did not understand what a half sister was until his mother said to just call the lady Aunt Sophia. Walter could only remember her as being older than his mother and somewhat loud in her talking. It was an absolute blank of memory as to how he, his mother and Aunt Sophia traveled from Saint Albans and boarded the Bremen Ship. As years past many recollections of the boat trip merged into black and white movies of boat travel. What was real, what memories were movies? Only a very few color images were retrieved from his memory.

Walt Fluegel

CHAPTER NINE: ON A BOAT TO GERMANY

On the first day of boarding that afternoon, passengers were escorted to their cabins. It was not first class accommodations for Emelie's position in life but it would have to do. They found that toilet facilities were down the hall and to expect to find delays. Delays occurred immediately. In the cabin, Emelie and Sophia had a problem to solve and Emelie had a double problem. It was a small cabin with bunk beds. Where is a small boy going to sleep? Where was his bed? Who was going to sleep in the upper bunk? It was a busy time for passengers and crew. They managed to get one of the stewards to help them. At first he brought a baby crib, assembled it and lowered one of the sides but Emelie noted it was too small for a big boy now. Finally the steward rolled in the smallest bed available and managed to squeeze it into place. The luggage was placed under the lower bunk and the chairs taken away to allow the bed to fit with space to move about. Sophia decided to take the upper bunk after all. She could manage for the five-day trip. On one night Emelie decided she could try sleeping in Walter's bed if she curled up and he could sleep in the bunk bed. No matter how or where he slept he felt and heard a low vibrational hum from the ships engine below. He did sleep well.

One particular memory of this boat trip is revived each time Walter sees a map of the Atlantic Ocean. He and his mother saw a map in the display cabinet near a door on the main deck. It was a map of the Atlantic Ocean with North America on the left and Europe on the right. Each day thereafter an additional pin with a large pinhead was stuck into the map to show passengers the location of the boat since the day before. It was not a new map because there were numerous pinholes in clusters across the map ocean. Walter could not understand how anyone could measure distance on the ocean. His mother didn't know either but said it might have to do with looking at the stars at night. The trip would last five days in bad weather maybe seven days.

SPEAK GERMAN?

When all one can see is water and a few clouds Emelie began reading something to Walter as they both sat in one of the deck chairs. Sophia was walking around the deck. A woman also in her deck chair next to Emelie was knitting something. She stopped her knitting for a moment to listen. She took it upon herself to interrupt Emelie and ask a few questions as to where she was going and for how long. Emelie at first told the woman she was homesick to see her mother. After more questions she only gave short answers, turned back and continued to read to Walter. Shortly after, the woman began to ask questions in German. Emelie answered in English at one time and German another. At one final interruption the woman began to chastise Emelie for not reading to her son in German or teaching him the language of his native born country. It was years later that Emelie told this story to Walter but did not indicate what happened after the scolding. The story was told after he acquired his own citizenship certificate.

At one time on a chilly late afternoon a steward came on deck with a tray filled with mugs of steaming broth. The mugs looked larger than the mugs Walter used to drink milk from at the Wartburg. The steward indicated for Emelie to take two mugs, one for herself and one for the boy, but to let the mugs cool just a bit before sipping. Walter noticed the other passengers were holding the mugs not by the handle but by wrapping both hands around the mug. His mother did the same thing and said it felt good in the hands on such a chilly day. (Her left hand was still in a protective glove.) Drinking that way at Half-B was discouraged because only babies used both hands to drink from a glass or mug. Besides, it did warm the hands and the broth tasted good too. Soups and such at the orphanage were usually

44

consumed with a spoon from a bowl. Some passengers were a bit noisy in their sipping and laughing with each other. But no one seemed disturbed to drink like a baby. They rather enjoyed the broth and each other's company.

There is no remembrance of what the food or meals were like on the boat except one stormy night; there were fewer passengers in the dining area. Emelie told Walter why he and many of the passengers felt sick to their stomach and some made messes that needed cleaning up. She called it seasickness due to the boat being tossed around in the storm. But why was Sophia very sick, more than Emelie herself?

"She is tipsy." From listening to comedy radio programs at the Wartburg, tipsy meant someone was drunk (As with Charlie McCarthy and W C Fields.) How could this be for Sophia? Emelie tried to explain that Sophia seemed to need more than their company and sought out other passengers also looking for wider acquaintanceship. She found some like-minded folks, one of which shared a bottle of high spirits with the others before the storm. Seasickness and tipsy were close companion words that made Sophia very sick indeed.

Hey Gunther! Why Are You Here?

Walt Fluegel

CHAPTER TEN: HEIL HITLER SUMMER OF 1937

The adventure of being on a large boat, finally making shore, disembarking, going through customs and finally boarding a train, may seem something to remember. But for a nine year old going to see his grandmother, most of the boat memory is still hidden. On the way by train to Bavaria however, one small incident flashes in memory. He remembers he was on a train at night snuggled upright into a pillow in his seat. The rhythmic clicking of the wheels on the track kept him in a delightful light slumber. In a moment this slumber was interrupted as the conductor opened the compartment door and reached for the ceiling. There was a central light shaded by a cloth-like dome resembling a clam shell. The effect produced a dim light. The conductor opened the clamshell dome part way to give himself more light and said something in German to Sophia who was awake. He looked at his clipboard while he talked. Emelie woke up too and said something in German. Soon Emelie and Sophia showed the conductor some documents. When he was satisfied, he closed the upper dome and slid open the compartment door and left saying something that sounded like, "Heil Hitler," Walter did not know it at the time but he would be hearing this expression throughout his trip into Germany. Each time he heard 'Heil Hitler' it reinforced his first time of hearing it.

There were other train trips to different parts of Germany all blending into one memory of train stations, swastika flags, public announcements of arrivals and departures and people milling around, getting on and off trains, and eating in small restaurants along the way

Hey Gunther! Why Are You Here?

and seeing a different Aunt or Uncle in a city. Sometimes Sophia was not with Emelie or Walter but when they were together they kept each other company and spoke in German while Walter napped after viewing scenery. Visiting relatives or in-laws took some time from Emelie's main reason for coming to Germany. She wanted to see her mother, she was homesick. Much of that vanished when they met after the taxi from the railroad station brought her to the bakery house.

Walt Fluegel

CHAPTER ELEVEN: GRANDMOTHER'S HOUSE: GERMANY 1937

Most of the visiting between Emelie and her mother occurred in one large room with a small kitchen on the far end. This large room seemed to be the main focus for family gatherings. From inside, the room with its large front window projected out into a flower garden, a wrought iron fence and beyond that one could easily see the town road. A smaller side window looked out at the entrance to the bakery. In that part of the room next to the large window there was generous space enough for a table and six chairs and one easy chair for grandmother Stoltz. In the back of this room a small wood-burning kitchen stove with an adjacent table and chairs told casual visitors to stay a while for coffee. There were two frequently used entrances into that large room. The main or formal entrance came from the bakery side of the house but closed off from the public with a lace curtain covering the door window. The other entrance at the back of the room also had a window door. But its view outside was quite utilitarian. The view seemed shaded and had a cobble or flag stone floor. The scene looking up showed a ceiling of open rafters, which descended to unused horse stables and a flight of stone stairs leading to sleeping rooms above the vacant stables, bakery ovens and the rest of the house. The cobble stone floor was wide enough to have wagons or carts make deliveries brought in by horses in the past. Now deliveries of coal or wood for the ovens and other supplies were made by truck through the stone archway.

An echoing effect from the stone structures and cobble pavement strengthened the reality one was in an outside environment. There were no doors on the wide arches. Further through the archway not too far from where the stairs and the cobble pavement ended one saw smaller structures away from the house. One for pigs, one for geese and one for goats. At a further distance from the house a large low building held stove-sized wood for the kitchen stove. On the main back or street side entrance the cobblestones came from the "T" extension of the main town road. The upper part of the cobbled T continued toward the neighbor, Frau Pup, across the road between the houses. However if the main roadway cobble continued it would have led down to a field, but it was a wide dirt path down one of the hills in the town.

ARMY IN TOWN

The large inner room had one more door leading into a formal dining room used only on special occasions. This dining room was on the opposite corner of the house from the bakery. Inside it had one big curtained window facing the garden and town road and several other curtained windows on the side-wall. Between these windows there hung one painted portrait of Bismarck, some works of art, one simple print of Jesus praying (same picture found at Half-B at the Wartburg) and one photograph of Hitler. On one special occasion when the whole town was involved this dining room became the center of attention at the bakery.

A cousin, Richard, was gone for a few days. One of his jobs was to keep firewood chopped and handy for the small kitchen stove but he worked double duty so he could accomplish something important for the family. This importance became evident because everyone including town folks were preparing a large amount of food for guests. At that time part of the German army was on maneuvers near the Czechoslovakian boarder and Richard managed to contact an officer in that exercise. The army was coming back in the direction of the town and Richard convinced two officers to stay overnight at the bakery house because they had two empty stables for their horses. The whole town also knew that the army was coming and many families were either assigned or volunteered to billet some men overnight. Previously Richard and a few other boys from the Hitler youth were delegated to make the contacts.

The bakery was busy that day with excited people exchanging information on how many soldiers might stay overnight at their place. Walter had only a brief time to see inside the dining area. He saw a familiar picture of Jesus praying, the same picture hanging in the dining room of Half-B at the Wartburg. Emelie pointed to a fancy framed picture of Bismarck and said that man helped found Germany similar to Washington who helped found the United States. Emelie was going to show Walter some more pictures she was familiar with when she lived in the house but Grandma Stoltz asked her to take cousin Wilhelm and cousin Margaret outside and keep them entertained while more preparations were being made.

It was only when Richard burst into the back door that anyone at the shop knew who from the army was going to be billeted. At the same time there were familiar horseshoe sounds in the cobble stone entry. Walter never saw a horse this close before and two of them! They were magnificent animals with shiny brown bodies and dark black manes. The officers had already dismounted before Richard came into the kitchen. Later Emelie told Walter that one of the officers allowed Richard to mount. a horse until they got close to town. He then joined the other boys in a car and slowly "escorted" the soldiers and horses into town. All the boys were wearing what looked like Boy Scout uniforms.

Several of the men began to use the outside pump to tidy up and were directed to the toilet facilities by Richard. After the formalities of introduction and meeting in the formal dining room a dozen men and the two officers stood behind their chairs. One of the men said Grace. When the prayer ended and they were seated, the meal was then served by the women of the house and everyone began to relax as they ate. Grandmother Stoltz, and two sisters brought in the food. At one time the dining room door was not fully closed. The curious boy opened it some more and stood in the doorway and stared at the candles on the table, the tablecloth and some fancy plates filled with food. One of the soldiers noticed him and talked to him. Walter did not understand the German and did not reply. Then when another

51

voice said, "Amerikaner!" Emelie heard that word too, then realized where Walter was standing. Faces turned towards Walter while Emelie quickly got up from the stove side table, took him by the shoulders, turned him around and shooed him into the kitchen while hearing some snickering.

FEATHER BED

After having his own supper with a couple of cousins in the kitchen Walter and Emelie went to the sleeping rooms above the stable. It seemed earlier than usual for him but Emelie explained that he would not understand all the talking by the family and the soldiers. He and she would just have to stay by themselves for the night. The bed they were to sleep in was large enough for two people so that night his mother would be sleeping near him under the feather bed. Her bed and other beds were going to be used by the soldiers. Walter was getting used to the feather bed since he arrived. Emelie explained what it took to make a featherbed. She also told him how she had to herd the geese to different places to forage when she was a young girl. Sometimes the geese rebelled and the flock chased her and poked at her real hard until she managed to learn how to use the special stick given to her by an older sister. He also asked her why the geese did not fly away. Emelie explained that geese need a long enough space to run before they can actually fly. If some of their wing feathers were clipped that would discourage flying away. He finally fell asleep.

All the soldiers and their horses were well taken care of by the town and had a hardy breakfast before departing early in the morning. Walter may have been dreaming of horses traveling but it was the officers and their horses that left early. They would have to march a mile or two out of town and board trucks that brought them to a train station. It was a mark of high esteem for the bakery or family especially for Richard that two officers were billeted in the same house. It was much later in an America civics high school class that Walter remembered that night. He found that in the third amendment of the Bill of Rights the army was not allowed to have civilians billet or house the army and that the military had to have their own quarters.

Of course that was inspired because of the British in the American colonies but in Germany that was acceptable with their own people.

A NEIGHBOR'S HEIL HITLER

The neighbor Frau Pup from across the entry road from the bakery was standing in her doorway on the cobbles. Walter was allowed after breakfast to go outside the back door, leave it open a bit, but stay within the arches of the house. He wanted to look at the places where the horses stayed overnight. But he saw Frau Pup for the first time since he arrived. He went as far as the arch and stopped. Frau Pup said something but he could not understand German so he just said, 'Hello,' and gave a short wave. She then made the Nazi salute and said, "Heil Hitler," Walter had been hearing that expression several times during his trip but only waved back to her. She seemed upset with him and began to wave her finger from side to side and then in his direction. Walter understood that sign language so he turned around and walked toward the entry door while she was still talking louder at him. Because the back door was still open about an inch Emelie heard the neighbor woman talking loudly at the same time Walter came into the back entry. Emelie asked Walter why that woman was yelling at him. As Emelie was about to close the door Frau Pup was at the door wanting to come in. She seemed upset but all Emelie could say was, "Good Morning," (in German).

Grandmother Stoltz became interested and invited her neighbor to come in and have a cup of coffee. That eased the tension somewhat until introductions were made. Frau Pup knew Emelie would be a visitor from America but was still upset that Walter did not respond properly to the salute. He should have been trained better she implied. This wasn't the first time someone complained to Emelie about her son but those people were strangers. This woman was her mother's neighbor. Later Emelie explained to Walter that if someone actually said, "Heil Hitler," to him he should respond in kind with at least the salute. It was almost like a wave but a stiff one in one direction forward. He understood. For the rest of the trip no one else complained to Emelie about that kid of hers.

Hey Gunther! Why Are You Here?

MILKING GOATS

Every now and then Walter could hear the goats bleating and one time asked his mother if he could see them up close. When he first came to see Grandma Stoltz and be shown quickly around the place there was little time to see much detail. He had never seen a goat before or even know anything about milking the animal. He knew a little about cows and vaguely knew how they were milked but he never saw any milking process except in pictures. An opportunity occurred when Emelie called to Walter to watch how Grandma Stoltz milked the goats. A few animals were restless and bleating. Grandma was on a low stool next to one goat and humming a tune in rhythm to her squirting milk into a pail. She and Emelie talked with each other as Walter studied the process then he looked at other goats. He tried to pet one but she objected until Grandma gestured he come and pet the one she was milking. Emelie told him to pet the goat on the head and between the ears only. The animals were not used to Emelie or Walter.

When Grandma Stoltz finished milking the goats she covered one pail with cloth and carried one pail through the arch on to the cobble and stopped near a door by the back ovens. She retrieved a large pot from this closet and poured the milk into the pot and asked Emelie to open a door that led directly into the bakery. The ovens were being used at the moment but soon it was time to take out some bread. When the time came an apprentice and Aunt Gretchen ignored the onlookers and did what they had to do to refill the storefront shelves. Grandma Stoltz told the workers she would close the oven door when the last loaves were removed. But before that she took the pot of milk and placed it in the oven and told Emelie this was the method of pasteurizing the milk. The other cloth covered milk container outside would be consumed at the noon-time meal. Walter asked his mother why the milk was put into the oven. She tried to explain in her own way the importance of pasteurizing milk that was not going to be used for some time. Maybe Grandma would think of making cheese from the milk soon. He knew that cheese was made from cow milk but now he began to realize that milk from other animals could be made into cheese. Later when he came back from Germany he told some of the other boys at the Wartburg about his adventures. He mentioned his Grandma's way of pasteurizing milk. Thereafter one of the boys who had a mental quirk kept calling Walter 'baked milk.'

RICHARD SEES HITLER

From time to time during that summer, Emelie would take her protective glove off and examine her injury. Sometimes she did it in public but in a quiet place. It often looked raw but she noticed slight improvement in the buildup of scar tissue. She was also flexing her hand as often as possible to keep the original strength. Whenever anyone, be they a relative or sometimes a stranger asked her what the problem was she just said she lost her finger in an accident. Early on she learned not to name the Cohens. In these early cases Cohen being a Jewish name became more inviting by the questioner to find out why she was working for a Jew. It didn't help that she said, "They don't practice it. It's just their name." When that didn't satisfy, Emelie avoided using the Cohen name altogether. She changed the name to Schneider. The questioning became less often when she wore stylish gloves on both hands during her travels. By tucking the left pinky glove finger into the rest of the glove the missing finger was never noticed but Emelie still had to be careful in how she used her left hand.

In the large room near the front window on a corner shelf up high was a large radio with very good volume. Only the adults were allowed to turn it on. When there was a news broadcast most of the household listened. During slack times if somebody in the bakery wanted to hear music, both front doors from the bakery and the large room had to be open. This seldom happened but when Der Fuehrer was making a speech it was mandatory for people to listen. Only one radio played in the house and what Emelie understood from the general conversation there was a yearly tax on every radio anybody owned.

Richard was absent at noon one day when the Fuehrer was making a speech in another city but Richard actually attended a rally of Hitler Youth in that same city where Hitler spoke. Richard and two other friends from the Youth drove up early to attend and would be back by

Hey Gunther! Why Are You Here?

suppertime. When he came back he was filled with joy saying over and over again. "I have seen the Fuehrer! I have seen the Fuehrer!" Reports say this scene was repeated several times in the summer of 1937 in many households in many towns and villages. At one time during one of Walter's nap times, Frau Pup was visiting and having coffee with Grandma Stoltz. She knew the Fuehrer was going to make a speech but insisted that Walter who could not understand much German be present during the speech.

Walt Fluegel

CHAPTER TWELVE: AUNT MARIE AND TELL THE DOG

The summer trip was coming to an end and Emelie had one more visit to make. The trip took an hour or so by train and in the final miles took a taxi to get to Aunt Marie's house. Mother and son would stay for one night before going back to the bakery house. As soon as the door opened and while the adults greeted each other Walter noticed a dog about his knee high just looking at him and coming closer then sniffing at him. "He wants to get to know you, let him sniff," Emelie said. The dog did not bark.

Aunt Marie said to Emelie, "That is a bit odd, Tell usually barks but when he sniffs that means he is getting to like that person."

For a moment Emelie was silent then asked Marie to repeat the name of the dog, "Tell, as in William Tell the Swiss bowman." While the two adults were talking, Walter instinctively reached down and patted Tell on the head, then his neck and back. Walter had only been acquainted with one other dog, a collie named Lassie owned by the director's wife at the Wartburg.

While Walter was getting used to Tell and his tail wagging and sniffing, Emelie's voice tenor changed. "I will have to tell you about a dog I knew years ago named Tell..." The conversation at the door then changed to chit-chat sort of greetings.

Aunt Marie quickly made some sort of lunch-snack during reacquaintance about old times and both summarized those 8 years of absence. Walter was almost ignored but after he ate he didn't mind. Tell brought an old rag that looked like an old pair of pants from his

57

play box and Walter seemed to know Tell wanted to play. "Try to pull it away from him," he heard his mother say. Walter got on his hands and knees and grabbed the chewed pants. The slight growling from Tell, with laughter, and screeching from a small boy signified a good friendship developing. After a few more attempts to gain the advantage the quantity of noise-making slowed down to an occasional just lying down next to each other possessing a part of the fabric. For a few moments the women thought they heard a slight snoring from the youngster and a uniform breathing from Tell. Both playmates had their eyes closed. Walter was also tired from the train trip.

CANARIES

Emelie heard a familiar bird sound in one room with a closed door she had not heard since she left the Cohens, "Do you have canaries?" she asked quietly. Marie and Emelie quietly got out of their chairs and both went to a side room filled with sunshine and two cages each with one bird. Emelie recounted that the Cohens allowed her to have three caged canaries in their house, one to a different room. Each night the cages would be covered with a dark covering to discourage the birds from singing especially if some of the guests did not appreciate their singing. In the morning the covers were removed and singing would soon begin. She told Marie that Trina in America had just one bird because Hans was nervous of having more of them around just in case they escaped. Marie had a name and age for each of her birds. So did Emelie.

"Who is taking care of your birds now?"

"I am taking a chance that Trina will do alright until I come back. Hans was not quite sure but agreed if Trina would always keep the room door closed especially on the weekends when he was home." Hans saw no reason to have a lot of birds singing.

Marie and Emelie came back to the living room and let the playmates snooze for a while. Marie announced that Ernst would be home from work soon, but their two teenaged sons were at a Youth summer camp and will not be home to meet their Aunt and cousin. As she said that her voice changed. Then she said something Emelie could not fully understand until a few years later. "Those camps may be good for their bodies, but I think their minds are being twisted. We are worried about them but there is nothing we can do now." Then with a little hesitation Marie said, "I will warm up dinner but you and Walter go outside and look over the garden while I put things on slow cooking I started earlier."

"We were glad to know you were coming."

TALK GERMAN POLITICS?

More conversation about family and slow walking around continued in the garden but whenever Marie talked about their sons and those Youth camps she whispered. Some neighbors windows were open. Tell was walking beside Marie but he suddenly changed direction and trotted toward the garden fence gate and gave one bark. "That is his signal to Ernst that we are in the garden." Ernst knew about Emelie but never met her. He however let the two sisters do most of the talking in the introductions and some at dinnertime. However, Emelie and Ernst compared notes on their individual apprenticeship adventures in their common trade of the butcher business. Ernst was somewhat hesitant to talk about the better economic conditions occurring in Germany but the politics bothered him. Emelie assured him she was so busy at her job in America she did not follow German politics or even American politics. So after dinner they listened to a comedy radio program for a while before showing Emelie where she and Walter would be sleeping in the guest room. When it got late; Walter did fall asleep on his own on the small sofa but Ernst gently picked him up and helped put him to bed.

ANOTHER DOG NAMED TELL

More conversation occurred about the family and each sibling's progress but Ernst tried to avoid talking about national politics, but it did come up occasionally. "Where is Tell?" Marie asked in a loud whisper. She got up and tiptoed toward the guest room, opened the door slowly, turned toward Emelie and pointed into the room. Marie came back to the conversation and said Tell usually sleeps on the foot of their bed and a few times on one of the boy's beds so this was a good sign. When he is on our bed he gets Ernst up early enough to take him outside to do his business. They agreed to let Tell sleep with his playmate and Emelie would probably get up too if Tell woke up Walter. In other words Tell would make the right signals for everyone. It was then that Emelie told of another Tell in her life and how just his name brought back some memories she could later review in different ways. One of those ways indirectly brought her to America nine months after Johan and his dog Tell died. She was contemplating becoming an American citizen soon but she never mentioned an American thought to anyone during this entire visit to see her mother. Not even with the stimulus of hearing a dog's name.

A few years later at the Wartburg, Walter contributed a short story to the "Wartburg Times," a mimeographed 'newspaper' telling about his adventure with Tell. The adult editor decided to change Tell's name to Bingo. The author did not know how to object but when people who knew him congratulated him on the article his objection faded but not the memories of being with Tell. The newspaper was sold for a small fee to relatives and friends who came on Visiting Sunday.

CHAPTER THIRTEEN: A PHOTO AND REMEMBRANCE

A day or two when Grandma Stoltz knew Emelie and Walter would be leaving to return to America, someone produced a camera and semiformal photos were made. Once or twice Walter was asked to "stand up straight." He thought he was always doing that for each photo with one or the other cousin so he exaggerated the pose until an Aunt took his left elbow to raise his shoulder a bit. He didn't know why she did this so when he was with his mother alone and asked her, all she could say was that his one shoulder was slightly lower than the other. It seemed like an innocent thing to have one shoulder lower than the other but he knew two other boys at Half-B in the Wartburg whose one lower shoulder was noticeably lower. Their back did not look like other boys backs either when it was shower time. He had no way to see his own back and it never occurred to him to compare himself to other boys except knowing that some had more muscles than others. John Atlas advertisements on the back of comic books were very influential in having boys try to make big muscles while preparing for the weekly shower.

NOT A PERFECT ARYAN

It was years later he learned that had he stayed in Germany he would not be qualified to be in the Hitler Youth because of his mild scoliosis. He did not have the "perfect body" of the Aryan race. That being the case many of these "misfits" were eliminated in one way or another.

Hey Gunther! Why Are You Here?

Grandma Stoltz who was adding some wood the small stove asked Emelie if she remembered where they stored their potatoes and preserved vegetables? Emelie knew. Her mother who handed her a string bag asked her to go down in the basement and get two jars of pickles—and by the way we put an electric light down there. The switch is just inside the door; Emelie asked Walter to come along. They went out the back entry and then past the ovens almost to the far archway.

HOMESICKNESS FADES AWAY

There was one narrow door, which Emelie opened, found a switch and turned it on. Emelie hesitated a moment to get acquainted with a new set of stairs and one side railing. Things were different yet the same. "We have to be careful now, hold the railing," she instructed Walter. She remembered as a child the experience of using a candle and holding it up high as she descended the first few stairs, high enough for the flame to make smoke trails on the slanted low plastered ceiling. Those smoke trails were gone now, covered by white paint. Gone too were the moving shadows of shelves from the candle flame as she descended the stairs. Now the wooden shelves were easily seen by the light from one large electric bulb. And the basement too seemed smaller because of this light; it was easier now to walk around. With a candle one walked slowly until the eyes became adjusted to the semi darkness and that seemed to make the basement a large room for anyone. It was chilly down in that room, it was chilly too when she was a girl. It was a good place to store root crops from the garden but now that summer was at its peak, last years crop was gone. Emelie showed Walter the one side wall, which will be uses just for potato storage. After that she found the jars of pickles and placed two of them in the string bag she brought along with her. The last remnants of her home-sickness were now fading away.

On the day of departure there were hugs, tears and promises from siblings nieces and nephews to write more often to and from Germany. Everyone was optimistic, times seemed to have a favorable future for Germany. Everybody knew Emelie as a grown woman with a child to take care of as best as she could. Past disappointments seemed forgiven and hopeful for more visits from Emelie. It was however the last time Emelie saw he mother for in 1937 events in Germany were headed in a direction that made other nations in Europe and in America nervous.

Hey Gunther! Why Are You Here?

Walt Fluegel

CHAPTER FOURTEEN: A JEWISH LEGAL PROBLEM

On one side trip on the way back to America, mother and son stopped at a law office representing insurance claims in the name of the Guild. The Guild had been informed earlier through the (New York Life) insurance company mail that Emelie would present them with some final legal papers to match claimed papers concerning the death of Johan. Letters were being exchanged between New York and the Guild. Both sides thought they solved the legal problems. All Emelie had to do was to present a sealed letter to the appropriate official and the final transaction would be complete. Nervously, Emelie finally met Mister Kepler, the proper official in his fancy office and was assured by previous letters she would be able to claim long overdue insurance compensation. He asked Emelie to sit next to his desk and wondered if Walter could be quiet.

The official had all the folders in front of him, glanced at one or two in greater detail then said in a quiet voice, "By the new law we are not allowed to do business with a Jew; is Mister Cohen a Jew? His name is Jewish."

Emelie did not expect this comment from an official representing the Guild but as when earlier people on her trip asked her this question she said calmly, "That is his name but they don't practice the religion." He asked her other questions about her working for him and as to who his friends were and did they celebrate Jewish holidays. She answered that yes many of his friends were Jewish and she thought those friends did attend the synagogue occasionally from overheard conversation. He then called his secretary on the intercom and asked her to summons his partner as soon as possible.

MISTER COHEN IS A JEW

While they waited Mister Kepler asked about Johan's death, their business, why she left Germany and how she liked being in America. She did not have time to answer about America because the partner was ushered into the office. The two men discussed the legal concept briefly but Emelie began to realize nothing would come of it. She was right. They said that their business would be severely fined if money without authorization was given to anyone living outside of Germany. And because Mister Cohn was probably a Jew the punishment would be very severe. The law partner left the office without any more conversation. Mister Kepler however, handed back the now opened letter Emelie gave to him and began to reach out to her for a handshake but lamely and quietly mumbled, "Heil Hitler," thus fulfilling an obligation demanded of these officials.

Sophia did not accompany Emelie and Walter on the trip back to America. As with his trip to Germany, Walter put all these memories into the same memory bank. It seemed to be one trip. There may have been one stormy day but was it the trip to or from Germany? It did seem that no one special chastised his mother about him not knowing German or any special thing happening on the boat. There was always sky above and water all around and seeing the pins inserted in the water of the Atlantic Ocean map. The hot broth in the mugs was a delightful late afternoon drink. He and his mother were together and walked a lot around the boat and talked with other passengers and exchanging experiences. He does not remember seeing any other children either. It all added up to a jumble of looking at everything, seeing and remembering nothing in particular. It appeared his trip back to America was uneventful.

Walt Fluegel

CHAPTER FIFTEEN: RETURN FROM GERMANY: THE COHEN'S HOUSE

Walter did not know there were procedures for reentry into the Wartburg. The rules required all children to be quarantined against communicable diseases for ten days but Mister Cohen arranged for an exception to the rules. He assured the director of the Wartburg that Walter would be living with his mother at his home in Saint Albans and no other children will be sleeping in the house. At the end of Walter's stay Mister Cohen's physician would examine Walter and certify on his health. Walter was not aware of these arrangements.

The very next morning after coming back from Germany, Walter heard singing canaries he had not seen the day before. Also he never saw these caged birds when he first arrived at the Cohens before he left for Germany but did hear them on the radio. His mother explained that the night before when he was asleep Uncle Hans and Aunt Trina came and brought the birds back to her. They were taking care of the birds until the trip was over. Uncle Hans was more than ready to return the birds. Walter remembered his mother on some Visiting Sundays telling him she had some canaries, but it made no sense at the time. As he got to know his mother better throughout the years that followed, canaries or budgies were always part of her soul and joy. Even when she began to live in Alaska many years later.

In those days of "quarantine" Walter learned more about the big garden and met the gardener who took care of the grounds; Walter listened to classical music on the radio (WQXR), tried to understand the Sunday New York Times and talked with and watched his mother straighten up the house, and cook and prepare food for the Cohens.

Hey Gunther! Why Are You Here?

Emelie did her duties and did not seem to be hindered anymore by not having her left pinky finger. In the meantime she did however discuss with Mister Cohen in private, the insurance money problem that occurred in Germany. Mister Cohen indicated that German politics may be headed for unusual times and he worried about what was happening to Jewish business between Germany and America.

During the following year Mister Cohen and Emelie had more conversations about her Germany trip and her thinking about her relatives and their feelings about the rise of Hitler. She let him know she was no longer homesick and was thinking about becoming an American citizen. When she wrote letters back to Germany she did not let any of her relatives know of her naturalization plans. She accomplished her goal in 1939.

DOCTOR'S OFFICE

A few days before they were to leave for the trip to the Wartburg Emelie had made arrangements to have Walter officially examined for communicable diseases. The doctor lived in the neighborhood and knew the Cohens and he was within walking distance. He looked after people in the neighborhood at least once a week but he also had an office in another place with other doctors and a small lab where some blood and urine tests were done. The examination was not new to Walter and to be told by the doctors wife to take his shirt off he complied without hesitation but he could not sit still. He kept looking and twisting around until the doctor came in. However, at the Wartburg the doctor examined one boy at a time in the play area and using the large table for his paperwork and big black bag. When finished with one boy he called in another until all boys were examined. Sometimes Miss Miller was watching, at other times she was within earshot of any requests made by Dr. Girard. The doctor in Saint Albans seemed to be the same age as Dr. Girard of the Wartburg. Walter knew he would be told to open his mouth and an AHHH stick placed on his tongue and have to say AHHH while the doctor looked in his mouth with a flashlight. The doctor also had a swab and streaked it over the back of his throat. He knew soon his eyelids would be pulled down and also told to follow the doctors fingers and to have the flashlight flashed in his eyes. The doctor also thumped his chest and back and listened to this part of his body and that part with the stethoscope and also hit his knees just below the knee bone. At the end of the exam he called in his wife who handed Walter a small jar and asked him to make some pee in it. He was so used to Miss Miller being around when he was on the toilet sometimes that he complied without any hesitation.

In the meantime while Emelie was waiting she watched the Doctor's canaries in the corner. She also answered some routine medical questions for the doctor's wife. The doctor also filled in some blanks on an official looking form.

SAYING GOODBYE TO THE COHENS

On Wednesday evening after supper the day before Emelie's official day off she began to pack a suitcase of Walter's clothes while he watched her and listened to her explain he would be returning to the Wartburg early the next day. They would be going alone but if the Cohens came home early that night he would be saying good-byes before he went to bed. If not then he would be awakened before they left for work in the morning. His sleep pattern for the ten day "quarantine" was that he could sleep as late as he wanted. He usually got out of bed around seven thirty. Emelie forgot that the first kitchen bell for the day at the Wartburg rung at six o'clock every day.

When it was Emelie's day off the Cohens were usually visiting friends and would come home late, but this time it was different. Fortunately the Cohens came home just before Walter got into bed. He quickly got into his bathrobe and recited what Emelie asked him to remember. Everybody met in the living room and Mister Cohen remarked to Walter it was a pleasure to have known him, and that was echoed by Mrs. Cohen. Other chit-chat occurred between the Cohens and Walter who then stretched out his hand as if he wanted a handshake from Mister Cohen and said, "I thank you for letting me stay in your house." They shook hands heartily. Then to the surprise of his mother and the Cohens he also said, "Thank you both for taking care of my mother." It was a complete surprise to everyone even

Hey Gunther! Why Are You Here?

Walter; it was spontaneous. Mrs. Cohen touched him on the shoulder and Mister Cohen shook Walters hand one more time. Emelie looked at the both of them as she drew Walter close to her. By the time Walter was awake the next morning the Cohens were off to work in New York City.

In the morning Walter saw that his Sunday best clothes were ready for him but he had to first go to the bathroom. On the way there he said 'hello' to his mother in the kitchen as he usually did each time in the days he stayed at the Cohens. On the way back he noticed his mother was dressed in her better clothes and not the uniform she wore every day. She indicated that time was important so getting dressed and having breakfast had to be quick. Emelie had plans to drop by a store before their long travel to the Wartburg. Emelie knew by heart the trolley, bus, and train schedules for the places or stores she usually wanted to be at including visiting her sister Trina (without letting Hans know.) This time she also had to concentrate on Walter and his suitcase.

When Walter was asleep Emelie packed a box of checkers and chess pieces Mister Cohen had given to her. Mister Cohen indicated the board was severely damaged years ago when someone spilled a drink on it. Also, he had lost interest in playing the game, so her son might be interested in playing with them at the Wartburg.

SOMETHING FOR THE BOYS AT HALF-B

So Emelie made plans to stop at the nearest Woolworth five and dime store to get a new board. She knew nothing about chess but she thought some of the older boys might. Right after breakfast and a trip to the bathroom they were on their way. They arrived at the dime store without any difficulty and purchased just the board. It was a bit unusual not to also purchase the checkers and chess pieces but Emelie indicated to the clerk that she would also buy other games as well. (At that moment Emelie flashed back to her earlier days of the encounters with customers at the butcher stores.) That night before, Mister Cohen took Emelie aside without Mrs. Cohen knowing and handed Emelie the box of checker and chess pieces and an envelope with money in it.

70

Walt Fluegel

He whispered, "Go to the store and buy the boys at Half-B some games." When she opened the envelope in the store she spent most of it on the new game of Monopoly, and familiar games of Parcheesi, and Chinese Checkers and three packs of playing cards. The clerk was willing to make a package of the games so they would be easy to carry on the train and trolley. While Emelie took care of the suitcase it was Walter's job to carry the games.

In the meantime Emelie did not make this day feel anything special. It was just the day he would be returning to the Wartburg. He would know what to do and know what was expected of him. Many years later Walter realized he always had the feeling that no one day was more important than another. Each day had to be lived as it happened, and at the Wartburg every day did seem like the day before except on special days that always came to an end and the routine would begin all over again.

Hey Gunther! Why Are You Here?

Walt Fluegel

CHAPTER SIXTEEN: BACK TO THE WARTBURG AND HALF - B

For Emelie the trip to the Wartburg was routine after years of doing it for the Visiting Sunday. But for Walter seeing urban scenery passing by was new and also seeing all the advertising displayed above the windows of the trolley. Some of these were familiar ones from the newspaper and magazine advertising and made more familiar from radio advertising of things like Ivory Soap, Quaker oats, Kodak, Hershey's, and many things to buy he knew nothing about. He had plenty of time to read the different kinds of printing and realized there was more than one way to make an H or a T or an S if he let his mind relax. He also had conversation with his mother when possible about the traveling they did these past weeks but most often every one on either the train or trolley or bus were quietly looking out the window or reading.

After traveling on the train for a while he was getting hungry so he asked his mother when they were going to eat. She searched her purse and found some cellophane wrapped hard candy lemon balls but told him they would be stopping at the station with a small restaurant in a short while if he could wait that long. He also said he had to go to the bathroom. Emelie did not want Walter to wait. She said, "We will take care of that very soon," then took his hand and they got out in the aisle. She saw the ticket-conductor in a back seat rearranging papers and got his attention. She explained that this was the first time the boy traveled on a train and had no experience going to the bathroom on a train, "Could you please help him?"

Hey Gunther! Why Are You Here?

"This way, young man. Stay here ma'am," In a short time Walter was escorted back to his mother. "It was a close call ma'am but he will be fine now." Emelie wanted to give the conductor some coins but he refused saying, "There isn't a day that goes by that some little boy needs to go—and in a hurry." Within another 15 minutes they would stop at a station, have some lunch and then take the bus to the Wartburg entrance.

The train finally stopped. Emelie managed to carry Walter's suitcase in her right hand and adjust her purse on her left arm and made sur Walter had the games package. At the station they had a ham sandwich with lettuce and mayonnaise and a glass of lemonade. It felt good on this late summer day. They caught the right bus to the Wartburg entrance but on the way Walter soon recognize familiar landmarks he had seen on the routine winter, spring, and fall Sunday afternoon walks. All the boys walked two by two down the city sidewalks. Older boys set the moderate pace followed by the younger ones and finally Miss Miller at the back of the line. The walks consumed about two hours of a Sunday afternoon.

The bus finally came to the Wartburg entry street. The entry with its two large stone columns was so familiar to both except for Emelie it was not a Visiting Sunday afternoon where lots of other folks would be walking up the wide sidewalk on the left side of the road. As they reached the top of the hill where it began to level off, Walter certainly recognized Half-B on his left and intuitively began to veer off the sidewalk and headed to the side door. This side door was one of the two usual doors all boys used to get into the house. It led into what some called the basement but it was a place for hanging winter coats, a place for toilets and sinks for washing up. Beyond another door was the furnace room. On the other side of the house or back-side there were very wide concrete steps that led to the wide open inside where most activity took place. The front door too was at the top of wide stairs and porch used primarily for assembly when ready to go to school or church. That front door also opened into the large open area or commons room.

Walt Fluegel

OFFICIALLY READMITTED

It was just not convenient for the boys to enter the house by the front door except for visitors and others not familiar with the boys' routines. But Emelie walked up the stairs toward the main front door, Walter following and they both entered. It was about two in the afternoon and Miss Miller was expecting them because Mrs. Gunther phoned the Wartburg the day before that she was bringing Walter back. Because Half-B did not have a telephone the message was delivered to Miss Miller the next morning but no time was indicated. The house seemed empty at first because most boys were in the woods or out playing ball in the field. There were greetings between Miss Miller and Mrs. Gunther and a handshake between Walter and Miss Miller. Mrs. Gunther gave Miss Miller a sealed letter with the medical information the Wartburg needed to allow her son to be officially readmitted.

A bit of laughter occurred when a gathering of boys began to congregate around one of the dining room tables where Walter's suitcase was being opened up. Mrs. Gunther first opened the package of games and cards on one of the tables and told the boys there that Mister Cohen her employer, thought they could have some fun. If they did not know how to play Monopoly one of the older boys would have to read the rules before they played. Miss Miller thought that Milton might be the best one to do that so she put that game aside. The Chinese Checkers and Parcheesi were familiar so Miss Miller said something to the effect it would be nice when more than one group could play when it came a rainy day. The empty checkerboard was a surprise until the box Mrs. Gunther put into Walter's suitcase was opened. It was a surprise to Walter too because he did not know his mother put the box there.

The boys knew about checkers, but they didn't know how to play chess, and there was no complete set available. But the biggest surprise were the pieces themselves, they were elegantly carved. Miss Miller immediately said, "They look expensive!"

Hey Gunther! Why Are You Here?

Mrs. Gunther then added, "They were Mister Cohen's set, but he did not play the game for a long time. Maybe one of the teachers could teach the boys how to play the game."

"Walter, you take good care of them from now on," rejoined Miss Miller.

"Yes Ma'am," he answered. Thus his answer to Miss Miller showed he was readjusting to the life expected of him now that he was back in Half-B. While Walter and the boys got reacquainted with each other Mrs. Gunther and Miss Miller conversed with each other but from time to time they spoke German. This was always a signal that it must be private information between the two of them. Good-byes were finally made. When his mother left to go on to Saint Albans, Walter was instructed to change from his Sunday-best clothes into his summer play clothes.

By supper time Walter knew that two of the Half-B boys were transferred to the Big Boys' house and three new boys entered Half-B. School would start in two more weeks. At school he would get to know several new boys or girls from the other houses or find that some others were gone from the Wartburg.

The usual Visiting Sundays and established routines at Half-B erased most of the Germany trip for Walter. It was another part of his life he could not really tell about. None of the others at Half-B or Miss Miller seemed curious about his trip to Germany. He did not realize or know about the importance of what was going on in Germany or the anxiety in the rest of Europe. What would a 9-year-old know? But for Emelie she was relieved of her homesickness and sometimes worried about her siblings and their families. More so after she was able to discuss her family thoughts with Mister Cohen who for business reasons and the politics in Germany understood what might happen. In the meantime working for the Cohens became a routine matter too except for two events that occurred in 1938.

Walt Fluegel

CHAPTER SEVENTEEN: TWO MAJOR EVENTS IN 1938

EMELIE BECOMES A CITIZEN

On February 3, 1938 Emelie became an American citizen. As Emelie understood it if the father of a family became a citizen then the entire family became citizens. Emelie explained to Walter it was different because it was not automatic for him to be a citizen, because the law applied to the man not to the woman of a family. So in the future he would have to apply. He became a citizen on May 2, 1946 when he was 18. But in 1938 it is not clear whether Emelie corresponded with her German family about the citizenship or not. If she had told them about the citizenship that would definitely block all insurance funds from being transferred to America.

HURRICANE IN SEPTEMBER

The second event of that year was an act of nature. On September 21 of 1938 there was a fast moving hurricane that swept up the Atlantic coast and veered inland to spread havoc from New York City and deep into New England. About a week before that storm, the Cohens went on vacation to Florida to visit one of their grown children. During the storm a large branch from a nearby tree broke off and landed on the Saint Albans' house. There was quite some damage to the roof tiling but not enough to penetrate the underlying structure. The branch had to be removed and the roof needed repair. Even though repair contractors were very busy at the time Emelie took it upon herself to get three contractors to give her a bid for the job. Emelie knew the Florida phone number where the Cohens were staying and related in her opinion of which bid to accept. She suggested the middle bid because the contractor seemed honest and seemed knowledgeable on what had to be done. The lowest bidder seemed vague and the highest bidder Emelie thought might charge the most because this was a more fancy part of town and the Cohens "could afford it." By the time the Cohens came back from Florida the job was almost done. When Mister Cohen was able to talk with the contractor he was convinced that Emelie made the right choice. Emelie was pleased with the praise Mister Cohen gave her.

Walt Fluegel

CHAPTER EIGHTEEN: NEW IDEAS FROM THE NEW YORK WORLDS FAIR 1939

DISHWASHING MACHINE

The following Spring everyone in Half-B knew the 1939 New York World's fair was becoming an important part of many lives. Boys in the band might play once at the NY fair and maybe twice and had to practice more often. Walter visited the Fair with his mother on two occasions. It was a new idea for him and at the end of the day with lots of walking and observing new things it was very tiring. He could recall one event for a long time his mother was interested in. It was about seeing a lady in a home kitchen using a dish washing machine while another lady was actually washing dishes at a sink. Walter told boys around him that he thought the lady at the sink pretended to poke her finger with a fork in her haste to get the job done. Both ladies finished at the same time but the lady at the machine who was reading a magazine did not look harried at all compared to the lady at the sink, who almost collapsed when she was all done. Everybody assigned for KP duties knew about dishwashing but never thought a machine could wash dishes without breaking something. A few days later when Eddie came back he told the same story so everyone then thought it was an act. No one at Half-B knew about or ever saw a dishwashing machine. It was something new displayed at the fair. No one at Half-B had any concept of this kind of advertising or the reason for the fair.

Hey Gunther! Why Are You Here?

Dishwashers were a new idea. Future technology occurred only in the comics, not in present 1939.

FIBERGLASS

And so for boys who were not able to go to the NY fair became very skeptical of the different tales told by others who were able to attend. One such case occurred after Walter's second trip. He and his mother visited an exhibit where a new product called fiberglass was being woven into a kind of cloth. Walter was fascinated and listened carefully to the demonstrator tell how the people at Corning began to make very fine threads of glass that did not break when bent. He remembered the man say you had to 'study' glass to understand it. He did not understand the word "study" used in this way. Study was done in classes but when the man also used the words 'investigate' and 'laboratory' Walter slowly realized he was accepting something entirely new. Much later in life the words, study, investigate, and laboratory were keys to understanding the world around him but he did not know it at that time. He only knew he had something very different and marvelous in his hand when little strips of fiberglass cloth were handed out as a souvenir to the people listening to the talk.

The boys at Half-B were very skeptical about fiberglass cloth too. "Glass breaks if you step on it! Gimme that," said Peterson as he grabbed it from Walter. He then threw it on the floor and stomped on it and only showed he could dirty the cloth and spread some of the weaving. Walter was laughed at and ignored when he picked up his souvenir as the crowd dispersed. He did not have the feeling to tell of another new thing he saw at the Fair, something so new ordinary citizens too were in doubt as to whether it was real or not. What he saw at first was a large movie type camera and off to the side there was a small box that looked like it had a jar inside with gray paint in it. Things were moving in this gray paint. Walter could not remember the name of the gadget he saw but could describe it. It was the beginnings of watching a small TV screen but because of what happened to him it stayed with him ever since.

Walt Fluegel

EARLY TV

There was a man near this gray colored jar in a box and he stood next to a microphone while talking to people. He asked them chit- chat questions such where they came from, what they liked to eat, and if they liked their mother-in-law. Everybody was having a giggly time of it because what folks saw was repeated in shades of gray, black, and white were of themselves. For each group of people he explained that the large cameras were taking their pictures and transferring the results to the fascinating gadget everybody was looking at. Walter and his mother were in line to be photographed. Walter was the only child in line.

When it was his time the questioner asked him to look into the camera then asked, "Does you mother ever spank you?" He did not answer immediately because the words 'spank' and 'mother' were never used this way in his understanding.

"Come on young man are you that good you were never spanked?" the man asked in a joking manner.

Walter knew the other onlookers were giggling too so he just said, "No she does not spank me."

"Ma'am you got off easy this time, thank you," and then the next person was being interviewed. But Walter realized the Fair was in a way a forerunner of the future and the question of being spanked or not just diminished into the fading spot when a future TV set was turned off.

ONLY IN AMERICA

At the end of a warm day of seeing exhibits at the Fair and listening to explanations many people including Emelie and Walter deserved a rest on benches while waiting for the proper buses to take people home. The elevated train above must have discharged some passengers because some of them descended the metal stairs and found empty spaces on the benches. Mother and son had to wait for the "C" bus. The "B" bus came and took on some passengers.

Hey Gunther! Why Are You Here?

While passengers were boarding there was a call from the top of the stairs, "Is that the "B" bus? "Hold it if you can!" The call came from a newsboy who was coming down the stairs. He increased his descent and suddenly tripped on the stairs while the "B" bus pulled away. The boy tumbled to the bottom. People on the nearest bench immediately got up and went to help the newsboy. Some of his newspapers fell out of his bag and the slight breeze began to scatter them. A man began to collect the papers while a couple of people knelt down at the boy's side. It was obvious he was hurt because there was a small gash on his forehead. A lady opened her purse and took out a small handkerchief and dabbed it on the wound while leading the boy to an empty bench seat. He seemed to be Walter's age. The lady stayed with him asking his name and trying to give him comfort. Other folks began to congregate around the boy who was trying to hold back some tears. The man who was collecting the blown evening newspapers asked the boy how much he charged for the papers. He gave the price and the man repeated what the boy said. "You heard him folks! Give this boy a chance! Come on now, let's buy his papers!" And everyone on the benches bought a paper. Some bought two papers, enough so that all were sold and the money was placed in the news bag. When the man returned, some people added more coins found in their pockets as they recognized the approaching bus to be the one they needed. There was still a gathering around the boy when Emelie recognized the "C" bus coming to a stop.

She and Walter stood up and Emelie said to no one in particular, "Only in America, America is a generous country." And then they boarded the bus. If his mother never said that expression again Walter would have forgotten about it while he dozed on the bus on the way home to the Wartburg. But occasionally through the years Walter heard his mother say, "Only in America, " on several other occasions of generosity, and this cemented his experience of seeing the boy falling down the stairs. As he was maturing from boyhood into manhood he began to realize his mother indeed began to be see goodness around her. A marked difference to her time in Germany.

Walt Fluegel

WAR TO AMERICA?

By this time Hitler's army had invaded Poland and the Second World War began in Europe. Emelie knew that all contact with family was completely severed and all she could do was to speculate on the fate of nephews who were Hitler Youth when she knew them and were enamored with Hitler. She had the feeling she would never see her mother again because she had no desire to go back. She was very Americanized too, and reading the Sunday edition of the New York Times during the week gave her a better idea of her new homeland. And she knew that America was preparing indirectly for war. But ever since returning from Germany before the war, Emelie got occasional phone calls from Trina asking her about siblings in Germany, then inviting her to visit on her day's off to talk more.

PLANS OF UNCLE HANS FOR EMELIE

It seemed innocent enough that Hans was interested too but sometimes he invited a surprise guest to have supper with them. These guests were older men from the meat processing plant where Hans worked. They were bachelors or recently divorced. Sometimes after supper Hans and Trina somehow left the living room to be in the kitchen or to be with Herbert. This left Emelie alone with the guest to engage in conversation. Some of these men were nice enough, suggesting that they should get to know each other better. One or two suggested they could take Emelie to his home in their car.

It was years later when Walter was in his mid twenties that Emelie told him about Hans wanting to marry his mother off to one of his cronies. "They knew I was a good worker. All they wanted was someone like me to take care of them when they got old." She then added, "I did think I wanted more children but not this way." Soon visits to her sister were only during the day with no stay for supper. When Walter became older he began to know his mother better and sometimes wondered why she told him these tidbits of her life. What was she trying to convey? Or did she just speak her mind to relieve her own thoughts?

Hey Gunther! Why Are You Here?

Emelie served the Cohens faithfully. Mrs. Cohen became softer in her personality towards Emelie and accepted that Mister Cohen would be talking with Emelie about the news especially from Europe. He would tell her about some of his European relatives or relatives of some of his friends trapped in German occupied countries. Emelie exchanged her family worries too and wondered if America would be dragged into war with Hitler. Mrs. Cohen had no known relatives in Europe that she was aware of. All ties were severed several generations ago she implied. In a small way Emelie was treated like family at these times but she was still aware that she was their servant. It also became apparent that Mister Cohen was having some medical problems, but not enough to keep him home from work in the city.

WAR ON BOTH COASTS

Visiting Sundays came month after month. On one December Visiting Sunday in the afternoon a certain general commotion developed on the Wartburg campus. People turned on the radio in the far end of the living room at Half-B. The radio was never turned to on Sunday afternoon but this seemed an exception. Some people had turned on their car radio and came into the house to make an announcement and shouted, "Pearl Harbor was bombed!" Many people did not know what or where Pearl Harbor was and who did the bombing. Or why. Some people in the know explained it to others but for Walter and the rest of the boys at Half-B it made no sense. The adults were concerned, others were confused but in the next few days by listening to the radio and reading newspapers, people realized America was at war across two oceans.

Because of the war atmosphere there were random air raid drills at night. Miss Miller blew a special whistle. Everyone became awake and had to put on bathrobes and go down the stairs from the bedroom and stay in the dark hallway and sit on the stairs. And wait. Miss Miller had the flashlight on only a few minutes. Every one had to be quiet. Everyone was quiet. During the daytime, older boys wondered if the Nazi bomber planes could fly the distance between Germany and the USA. Some argued they couldn't because an Uncle or grandfather said they could not and besides there would be no fuel to

84

fly back. Japan was too far away but aircraft carriers also needed fuel so where will they get it from? Most people thoughts from the Atlantic Coast of America were on Germany. Also, according to a mechanics magazine they said no airplane in the world could fly from Europe to America and back. But Walter's mother in Saint Albans could not think about air raid drills or bombing or other civilian calls for the war effort. One day she found Mister Cohen dead in his favorite chair next to the radio. Open newspapers were at his feet. Mister Cohen's death changed everything for Walter and his stay at the Wartburg.

MISTER COHEN DIES, PLANS CHANGE

It wasn't long after Mister Cohen's death that Mrs. Jane Cohen decided to move to California to be with her brother. That meant the Saint Albans house was to be sold and Emelie had to find other employment. Mrs. Cohen appreciated having Emelie for all these years and mentioned that Emelie would be in her will and they should keep in contact. After about three or four letters, contact was lost, Emelie shrugged it off until accidentally meeting Mrs. Cohen's brother in Alaska. That was a time when there was a flood in Alaska and Mrs. Cohen's brother was some kind of administrator for the federal government. But that would be in several years from the time Mrs. Cohen departed for California. In the meantime Emelie would look after the house and keep it tidy until the real estate agent could sell the house. It was he who suggested that Emelie could be more independent if she cleaned house or be a cook or do day work for individual households. She did not have to be a live-in domestic. He told her he had a sister in Mount Vernon who needed someone at least once a week to clean house and occasionally cook for a large number of people. That was all the incentive Mrs. Gunther needed.

Hey Gunther! Why Are You Here?

Walt Fluegel

CHAPTER NINETEEN: CULTURE SHOCK

LIVING WITH MOTHER

Walter's mother soon found an apartment on the third floor of a large house on North Fulton Avenue in Mount Vernon. The house was owned by middle-aged sisters—the Brockmans. The apartment had two bedrooms, a bath, and a kitchenette. This was a few weeks before school would start, and a new life for Walter and his mother would begin anew. The Wartburg life ended when Byron Hendrickson of Half-B shouted to Walter, "Hey Gunther, you don't belong here anymore!" (That was the title of the first book in this series—Hey Gunther! You Don't Belong Here Anymore.)

It took almost 14 years before mother and son—Gunther—would be living with each other again. Neither one really knew what the separation of those years did to each other. Walter knew or thought of his mother as a "friend" who visited once a month on Visiting Sunday. His mother saw her son grow slowly from an infant to a 14 year old but did not know his personality. Who were these two to each other? In another five years or so, the need for a young man to explore the rest of the world such as Alaska would be another turning point in both their lives again. But in the meantime, Walter, would have to live in another world of bus and trolley schedules, locations of stores, the library, a church, the way to the public schools, and get to know some of his neighbors, have an allowance, a key to the house, a wallet, and perhaps get a small job. Also he had to get to know his

Hey Gunther! Why Are You Here?

mother as a mother not as a housemother to twenty or more boys and not to be with those boys and the routines dictated by the bells that kept the Wartburg synchronized.

Mrs. Gunther had no easy way to talk to Walter about his new school, a junior high school, the Wilson, nor he with her. What should she ask, what would he tell her or compare. And Mrs. Gunther had to make sure she was fully employed so she could pay the rent and buy the groceries. She had to make sure she had a reliable steady list of clients for each day of the week. Both mother and son had to make adjustments relatively fast. In a sense it is now known as cultural shock but its toll became manifested in Walter.

At first it was exciting to be "free" of constraints imposed on anyone from the orphanage such as walking to school on your own about a half mile or more, being with strangers in school with both boys and girls for just a few hours of the day, getting to know different classmates at different times of the day, being free to take chances on going home from school on a different street, knowing you are the only boy wearing corduroy knickers instead of long pants, having lunch in a cafeteria and sitting in different places in the lunch room, and at a dance seeing boys and girls actually holding hands for the dance or having a boys hand on a girl's waist. Learning how to dance never occurred at the Wartburg. No social skills were taught but what was taught made the orphanage run smoothly. Mrs. Gunther was not aware of these things so she had no idea that this cultural shock became a form of stress (as we know today) that affected Walter's health. Stress is now known to affect the immune systems ability to fight off illness. It was compounded by meeting a new population of others in your age group and different adults who had an immunity to each other. But it was new to Walter and it made him prime for getting pneumonia. It occurred within 2 or 3 weeks of being in a new school.

The only thing Mrs. Gunther could do at the time Walter become ill was to have him stay in bed for the day while she went to work. She asked her landlord ladies, to look in on Walter and see that he would drink his soup at noon if one of them would heat it up. The sisters lived on the first floor with their older brother and elderly mother but had a small sewing business on the second floor also occupied by a cousin of about their own age. Previous to owning the Fulton Avenue house they had an upscale dress making business in New York City but the stock market crash wiped them out. They set up a new much smaller business on North Fulton Avenue, altering dresses and business suits for former women customers also affected by the crash. Mrs. Gunther and Walter were their first rental costumers but they took a chance on having a young boy of 14 from the Wartburg being in the house. Also, because the boy is under the care of his mother. At noon Walter did not respond to wanting any soup and he seemed to be having a fever. Miss Evelin B decided on her own to call her family doctor who looked after her mother to take a look at Walter. The doctor managed come later in the afternoon. After an examination he suspected that the boy had the beginnings of pneumonia and wrote out a prescription and told Miss B to keep the boy in bed for more days and to inform his mother this could be serious and to report any changes in the boy's condition. When Mrs. Gunther came home after work and got the prescription she immediately walked to the South Fulton Pharmacy across the bridge that spanned over the railroad tracks. At that time pneumonia was one of the leading causes of death in the country and Mrs. Gunther was grateful to Miss E. B. for calling her doctor. The prescription was for a new "miracle" medicine called sulfa. (There was a Nobel Prize given to Gerhard Domagk in 1939 for the discovery of this drug. But the Nazis disapproved of the Nobel committee also giving a prize to a German pacifist thus forcing the rejection of receiving the prize. It was accepted after the war in 1947.)

WALTER IS A TRUANT

A few days later a stranger came to the door of the Fulton Avenue house. He was a school truant officer and had to make inquiries. He had to see the boy himself to confirm illness and noticed that Walter was in bed but had a bloody handkerchief to his nose. He remarked to Miss E. B. that his daughter had the same bloody nose condition after taking a new drug for a minor cut on her hand that got infected. He asked to see the prescription bottle. He said it was none of his business but urged Miss E. B to call her doctor and tell him about the bloody nose. The new miracle medicine affected a few people this way but he found out that it helped lots of wounded soldiers on the battlefield during the war still going on. However, before the truant officer left the house he dropped a warning to Miss E. B. to tell the boy's mother to phone the school next time the boy was ill enough to stay home. He fulfilled his duties but emphasized with the situation when Miss B related highlights of Emelie and her son. After Emelie came home from work she met the doctor who had also just arrived. He indicated to Emelie that, "We know the medicine is working." And before he left, the doctor gave other instructions to Mrs. Gunther on what to do for her son. At that time in the 1940s roughly 60% of the pneumonia cases were diagnosed and treated in home situations by a family doctor. From thenceforth whenever Walter had to fill out a medical questionnaire wherever he went in life, 'Sulfa' was always inserted in the space where it asked about allergies. It always flashes an image of a bloody handkerchief in the visual field of memory.

(Note to readers: In the early paragraphs of this story of mother and son the philosophical question of — Why am I here? a number of "here" were explored. So far I have mentioned the death of Walter's father. This indirectly removed Walter from an industrial center of Germany that were heavily bombed during WW2 thus making a new 'there' or even death. Also it was intimated that his body with scoliosis was not the kind to be part of the Hitler youth, another possible death because perfect bodies were prized. And now with the pneumonia under control with a new medicine possible death was averted. Thus another 'here' was planted and continued by events that unfolded.)

BACK AT SCHOOL

In time Walter would be going back to the Wilson school for the 7th and 8th grade without any medical reason to stay at home. Mother and son were slowly getting to know each other and they in turn were being known by the Brockman sisters and their brother. He was retired but had a half time job in a war industry machine shop within walking distance of the house. At school Walter adjusted to his new situation of classes, lunch, recess games with others, and the cafeteria routine. The cafeteria was small for the size of the entire student body so different home rooms of students had to wait in the Assembly auditorium in assigned areas. As a number of students finished their lunches and left the cafeteria a student monitor announced which row of students in the assembly hall were now allowed to enter the cafeteria as some other students left.

During this cafeteria waiting time Walter slowly absorbed the cultural norms of others his age. Most of the time he just listened as he did at the Wartburg, participating only when it seemed appropriate. He heard jokes he never heard before, he listened to other boys discuss the latest car they saw, or the latest gizmo seen in Popular Mechanics, or maybe talk of the Yankees versus the Giants or the Dodgers, or maybe what it was like to have a job with your father at the corner grocery store. Radio programs of the Lone Ranger, Jack Benny, The Shadow, Charlie McCarthy, Bob Hope, and others were discussed after the day's broadcasts. The girls segregated themselves from the boys at this time and besides if any boy talked at any length with a girl he was teased for a few days. But as with the Wartburg environment some students were smarter than others, cliques developed between those more inclined to want be in school and those who were reluctant to be there. None of his classmates seemed to have an interest in Walt's former life at the Wartburg. He was just there. Some knew and didn't mind that he was on the edge listening in, others who didn't know just accepted him as another transfer into the school while most of the students knew each other from earlier grades. But some of his teachers began to know of Walter Gunther. But his mother did not know about any of the teachers because she did not ask about the teachers. And Walter was not inclined to say anything about school except he liked school and he had reasonable grades in his first year with his mother.

SCHOOL LESSONS NOT IN BOOKS

At Wilson it was customary for the home-room teacher Miss Roget to require her students to learn how to express themselves. She helped Walt overcome his difficulty in public speaking before his classmates. Each student had to tell of something he knew that was not regularly

91

Hey Gunther! Why Are You Here?

taught in class, maybe something he or she read in newspapers or magazines, or heard on the radio. The talk must last no more than three minutes. He had just the right subject he thought. It seemed more important than what others were telling about. He was the last speaker. His topic was 'What kind of toothpaste not to use.' He had read an article in the newspaper telling about the dangers of using toothpastes with a large amount of abrasives in it because that would wear down the tooth enamel too much. And more cavities would develop. It was his first public talk ever. As he was trying to tell what he found he slowly began to tear up. He did not look at the other students but at the skylight above. The tears came, hesitations became evident, and he heard Miss Roget shushing the other pupils, but he finally finished within the three minute allowed. He wiped his tears and blew his nose before he sat in his seat.

Miss Roget did not allow any short discussion this time and fortunately the hall bell sounded for class change. Walt was set to go to the library for book reading time, but Miss Roget stopped him. She asked what class he was going to go to and asked him to sit down in the desk next to her desk. She wanted to talk to him about his talk and said she would first give him a note to give to the teacher in the library telling why he was a late arrival. Walt thought Miss Roget would scold him on crying but was surprised when she explained about the facts of what he talked about. She too read that same article. She pointed out that the article was an advertisement meant to guide people to a certain brand of toothpaste. But in essence she helped Walt to be more careful of what he read. If he was going to read these types of articles he should try to find other articles from other sources and compare notes. Don't take information from only one source she stressed. Little did Walt not yet 15 years old realize that that three minute talk and Miss Roget would set him on the intellectual journey towards a future in Alaska and later in academia where he would be talking at times for a living. He took his note from Miss Roget to the library and gave it to the teacher monitoring students who were busy reading their books.

Walt Fluegel

OUTSIDE LOOKING IN?

By the time his first year at Wilson was coming to a close Walt seemed to distinguish his public school learning from books and teachers to learning about other students in a student life. He had his own life outside of school that others did not know about because he seldom if ever volunteered this information, and he did not know how others lived because he never asked anyone about their home life. He never had this kind of practice at the Wartburg. This kind of pattern of not being too inquisitive about others and not volunteering about oneself with others seemed the most comfortable for Walt. It was this way into adult life. Some folks think of this as being a loner, but to Walt he knew he was everyone's equal or just like him. He wasn't disliked but he found out later in life he became an acquaintance to many around him. Students and many adults knew him but not about him. At the end of the school day when everyone was going home a bunch of boys would leave together in one direction. As each one got closer to their own residence they peeled off and went into their house or apartment. The last one then was Walt himself going alone to North Fulton Avenue or the public library. At the library he began to check out books to read about Arctic and Antarctic explorers, books by Luther Burbank, Washington Carver, Robert Service, Jack London, Roy Chapman Andrews and other adventurers. This kind of reading progressed into high school but in an indirect way. At the end of the first year at Wilson each student was required to fill out a short form to indicate what books they read. Walter filled in just four books making sure he included the author.

Within a day or two when he submitted his list, Miss Roget asked him to stay a moment after class. She showed him his list and said something to the effect he should read more. She said he seemed to know things others did not know about in general home room discussion times so how did he know these different things. Walt (he was now being called Walt by other students.) said yes he read outside books but he thought the list was for only books he read at school. School reading was different from personal reading, but Miss Roget assured him that school was not the only place where someone

93

learned things. He then told her he used to check out books from the bookmobile at the Wartburg that came every two weeks. From then on he found it easy to talk with Miss Roget and his other teachers and be encouraged by them. Except one time Miss Roget admonished him when there was some talk about the Pope in Rome or something having to do with religion. "I don't care what flavor your religion is so don't bring that topic up in class or in public again!" The word "flavor" was long remembered and her 'flavor' statement was a lesson applied many times within other parts of society throughout Walt's life. Miss Roget was Roman-Catholic. She did not hold a grudge to anyone but was generous with her time.

PAVING STONES

In a junior high school General Science class Miss Hardy never explained what science was only that biology, chemistry, physics, geology and words like astronomy were called sciences. As such Miss Hardy did her best to explain that everyday experiences or observations could be grouped into these sciences. When Miss Hardy gave many examples it slowly impressed on Walter that he too could do the same thing. When she demonstrated the concept of metal expanding when heated he realized he understood how the mercury thermometer worked. But when it came to understanding geology the concept had a profound influence because of its immensity. The whole world was involved along with the concept of time, time in millions of years. It made information about dinosaurs he read about in books from the bookmobile at the Wartburg more understandable. And wouldn't it be interesting to be a scientist like Roy Chapman Andrews who dug up bones preserved for so long. Also when photos of the Nile Delta, and the Mississippi Delta alluvial fans were explained as an ongoing process of the earth that held a fascination to want to be a geologist Walter was not aware that this General Science class was the time when paving stones were being placed before him leading to his future in academia.

CHAPTER TWENTY: MONEY MAKING JOBS BEFORE COLLEGE

Walt also did not know that Miss Hardy was a neighbor who lived in the large brick five-story apartment building across the street on North Fulton Avenue. Soon after the second semester occurred she contacted Walter. She had an apartment on the first floor shared with Miss Roland who also was a teacher but in a different school. Miss Hardy wondered if Walter could give her a hand in correcting papers! As one of her former students he knew that Miss Hardy gave several exams during the semester and she thought she could use some help. She would pay him some money. His first job was to "X" off the incorrect words on a list of words that did not match the list she gave him. If the spelling was incorrect it was a 1/2 off "X." She also required good handwriting, so if Walter could read it he did not have to consult with her. The exam looked familiar, there was a short sentence answer section, a multiple choice section, but it was the vocabulary section Walter would have to correct. Most of the exam was already corrected by Miss Hardy. When all exams were corrected and scores added there was time for chatting and some cookies. At times Miss Roland listened in and both teachers seemed to want to know more about the Wartburg too. Miss Roland had a hobby of making Jewelry and gift cards made with very small seashells found on Florida beaches. In time she showed Walter some of these jewelry pieces and other works of shell art. She wondered if he would be interested in doing this as a hobby for himself. He thought so, so she gave him a catalog from a company that supplied materials. It took a while before he could make acceptable jewelry for sale but in the meantime, on Saturdays, he had another job of working in a green house.

IN THE GREENHOUSE

His mother somehow met Mister Evans who owned several greenhouses on the outskirts of town at the end of the city bus rout. He supplied some cut flowers to local floral shops and also occasionally supplied a Woolworth store in New York City with easily grown houseplants. He hired two men who did most of the hard physical labor of mixing soil, loading flats, repairing broken glass, making flats, watering and general upkeep of the green houses. There were three women employees: Mrs. Helen who was the bookkeeper/sales person for drop-in trade, Miss Carolyn was an older woman and Miss Janette was a younger woman perhaps in her twenties. Their jobs varied from making floral arrangements for funerals, birthdays or special events to controlling weeds, planting seeds, or pruning vines. In late winter they too aided in doing a lot of the transplanting for the spring demand. Mister Evans always hired others with nimble fingers for this tedious job.

Walt was ushered into the work area of the greenhouse by Mister Evans and introduced to the other workers. He had never been in a green house before and told Miss Carolyn his 'boss' he was willing to learn what to do. The job was simple. There were flats filled with a particular type of soil. Miss C took a plywood board with uniformly spaced pointed dowels and turned it upside down and pressed the dowels into the soil. When this dowel board was removed the soil was smooth except for the holes made by the dowels. Seedlings were going to be placed into these holes. Miss C showed each step. By using another dowel, soil around the hole was moved into the hole around the seedling roots and gently pressed down. When the flat had all the holes filled with seedlings they were watered and carried to a bench for one of the men to distribute into the proper greenhouse. Each dowel board had a different number of dowels for the type of seedling to be transplanted. At first Walt was given large seedlings to transplant and that had strong roots. He also had to learn how to remove the small seedlings from their original flat. Each kind of

96

seedling tray had its individual seedling property so he had to learn by trial and error how to remove clumps of seedlings. From the clump he would take one plantlet in his fingers, separate with a pencil like dowel the entangled roots without doing too much damage and transferring the plant to the new flat. He did this all morning until lunch time. Walt had brought a brown bag lunch his mother had prepared for him. 'He did a good job for a beginner,' Miss C said. The 30 minutes lunch time seemed too short with talking and getting to know each other.

ACCOUNTING

Each time at the end of the working day Walter would be paid. He would be tired but he had to walk to the bus stop then wait. Usually he would be home within 45 minutes trying to relax on the bus. At home he showed his mother what he earned and sometimes she asked in a chit-chat way what he had to do at work while they were getting ready for supper. But one Saturday he came home an hour late and did not volunteer showing his mother what he earned. "Your supper is cold, what kept you? I was worried."

"I had to work a little late so I missed the bus," answered Walter.

His mother asked, "How much money did you make?."

He emptied his pockets and showed her what he had but when she added up the coins and bills it was at least fifty cents short.

It was at this time both mother and son began to show a different side of themselves to each other. Mother sounded a lot like Miss Miller who wanted to know the truth and the accused wanted not to tell by making up excuses or evading the questioning. Eventually Walter gave in almost in tears. He reached into his other pants pocket where he usually had his folded well used brown lunch bag. "I wanted to surprise you with this." (He was late because he stopped at the floral shop nearby and spotted little ornaments.) He opened his bag and pulled out a tissue wrapped glass object. It was one of those blown glass ornamental swans about an inch and a half tall but in an orange color. "I thought it would go well with the other swan on your nicknack shelf." His mother was stunned, and did not know what to say as Walter went into his room and fell on his bed. Eventually they had supper together in silence but ever since then Walter's mother never asked to see how much money he earned on his job and future jobs. It took a long time before there were any surprise gifts from son to mother.

SERVING CUSTOMERS IN THE GREENHOUSE

Spring Saturdays and Sundays at the greenhouse gave Walter a chance of helping customers wanting 'to make their garden grow'. Today young plants come in individual plastic containers or a six or four plant pack. Customers now help themselves. But in the '40's Mister Evans had temporary tables set up near his parking lot with a wide selection of flats. There were assorted vegetable or flowers to choose from and different ages of maturity. Depending upon the plant type there may have been as many as 25 or more plants in each wooden flat. A gardner would approach the tables and someone on staff would be ready to help. Either a trowel or bare hands were used to take a plant by the root and remove it from the flat. It was easy to do because the soil was very soft and newly watered but this sometimes meant it could be a sloppy event. Strips of old newspaper were handy to wrap each plant at the root end and then placed in an empty flat. When the customer had what he or she wanted the selection was brought to Mrs. Helen who had her cash register by the main entry. A large selection was placed in an old cardboard box and taken to the customer's car. Smaller selections of plants were consolidated into one bundle of newspaper wrapping for customers to take with them.

At times a customer asked for advice on planting and occasionally Walter knew what to say. "If you lay the tomato plant a little more on its side and a little deeper when you plant, it will encourage more root growth from the stem. Your plant will be stronger that way. Don't worry about the plant, it will bend on its own and grow upright." Walter never grew tomatoes before but somehow he must have heard this advice earlier from listening to one gardener talking to another. Mister Evans confirmed this advice and did not mind when Walter sometimes gave a customer an occasional baker's dozen especially when an extra plant was rather scrawny.

BEING A CADDY

By the end of the planting time Walt was no longer needed at the greenhouse but at this time school was over until September. He did not need extra pocket money except if he wanted to go swimming at the county pool. He knew how to get there from his time at the Wartburg and went at least once a week. But the lure of having more pocket money was strong enough for him to take a chance on trying to be a caddy at a nearby country club golf course if he took a bus. This was a time when golf bags did not have wheels, and bags came in various sizes and weights. When the assistant caddy master saw Walt he was doubtful if Walt could walk and carry a bag for the 18 holes. Fortunately, at that one time there were not enough caddies available. Players usually went in pairs so Walt was paired with a veteran caddy who instructed Walt on what to do. And fortunately too this first time the golfer had a light bag to carry. Walt was a quick learner, meaning keep his eye on the ball, speak only when spoken to meaning don't give advice to the player, just follow the player until near the ball, and be ready to present the golf bag for the player to make his own selection of club. If the ball landed into the rough the caddy walked faster to search for the ball before the player arrived.

Only older caddies could make suggestions, and only to experienced low par players. It was a different kind of working but this first time Walt also learned from other caddies to come very early in the morning before the assistant caddy manager arrived. Anxious early eight o'clock players were very ready to register after they played a round or just a nine hole round and took an early caddy too. The pay was good compared to working in the greenhouse, and sometimes there was an extra tip if the player won the game against his partner or partners. Any caddy job for Walt after nine in the morning was a waiting time until around late afternoon when players coming off an office job wanted to just play only nine holes.

Hey Gunther! Why Are You Here?

But school came soon enough. Was it two spring times at the greenhouse and two summers at the country club or only one? And how often did he caddy early during the week? It didn't matter in making pocket money for odd things and by this time he did not need or want an allowance. He had the habit of either depositing money in the bank or buying war bond stamps. In the fall, his mother's clients may have wanted help in raking leaves or tidying up their gardens, and so did their neighbors. So after school or fall Saturdays there were numerous small jobs that paid bus fair and for the small carton of milk at lunch time. But by doing some calculations he saved money if he brought a lunch 'bucket' with a thermos and filled it with milk from home. By this time Walt was in high school and like all transfers had to learn the school culture and understand the new teachers.

LESS THAN 10%

The WW2 was still going on in Europe and the Pacific but other than regular news reports and buying war bonds or stamps, students at A B Davis prepared themselves for the future. Less than 10% of the national student body in the 1940s had an inclination to go on to college. But how many from Davis? Higher than the national average, Davis was known as an academic high school, which differed from Edison on the other side of town and known as a vocational high school. Most Edison students went into the trades. From conversations the college bound students were destined for certain colleges chosen by parents who could afford their alma mater or required prestigious institution for entering law, business, or the medical profession. No one seemed to indicate other reasons or methods of choosing college. Walt seemed an exception, especially in the senior year when going to the University of Alaska in Fairbanks was finalized.

PULLING UP THE BOOT STRAPS?

So in high school, Walt was saving college money from jobs (and a small business) and had a strong desire to learn about farming because biology seemed the logical choice. It was seeing living critters under

100

the microscope in Miss Landis's class that cemented biology above all the other sciences he was interested in. Geology seemed daunting because rocks were heavy and how was any one going to make money for a living by bringing rocks home to examine. He did not know that being a geologist was a profession. (He did not realize it that his homeroom seatmate Gray Robinson at Davis was going to study geology in college.) Astronomy was interesting to know, but how was one going to earn a living looking through a telescope? Chemistry did not appeal to him, and physics had a lot of math to know. He knew his problem with transposing letters and numbers gave him difficulty. He did not know that there were all sorts of biologists for example because the only biologist he knew about were his teachers. They did instill the love of learning that came very easy for him anyway.

At that time if a student decided on a career direction in life, counseling, as we know today was not needed. Determination, grit, and the Horatio Alger mystique was all that mattered. The student counselor and also the vice principal Miss Lewis admired his determination to go to college especially since they knew of his Wartburg experience. They also knew because of certain standard tests he had enough intelligence to succeed in college if he applied himself. So when Walt decided to become a farmer that set the stage for going to college and this produced difficulty at home with his mother. It seemed that the only practical way to earn a living by knowing biology was to grow plants or animals and sell them. Reading about Luther Burbank, the horticultural wizard and his own greenhouse experience, were logical directions to find a college.

ADVANCED SCIENCE CLUB

But by being in the Advanced Science Club (ASC) did this mean one was destined to get into college? For Walter, a few years from being in an orphanage, this was not the reason, it was just being with other like minded serious students in the sciences. Everybody seemed serious in wanting to learn more. As such for Walter there was a chance to spend a couple of afternoons a week with lab technicians at the local hospital laboratory. Other club students spent a couple of afternoons after school with other professions, such as a chemistry student being with a druggist, someone liking engineering being with the city planning people and so forth. Walter and one other student watched and talked with the medical laboratory technicians at work examining urine samples, petri dish throat swabs, counting different cells in a blood smear, and occasionally the rabbit procedures used in determining pregnancy.

Actually being allowed to examine stained blood cells under the microscope and actually seeing differences in cell types made biology more interesting. Also the speed of the technician in determining the kind of cell and counting the cell types on a special counter made lab work very important. It was more important too that the doctor relied upon these laboratory results, It was also important for the doctor to know the condition of recently acquired urine samples right there in the laboratory to determine the health status of a patient. Walter was allowed to see differences and to listen to the explanations of the laboratory technician, during their working time, not in the classroom. But later when explained to the ASC students about urine samples this elicited a yuck response. Mister Stokes the science advisor to the club managed to put this into perspective for each part of science having a negative to the layman's view of a profession. For Walter, a negative occurred when rabbits were killed in order to determine if a woman was in early pregnancy. He heard of guinea pigs, mice and rats used in laboratories but never rabbits. So when he saw one being killed by the technician injecting an air bubble into a blood vessel it had a profound influence on him. Would he want to kill an animal to find an answer to a question? Apparently it was routine in many places. He had to get used to the concept of animal "sacrifices" for knowledge. It grew on him, but he always knew animals were killed for their meat but to learn by killing and examining parts of a body just for knowledge was different. When it came time for him to kill an animal a few years from that experience it was in Alaska when he had to shoot a pig in the head. Students in Alaska had to learn how to butcher animals for their meat and prepare the meat for selling certain selections.

For the students in the ASC it did give a better preview of future occupations in the sciences, but there were no examples to go to

102

concerning farming which seemed predominant in Walter's thinking. But what college? Because Mount Vernon was in New York, the nearest agricultural college Walter heard about was Cornell. He did not know where it was or anything about colleges but knew it was one step up from high school, thus more knowledge. He did not understand that there were different grades or "better" colleges than others. In other words he was naive but enthused.

NOT CORNELL

When he mentioned to his mother he might want to go to Cornell college there was an awareness his mother began to object. It would cost a lot of money but he assured her he could give it one year's trial and maybe he could get jobs in the meantime and save money for college. After a few days when he told her, she almost said no he should not go to Cornell for the reason he would have to visit with his Uncle Hans and she did not want that. It did not make sense to him but there was friction because of it. In all this time Walter was still reading about arctic adventurers and happened to read about the Matanuska Valley in Alaska, a colony in the 1930s sponsored by the New Deal program of the government. Huge heads of cabbages and other crops were grown there and the mention of the University of Alaska in passing was another spike of interest in college possibilities. The Horatio Algier pull yourself up by your own bootstraps mentality was strong and encouraged by adults around him, and by a smattering of disbelief, 'crazy' comments by other students which he selectively ignored. Thus more concentration centered on the Alaska possibility. Somewhere he read about musk oxen and the thought of domesticating them. They did not need shelter like cows and they produced very fine wool that the natives in northern Canada used in making warm clothing. Could they be brought to Alaska and be domesticated? It was a passing thought: could he be involved in that venture? But at this time other interests made themselves known.

Hey Gunther! Why Are You Here?

BLUE PRINTS AND RELIABLE SPRINKLER

To pin down a date when Walter began to attend night and Saturday morning classes in mechanical drawing class is hard to come by. Also why? Because WW2 was still going on, the class was free in an attempt to encourage youth to learn skills needed for the war effort. But that was a class where Walter learned to make perspective drawings of ordinary objects seen on an everyday occasion. These classes were given in Edison High School. All this was new but vanishing points, mechanical pens, compasses, micrometer rulers, making blueprints, kinds of ink, velum or transparent type paper cloth, and other supplies were part of this school vocabulary. His teacher was very liberal in his approach to students and when looking over the shoulder of his working students there was a general sense of being helped on a specific problem rather than being admonished on making an error.

The last assignment for the class was to make a final blueprint of a small object. The term blueprint was a common term in those days and this is the first time Walt saw how it was done. For a last part of the course, Walter decided to draw the details of all the parts of an old lock and key removed from an old door he found in the basement of the North Fulton house. He was pleased with the choice of object and also pleased to be commended by the teacher of the class for choosing this item. Of course other students had other objects too they wanted to draw or choose something available on the front desk. He had two choices. It was either making a detailed drawing of his razor and blade or the lock. At first because he was seriously starting to shave he thought he might forget to bring the razor home but it was easier to leave the lock at school in his assigned cabinet so he concentrated on the lock. For some reason this led to getting a job at the Reliable Sprinkler Company (fire sprinklers) factory about 10 minutes walk from the Davis school.

Walt Fluegel

CLEANING LINKS AT RELIABLE SPRINKLER

Two main reasons why Walt did not become a draftsman for the company were apparent at the start. He was still a student in AB Davis and the company needed someone full time and the previous draftsman somehow returned early from the army and resumed his old job. But somehow Walter was taught to clean the fire sprinkler links needed to make the sprinklers operate when the room temperature reached a certain high degree. The job included using harsh and possibly dangerous chemicals. These were housed in a room with a powerful suction hood to vent the room. This fume hood was turned on as the first thing to begin the day's work. The vent was as long as the sink and a few inches above the containers of cleaning chemicals. These chemicals were in large crocks lined up at the back of a large soapstone sink under the fume hood and filled by the foreman only. Walt did not know what the chemicals were but was cautioned to always wear long thick rubber gloves, a face mask, and a familiar type lab apron. He also had to roll up his shirtsleeves so they would not get wet. All these personal safety chores had to be done before selection of the links.

Links were placed into a two quart sized ceramic container with many small drain holes along the sides and bottom. This was called a washer. When the washer filled with links was inserted into the first batch of chemicals and swished from side to side or in an alternating circular motion the chemical reaction began between the copper of the links and chemical. That reaction produced dark colored fumes that were immediately sucked up by the hood. A silent count to three, remove, drain, and into the next crock and on to another one or two and a final crock being filled with running water ended the cleaning process. But the links needed drying before they could be soldered together. The solder was of a metal formula which melted at a certain degree in a fire. The design of the sprinkler allowed the sprinkler to be screwed to a water pipe under pressure. If the solder melted, the links would separate and underlying water pressure would gush out spraying water into the room below.

Hey Gunther! Why Are You Here?

The link drying process was ingenious to Walt, never having seen anything like it. The cleaned wet links were dumped into a shallow square wire screened tray basket that could slide on two angle iron rails. These rails spanned the length of a long table with sides and holding dry sawdust. Dry sawdust from the table was scooped on to the wet links and mixed by hand. The sawdust took on the water and depending upon how much sawdust was used the links began to dry. The wet sawdust fell through the screen and when shaken from the links new dry sawdust was applied and mixed. When completely dry the links were placed into a crock and brought next door to the soldering room. In that room about nine women applied the solder in various stages of assembly until the links were ready for further assembly into the final sprinkler product. Walt was able to produce more than enough links to keep the soldering room busy for the day. There was time for 'visiting' with the women next door and sometimes with other employees in the factory. However most of this 'spare time' was occupied by odd jobs assigned by Dave the foreman. It was an all day summer job with half days on Saturday morning. Walt's pay was very good; work was pleasant, and much better than caddying the summer before. It was sometimes possible to work during the winter after school for a couple of hours or during the holiday breaks. His college funds were growing. His mother never asked him about his wages but was curious about his college fund. But by this time she knew he was interested in going to Alaska sometime to see what it was about. Cornell, and Uncle Hans was no longer mentioned. Neither had his wanting to go to Alaska until he received and filled out an application to the University of Alaska.

Walt Fluegel

CHAPTER TWENTY-ONE: THE JEWELRY BUSINESS

In the meantime his initial meeting with Miss Roland and his developing interest in sea shell art began to occupy more of his evenings after doing home work assignments. He could easily concentrate on the art while listening to radio comedy or variety programs or just music from station WQXR. The catalog of seashell supplies showed findings for making earrings, pins, broaches, necklaces and suggestions on making decorative cards. Once he asked Miss Roland for advice on how to get started on techniques it seemed very natural to take chances on various design and color modification. Some packets of shells were natural colors but other packets were stained in a variety of colors. Size ranged between a quarter inch to half inch.

At one time when he was in the Woolworth five and dime store he saw some custom Jewelry and examined them carefully. The earrings were made of something other than seashells but looked very similar to what he was doing. What impressed him about his own work was the realistic look of the flowers, small delicate flowers, and the glue holding the seashells together was not visible. This impressed most of his future costumers who were willing to pay $1.25 for a pair of earrings. In those days that was a lot of money and this made the college fund grow.

There were times when Walt remembered the care he had to take when he transplanted seedlings into flats. He had to have nimble fingers. However, when working to pick up small shells he still had to be nimble when he used curved and pointed end forceps. Too much pressure with the forceps and some delicate shells would break. He had a choice of using tweezers or forceps but tweezers seemed clumsy in comparison. The artificially colored shells were robust shells. This hobby became more concentrated with the accumulation of earrings and matching pins. Miss Roland accepted some as 'payment' for her help but what would happen if Walt could also sell them to total strangers? Miss Lewis the vice principal of A B Davis was interested in seeing Walt's progress. She bought a few for her young nieces. It became possible to make more and more Jewelry because bouts of getting colds and school forced Walt to quit working part time for the Reliable Sprinkler Company and spend more time at home. But if he was ever to sell seriously he had to find a way to carry or display his wares. While these thoughts were present, other events such as becoming an American citizen vied for attention.

BECOMING A CITIZEN AND CONFIRMATION CLASS

On special times today such as the Fourth of July we see TV news snippets of people in a courtroom setting being given small American Flags. Sometimes people would raise their right hand and then repeating words said by an official, or once the words were said a distant voice announces that the people we see are now American citizens. Joy, waving the small flags, hugging each other, or showing the naturalizing certificate with a TV voice-over announcing something to the effect that so many people in America are now new citizens. And then in an instant later a different news item is presented. With these similar images seen year after year, which one accompanied Walt's proceedings? The official time was May 2, 1946, but TV was not known then. There were black and white movies. WW2 was still going on. What was the setting at his time? Who was there to witness the event? How did he feel now that he was a citizen? Was anyone at A B Davis interested? What did this piece of paper mean? The paper that gave a description of hair and eye color and said he had a scar on his chin. Did he feel different from others around him? This is a mystery of blended memory. However, he remembered he did not feel different. He did not have any allegiance to any foreign power before he applied so he did not have to regret or think of his past. He thought he was always a citizen as much as anyone else in school. It was almost akin to the previous time a few years earlier of his religious confirmation class into the church.

Before he left the Wartburg, Walter's mother promised Miss Miller and the Wartburg to have Walter confirmed into the Lutheran Church within the next year. He would now be 15 years old. One afternoon a week, (Wednesday?) some students of this age were allowed to be dismissed one hour earlier to attend their church lessons prior to confirmation. One lesson remembered by Walter was very impressive. The pastor was instilling the idea of sin and its lasting mark on the soul. He used a closet door and pretended to have a hammer and a nail. The door was the soul, the nail was the sin, and the hammer was the temptation or situation that made the hammer drive the nail or sin into the soul. Yes, the nail could eventually be removed, but the resulting scar of the nail or sin was now on the soul. Forever. But on Judgment day the scars could be counted. As his years progressed into adulthood he wondered on this analogy and the idea of starting all over again and not being marked a "sinner" forever. Was a simple mistake a sin he wondered? Can we learn from our mistakes and who is to judge what a sin was? During the lessons he never questioned his pastor but he remembered his own questions and other thoughts about them from time to time. Confirmation day did come. He was now considered a Christian. A confirmation class photograph was taken with the preacher. On that same day Walter and his mother visited with friends of his mother in the afternoon and that was that. Nothing out of the ordinary happened. No special feeling about being confirmed. No celebration. No understanding as to the meaning of being declared a Christian. He did not change his daily routines. However, it did not stop him from thinking about other religions and their philosophies and why there were so many different religions in the world.

ACTUAL SALES OF JEWELRY

But beyond middle teen time, Walter could not dwell on any one topic for long such as religion or patriotism, but on going to school and doing school activities or having a job to earn college money and realizing he was growing up. At the Sprinkler factory and at high school he began to take more than a casual interest in the women and girls around him. At the factory some of the women would tease him and ask if he had a girl friend and at high school the other boys hinted that they did have a girlfriend. Attempts at having a date had its complications; a notable one being that some of his girl classmates did not date boys younger or shorter than themselves. He never looked his age and it did not help to have a short stature. Other times girls shorter than he accepted his invitation to be taken to the latest movie with a soda after and a walk home. Sometimes one of his dates wanted to go bowling especially if her parents also wanted to bowl.

During this time he managed to make a display case for his seashell Jewelry. It could hold up to 25 or more pairs of ear rings on the upright side when he opened it and several pins and clasps on the horizontal section when he opened his case on a table. It was sturdy enough to be carried on a bus or trolley but it had to be held by a handle upright all the time. At his mothers suggestion he also had a pocket large enough to hold a 4 by 5 inch hand mirror. With his mother's help the case was covered in dark denim cloth and on top held together with a window lock near the handle. It was very plain on the outside in comparison to when the case was opened. The contrast between the dark outside and inside colorful contents always surprised the potential customers. And who were the customers? He took one big chance on seeing people he already knew.

It was early spring when he visited for the first time the Reliable Sprinkler Factory after being absent all winter. He arrived at noon when he knew many of the women employees had their lunch break outside at a couple of picnic tables. They were pleased to see him and curious about what was in the case he carried. When he opened it some women exclaimed at the beauty while they also instinctively reached for the earrings mounted on their thin cardboard holders. They asked each other how the color looked on each other. When Walt saw some reach for their purse to look for their makeup kit he directed them to use his much larger hand mirror. It was just by accident that the day before was payday and there was "spare change" for such an impulse purchase. At that time in the 1940s no one seemed to mind paying $1.25 for a set of earrings. Some of the solder room women asked him all sorts of questions. Some were personal questions.

Yes Walt, did have dates with girls and one 'steady' girlfriend, which seemed to please some of the older women. Yes, he was trying to save enough money to attend college for at least one year. But why Alaska? Hard to say, but adventure and travel were acceptable reasons. He also heard, "I have a sister working in such and such a place and she would love to see your things. Do you know where that place is?" And thus Walt found out where other women worked in a factory or in an office as a secretary and bookkeeper. He began to know when payday occurred and thus his college fund grew. In a way making and selling the Jewelry gave him more time to visit the county swimming pool on hot days for an afternoon swim or visit the library more often. Also it was nice having a 'steady' girlfriend he could take to the movies and smooch with after.

Hey Gunther! Why Are You Here?

Walt Fluegel

CHAPTER TWENTY-TWO: NAZIS AND GRANDMOTHER

The outside world was more important to the adults, especially Walter's mother. WW2 finally ended and with letters or phone calls to Aunt Trina in Long Island, Emelie got bits and pieces of news from Germany. Relatives in Germany did not know that Emelie moved to Mount Vernon. Trina was the only direct American contact. The Chicago contacts were lost.

CARE packages and letters were sent to Germany to a sister or brother in hopes of gathering more news. It wasn't long after the CARE packages were sent that return letters reached Trina first and sent to Emelie soon after. And then later, letters came directly to Emelie. The news was mixed; some relatives survived the war others died. Emelie's mother, Walter's grandmother had died during the war. But as more letters arrived a paragraph or sentence from one brother or sister told the complete story. It seemed that during the war there were occasional food shortages. Food went to the army and productive workers, good German workers. Older people such as Emelie's mother who no longer could work were denied food but in the case of the bakery family someone had the doctor put her to sleep. Emelie did not know who, but found out through other letters, several members of the family signed the legal papers permitting this procedure. It was a practice repeated in several families in Sparneck, Bavaria. Emelie made no more contact with her German brothers and sisters after knowing the whole story. For Emelie that ended the Nazi era. And being an American citizen she no longer belonged to the

Hey Gunther! Why Are You Here?

country of Germany. She did not tell Walter any of this until years later when they were both living in Alaska.

Walt Fluegel

CHAPTER TWENTY-THREE: ADVICE; LIVE NOW NOT IN THE FUTURE

When he became more and more determined to go to Alaska it seemed to others nothing could change his mind. Miss Lewis made suggestions that he live in the present and not in the future by thinking about Alaska so often. Walt tried to vary his social experiences in school. The Advanced Science Club was one diversion in time and being a Marshal (Hall police) occurred only during class change time. Miss Lewis wanted him to be more social. He tried to go to informal dance times in the gym but an old lack of following rhythm—(as in the band practice in the Wartburg) closed off this activity. Not too many boys were interested in the Punching Bag Club, but here the fast rat-a-tat bounce and punch rhythm was mastered to a degree. But muscle power needed to sustain the activity dwindled. If three or four other boys were waiting their turn in rotation a good hour or more of fun filled the rest of the afternoon after classes. But not everyone in the club participated often enough to keep it going for long. The punching bag was hung on a hook in the alcove leading to the gym.

THE GYM TEAM

Next door, members of the Gym Team did their exercises and challenged each other on the parallel bars, high bar, rings, rope and other exercise apparatus. The John Atlas syndrome pervaded many of the youth desire to have big muscles at that time. (No body wanted to be 98 pound weakling.) In a sense these fellows were in good muscular shape but Martin was an exception. His upper body was in fine form, but he had skinny legs. Try as he might he could not improve his leg shape hence leg strength, but he could do bench presses equal to the others. Howard was very good on the high bar doing rotations but he being taller than all the others had to make sure his knees were slightly bent so he would not bang into part of the slanted ceiling during the height of his rotation. Every now and then the rope was lowered and each member was timed to see who shimmied fastest to the top.

One day while Walt was watching from the gym door, Johnny, spotted him and said, "Hey Walt, can you climb the rope?" Walt walked into the gym without saying a word and looked up at the rope as it met the high ceiling. He knew how to shimmy but instead he grabbed the rope and hand over hand began to climb. He did not use his legs as required in official competitions. He reached the top and shouted 'good.' He was surprised at his accomplishment, but once up there he had to be careful on how to descend. He did not want to slide and burn his hands on the way down. It seemed his punching bag 'training' helped him in grip and arm strength. Also his body was small and not very heavy. So when the others tried to climb they had to resort to shimmy using their legs. This rope climbing made Walt an unofficial member of the Gym team. At one time they ganged up on him while he was watching them. They asked him how much he weighed. "115," he said. They picked him up and passed him around over their heads. After this first time he got used to this antic. They never dropped him. When they got tired of passing him around he was placed on the gym mats with a good laugh. Sometimes one or two of the gymnasts went to the punching bag and rat-tatted for a while. (As a note in passing, every time the Olympics are shown on TV, Walt makes special note to watch the gymnastic events.) However, in general Walt did not have the kind of body for the high school sports world to admire because of his scoliosis and lack of sustained intense muscular effort. Track / field and swimming sports were so intense for him that he dropped out early and just admired his classmates.

Walt Fluegel

A STEADY GIRL FRIEND?

Aside from after school life of clubs and social life for students of wealthy backgrounds there was hardly a distinction. However, many other students had part time jobs during the week so the social life or dating life between boys and girls was geared to a new movie that came to town, occasional dances, or maybe a church function. In his senior year, Walt occasionally met the parents of his 'steady.' While Walt was a senior to graduate in June, she would be graduating in January, a half year later. It was common to walk with a date to the movie theater. Sometimes if the weather was about to rain, her folks would drive them to the movie, and come back for them later at the soda fountain near by. One time his 'steady' parents invited him to a supper meal.

Conversation was cordial but mostly with her father. Her father was a self-made successful businessman and was interested in Walt's Jewelry business and plans for Alaska and his further education. But as the meal was progressing Walt noticed his steady's mother was done with her meal. When he looked in her direction she just pointed to Walt's plate, not saying a word. Walt stopped talking and finished soon after. Walt was pleased to realize that with his 'steady's' father, someone, some other adult outside of school activities understood what his goals were. But his 'steady' became less steady as time came towards graduation. It seemed she became more interested in a home-room classmate of Walt. They had more classes in common and therefore could converse or visit during class rotations in the hallways while Walt was doing his Marshal duties. Consequently by graduation time Walt did not attend the prom and because he still could not, or did not dance, that function was never planted in his memory.

GETTING READY TO GO TO ALASKA

As summer progressed and college money was accumulating from the jewelry business details of making travel plans became more serious. From New York City to Chicago then to Salt Lake City to see the Mormon Temple was part of the plan. After that, on to Seattle, and then on a plane to Fairbanks, Alaska. During early summer Walt got curious about the Mormon faith and searched the Mount Vernon library for reading material. The pioneering spirit against lots of odds and the founding of a new religion here in the USA appealed to his own sense of adventure. Only this time it was by train and only one person satisfying his own curiosity, not wagon trains with lots of people following a charismatic figure across the open plains. About two weeks before the University of Alaska began to accept its new enrollment of students Walt was ready to travel. A duffel bag of clothes had already been shipped to the U of A earlier. A small suitcase was prepared for the immediate train travel across country. Traveler's Checks were purchased and would be hidden in different places on his person and in the suitcase. During all this last summer time his mother never indicated how she felt about his leaving for Alaska. But she did not appear happy. His plans were to start traveling across the country within two weeks and be at the University of Alaska to register at least three days before classes started.

Walt Fluegel

CHAPTER TWENTY-FOUR: TO THE TRAIN STATION ON THE WAY TO ALASKA

Because less than 10% of high school students ever went to college in those days, Walt's mother basked in the realization that he must have been an exceptional person. All the people she knew indicated as much, but she was conflicted. She only knew him for about five years, not the detailed years of childhood but of a boy becoming an adolescent. He seemed confident in handling his life, the making of money, meeting people, supported by his teachers, getting interested in girls (which was a problem for her) and charting his own course all within the short time from being in the orphanage.

They did different things together during the various summers on weekends when she was not involved with her clients. But the day arrived to say final good-byes to Miss Hardy and Miss Roland across the street in the apartment house. Other neighbors also knew what was happening too, including the Kruger Family who lived across the street next to the apartment house. Patsy Kruger graduated high school two years ago and was working in an office; Haze K returned from the army and was in college studying to be a physical education teacher. Mister Kruger was a self-employed carpenter 'handy man' and Mrs. Kruger also did day's work but did not have clients who needed someone who also did cooking. The landladies said their good-byes but expected Walter would visit next summer after the first year. Mister Kruger gave Walter and his mother a ride to the Mount Vernon train station in his rickety pick-up truck late in the afternoon. That train went directly to Grand Central Station in New York City.

119

Hey Gunther! Why Are You Here?

All this time on the train, mother and son said nothing to each other, each wrapped in their own thoughts. They had supper together in silence in a restaurant near Grand Central Station.

On this night Walter did not remember if they had a supper in a restaurant at the Station or at a nearby (Horn and Hardart) Automat on the way to the theater. Whenever they went into the City it was routine to go there without being rushed. His mother seemed to know how to time everything because trains, busses, trolleys and movie shows were always on time and she could estimate how long a meal-time would be. At the Automat individual sandwiches, bowls of soup, even pies were displayed in little cubicles lining the walls. A whole section would be devoted to different sandwiches for example. By placing the right coinage in a slot and rotating a handle one could lift a glass door lid to the cubicle and take out the sandwich. Almost immediately the door would shut and behind the door one could see that the cubicle would rotate around and a moment later return with a new sandwich. It would cost more coins to get another sandwich. It wasn't the fact that someone had to fill the empty cubicle that gave a certain lasting impression on Walter but the women in the glass booth dispensing coins in exchange for dollar bills.

Not everybody had loose coins available, but these change makers had a certain skill of reaching into a deep coin filled tray grabbing nickels and sliding just the right amount of coins towards the customer, all in several quick motions. They were always correct and after a while regular customers including Walters mother never counted the coins. To add to the wonder of instant counting was the look of the fingers of these skillful women. Were they wearing a kind of fine glove or was it metal dust that rubbed off the coins that made their fingers look dark and gray? This curiosity was never satisfied. Starting on this night waiting for the train these routine things and thoughts were slowly being embedded in distant memory banks pushed along with new thoughts of coming adventures.

120

Walt Fluegel

IN RADIO CITY MUSIC HALL

Grand Central Station was familiar to both of them with its large open space and its famous clock, the tall ceiling, the ticket counters, and the distant sounding of train departures through the loudspeaker system. Outside the station it was a different world with its tall buildings. Since leaving the Wartburg, Walter and his mother sometimes walked from the station to Radio City Music Hall to take in a movie followed by a floorshow. When she first told him the theater could hold almost 6,000 people it amazed him. He got used to it after several visits in those few years between living in the orphanage and living with his mother.

When it was possible they would take in either a Christmas or the Easter show depending upon what his mothers' client needs were for those holidays, or just go into NY City now and then to see a show. Throughout his later life every time the Dunkirk war episode is mentioned either in the news or seeing an incident in a movie a flashback of Radio City comes to mind. That movie was Mrs. Minniver. But the most impressive long lasting remembrance for Walt occurred because of one impressive floorshow music.

BOLERO

When Walt in later life began to routinely have his radio tuned to a classical music station he sometimes heard the ta-da—dmm-dmm-dmm: ta-da—dmm-dmm-dmm of Maurice Ravel's "Bolero." It opens up memory of a spectacular routine displayed in the Radio City Theater. He does not remember the floorshow of the particular event but does remember those snare drums beating to the cadence presented by the Bolero! There was a certain repeat of the music again and again but never quite the same in the repeat musical phasing. All the drummers, 20 on each side of the theater were aligned along the right and left side walls with their snare drums beating. Six thousand people heard the snare drumbeats above the music while Walt's eyes were riveted only on the drummers. Never mind what was on the stage. The music came from the orchestra pit and the drummers were imitating the rhythmic chords of the music. It was loud and impressive and long lasting. When the Bolero was finished and the drummers departed with applause; the floorshow continued with other routines.

As usual any floorshow always displayed the Rockets with their tap dancing. All the women dancers, stretching from one side of the stage to the other, seemed to be the same height and form. All were dressed in modestly revealing costume that usually included fluff of some sort, and plenty of reflective glitter on the costume or on dancing shoes. What impressed Walt's mother was the ability of the dancers to kick their legs high without losing balance and being very precise to the music being played. In special dance maneuvers the music would become low volume, or pause, allowing the tap-dance rhythm to spread over the audience. It wasn't the precision his mother saw that impressed Walter, but just seeing many young women dancing that way. He never saw that type of dancing at the orphanage and in any other place except at Radio City Music Hall. But, shows come to an end and of course when the days outing came to an end it was always a walk back to the Grand Central Station.

But in this last trip to Grand Central Station they remained quiet by waiting for the announcement for the overnight train to Chicago. University would start in the middle of September, a bit later than the usual public school times that started the day after Labor Day. So his journey to Alaska would start from the Station that night. Mrs. Gunther made sure Walter had his train tickets for his entire journey to Seattle. Walter also assured his mother that he could figure out how to get to the airport in Seattle to fly to Fairbanks, Alaska. He knew what the plane fare was and had Traveler's Checks for the amount. Finally it was announced for passengers to board their train. There was a kiss and hug followed by a picking up of the small suitcase and the turning around to follow other passengers. Walter never turned around to get one more last look of his mother. He would not see her again for three, maybe fours more years.

Walt Fluegel

CHAPTER TWENTY-FIVE: ON THE RAILS AND PLANE

Walt settled into a window seat and watched the scenery blink, blink, blink by. Because it was near the end of summer the remaining daylight seemed to fade fast and more so because of the mesmerizing rhythm of the wheels clicking over the rails. Occasionally the train stopped to pick up more passengers. Somehow he managed to get a pillow from the porter so he could rest his head against the window and fall asleep sitting up.

As with other times where memory of actual events and seeing movies of people on trains blend into one another over the years which image should he described. Which is the real event as witnessed by Walt Gunther? What scenery held interest to be embedded and not confused with another? How could one distinguish one cityscape from another just from looking out the window? And how could one farm speeding by be able to distinguish one from another? How and what kind of decor did the passenger cars differ from the dining cars? How was the service in the dining car compare with the cafe type car? Here is where memory may prove to have been altered over time but assuming there was such a thing as a cafe car the memory seems clear. It seems to have occurred on a train because the memory scenery keeps moving along too. The cafe car was designed for those passengers who wanted a quick meal. Something from this trip had to pin down a memory, an unusual memory distinguishing itself from the grand mixture accumulated over a lifetime. It was an incident in the cafe car that distinguished itself because of a definition of something on the menu.

Hey Gunther! Why Are You Here?

I'LL HAVE IT

The cafe car was designed in the manner of a drugstore soda fountain and snack bar. The quick-order cooks handed a menu to a customer to check off what they wanted from the limited menu. Cooking was done behind the counter where customers could sit on mounted stools but there was plenty of room for other people to walk next to the window and perhaps wait for someone to leave when finished. When Walt entered the car all seats were taken so he waited next to the window in the middle of the car. Three other people were also waiting, but were concentrating on an argument between one of the passenger-customer and one of the cook staff. "But sir, you checked off beef burger on the menu, and that is what I fixed for you."

"But I don't want that, I want a hamburger. This thing's got gravy all over it and other stuff!"

"Sorry sir!, you did not check off hamburger."

Again another protest from the customer, "What's the difference between a beef burger and a hamburger anyway?" It was enough of a ruckus where all eyes were either on the cook or the customer. Then when it seemed that the head cook had to come to settle the dispute a loud voice came from one of the waiting passengers: "Mister Cook if he does not want that, I'll have it." All eyes turned to the window where Walt was standing.

"Young man, I have to hand it to you. I'll be done in a minute so you can have my seat," said a middle aged man to Walt. The cook looked relieved too because he was going to the garbage can with the disputed order and stopped in mid stride and also looked toward Walt and made a grin. Walt did not worry about the difference between a beef burger or a hamburger. He took a chance and satisfied his hunger. At this stage in Walt's life he was willing to try new things in new places. In Alaska he would hear, see, taste, learn, and have many different experiences; different from his adolescent life in Mount Vernon NY. Things much different from his sheltered life of the Wartburg. He was all of 19 at the time, and eager to learn.

Walt Fluegel

CHICAGO AND SALT LAKE CITY

At the time of a day or two of being a tourist in Chicago seems not much different from being in New York City with its tall business towers and stores. Yes, the city was next to a lake but New York also nestled next to a body of water. However, the Field Museum of Natural History in Chicago was the main attraction for Walt. He wanted to make comparisons to the New York American Museum of Natural History that he visited from time to time with his mother. But because each museum rotates their main attraction it was not a serious comparison, only a wonderment to experience again in a different city. The large and small fossils of Prehistoric creatures were never a dull moment at the American Museum nor the dioramas depicting their time. It was a big difference from seeing pictures from National Geographic or books from the bookmobile and actually seeing the real thing a few feet away. These few visits to the American Museum or the Hayden Planetarium to see sky shows were accompanied by his mother. But now in Chicago in a strange place he was on his own time schedule and coming to the realization that he was absorbing knowledge or information by his own searches into the world around him.

After Chicago the next train stop for Walt was Salt Lake City. He had an interest in following up on his reading of the Mormons. As with the Chicago stopover he checked into the YMCA for the night and inquired about trips to the Great Salt Lake and visiting the Mormon temple and take their tours. During that first morning while waiting on the bench for a bus that would take him the Great Salt Lake he noticed a drinking fountain near the bus stop sign that kept spouting it's water. Occasionally a passerby leaned over to take a sip but not make any attempt to turn the water off. There did not seem to be a way to stop the flow. Someone else came by, took a sip and just as he was about to leave, Walt asked him how to turn off the water. "They keep this flowing during the tourist time to remind folks about the early pioneer days. They say the water is in honor of Brigham Young and him saying "this is the place." You must be a tourist?" Walt nodded a yes. "This is the place,'" echoed in his mind from reading about the Mormon trek and Brigham Young. A few more comments about Salt Lake City were made by this pedestrian which gave Walt the impression he would have a good day ahead. Just then his bus arrived.

He asked the driver just to make sure and the driver responded that this being the end of the tourist time there will be very few people at the lake. "I just want to see it, I have read a lot about this country, it is all new to me."

GREAT SALT LAKE

It was new. A lake was not new, but a very salty lake was new. Seeing a lake with mountainous terrain was not new either because he had seen many a lake in upstate New York on hitchhiking trips, and having seen many a National Geographic magazine photos. But the stories about the great salt lake were new. In the tourist information area at the lake, Walt saw photos and read their captions. He also learned about the brine shrimp and brine flies and decided he did not have to try swimming in the concentrated salt water. Besides it was a chilly morning. The little whiff of marine smell did not bother him because he was use to the marine smell when he went swimming or row boating at Rye Beach not far from Mount Vernon. His stay at the lake was brief but he was pleased with his visual exposure.

But exposure of his mind to an entirely different thought from some 'official' Mormons on Mormonism was becoming a reality after his initial curiosity of reading books a few months before his trip began. A whole afternoon was spent listening to several speakers talk about the origin of the religion itself, the establishment of groups in one town or another and being chased out, then moving on and looking after each other as they finally settled down in what is now Utah. For the moment that afternoon Walt did not bother ruminating about the origin but what are the Mormons doing now in their own society. He was impressed by their tight social commitments to each other and care of the less fortunate. Their commitment to education at all levels made itself known when each of the young speakers told of their background in what colleges they were attending and what kind of degree they hope to earn.

126

Walt Fluegel

Questions from the audience were answered without hesitation. The most favorite one being about polygamy. In one case the young man said one of his grandfathers did have several wives and he was descended from one of those wives but now the church does not permit polygamy. Questions about the temple, how it was built, and going inside and being a Mormon were all answered, even questions of who spoke for the church and the obligation of being a missionary to spread the faith over the world. But as in many a time when Walt began to dig deeper into a subject he needed time to think about all this new information. At the end of hearing these small talks it was getting late and the day was ending. He also did a lot of walking to see the various monuments around the city dedicated to the pioneers who eventually created the state of Utah.

One more Salt Lake City obligation Walt set for himself was to visit the Mormon Tabernacle and listen to the organ play while its music was on a national radio broadcast. The Tabernacle was open to the public earlier than the official broadcast time to allow an audience to assemble. If the choir was going to sing perhaps the attendance would be at full capacity. Before the broadcast started an announcer told the audience about the making of the building, the acoustics, and the citizens who sang in the Tabernacle Choir. It was an impressive talk, but when the music began to play Walt realized his interest in organ music was not as keen as his interest in the nature of the religion that nurtured this expression. He was polite and remained seated until the program was finished. When he finally left Salt Lake City heading towards Seattle, Washington his thoughts did not dwell on the intricacies of Mormonism but the Alaska journey ahead. He was not aware that there were some Mormons at the experimental station at the University of Alaska and other Mormons living in Fairbanks.

The passage of time from Mount Vernon to Seattle was in a way a blending of being on a train for hours going from East to West with few major stops, a lot of different scenery passing by, and reading paper-back book science fiction stories. Sleep on the train was mostly in an upright position with a rented pillow for the night. Meals were routinely adequate, and other passengers were a blend of ordinary folks, and none of them wanted to know why Walt was traveling in the same direction they were traveling. And he too, kept his curiosity about them to himself. Before he boarded the commercial Alaska Airlines plane, from Seattle to Fairbanks, he did send a postcard to his mother telling her all was going well. There were no details.

FIRST TIME ON A PLANE

It did not bother Walt that this was the first time he flew on a commercial airplane. This travel had to be done and if other people traveled this way why have dark thoughts about it. In some of his reading about travel in Alaska it was common to use a bush pilots transport in small planes to get from one town to another. There were no roads to speak of between towns in the Territory of Alaska. Another way to get to Fairbanks would have been to take a boat from Seattle to Anchorage and then a train to Fairbanks. But all that would take more time than he had planned. The hum of airplane engines was constant compared to the click-it-ty-click of the train travel across country. The plane's movement did not seem bumpy or have a swaying motion either. Even though he flew over mountains, everything below looked flat and reminiscent of seeing air photos of rugged landscape. Walt found out later this particular plane he was on was from WW2 surplus but converted to civilian use. The cabin had the barest essentials for sound deadening but was comfortable. It took about 8 hours to get to Fairbanks from Seattle. He was now many thousand miles from Mount Vernon in the last frontier, the Territory of Alaska. Population at the time was about 130,000 in a land mass about half the size of the lower 48 states.

SPARSENESS

Upon landing he was not prepared for the lack of bigness and activity or the abundance of sparseness. The airport buildings seemed far apart, and the ride from the airport to downtown seemed closed in by spruce or aspen or alder trees. The leafy trees were already turning yellow. It was very rural. In comparison to what he was familiar with in Mount Vernon. The bus service from the airport dropped Walt and several other passengers off at what was the main bus stop in town next to the local movie theater. This terminal had no resemblance to what he was used to back in Mount Vernon or New York City. As weeks passed the bus schedule and timing was very familiar. The road too was not paved but was a gravel road that occasionally needed regrading. He soon learned that if he missed the bus he could walk three miles by train track or hitch a ride on the road but that was a five mile gamble. In winter there was no hesitation in getting a ride into town. If you were lucky enough to have a Saturday night date with one of the women students on campus one always took the bus. Very few students owned cars at that time. Although most students lived on campus the total enrollment would be near 200. Only 20 of them were women students.

Hey Gunther! Why Are You Here?

Walt Fluegel

CHAPTER TWENTY-SIX: AT THE UNIVERSITY OF ALASKA

In that same week of arrival, dorm rooms were assigned but returning students had first choice. Most rooms provided for two roommates, but a few held three beds or only one bed. Walt asked to be placed with a former student so he could learn the ropes faster and get familiar with routines. Walt used to have a roommate on the New Farm at the Wartburg but Jack H was so different from anyone he ever met before or since. When Walt and other fellow dormers had bull sessions and someone mentioned Jack H there usually was a groan from someone. Jack H did not mind openly castigating "the Judge" who happened to be the president of the University of Alaska. But in summary most others thought of him as a malcontent or agitator and wondered if he was a Communist. That was a time all "misguided" people were called Communists if anyone doubted someone in authority. In private, George G whom most older students respected, quietly explained that among other things not to like about the "judge" he owned many acres of land around the university and set a high price for anyone wanting to buy a small lot. So before any real formal education began at the university Walt was slowly beginning to learn about the "frontier" of Alaska in the political as well as the geological sense. He learned a lot just by listening and by not being too inquisitive about motives, only facts.

In those first days of being on campus Walt became well aware that the university was relatively new compared to universities he heard about while he was in high school at A B Davis. The Main classroom building of wood frame construction was perched on a knoll that

131

overlooked the Tanana valley and below the knoll lay the College flats. On campus there were several wood frame dormitories and only four buildings made of concrete and a fifth one being built, the Geophysical Institute. The other concrete buildings were Hess Hall (the women's dorm), Eielson serving in part as the administration building, and next door to it was the gymnasium. Further out, on campus was the power plant. This building supplied water, electricity, and steam heat to all buildings. A campus laundry was nestled in the back area of the power plant. The cafeteria was in the basement of Club men's dorm, but Walt resided in the Main men's dorm. The Vets dorm housed returning WW2 veterans taking advantage of the GI Bill. All the men's dorms were of wood construction, sheet rock wall paneling and generally thought to be former army barracks. Most rooms were painted an institutional green but some were painted colors preferred by the last occupant. Warmth was no problem in winter. Away from the general cluster of buildings, married students were housed in several trailers, also supplied with water, electricity and steam heat. Some faculty families rented small homes not too far from the Geophysical building. But to inquire about the history of the place was not as important as to being there for a higher education.

REASON FOR BEING THERE

The "real reason" why some students were in Alaska rather than going to well established schools were revealed little by little over the tenure of a few years. Walt's first roommate, Jack H for example, probably was trying to hide from the law in another state. He understood from letters back home that so long as he remained in that god-forsaken place in the Alaska territory no one was going after him to return. Another room mate Jeff T, happened to "put a bun in the oven" with a high school girl in Newark NJ. He was at the U of A to study mining engineering, but within a year the girl's father enticed him back with a generous offer of paying for his college if Jeff married his daughter. Much later after Jeff T left, George G met a former woman student wheeling a baby carriage on the streets of Anchorage. Jeff T had promised the girl he had an emergency at home and would come back to resume their friendship and their studies.

Walt Fluegel

After her baby was born all her letters to Jeff T were returned unopened. A few students came from coastal towns of Alaska and had worked in canneries and knew that a college education meant a better life than factory life and what else was there to do in winter. Many others knew that gold was not the only mineral to be mined in Alaska and knew the mining professors could direct them towards other mining ventures. Anthropology transfer students thought Alaska a good outlet to round out their overall studies and stayed only a semester or two. Agriculture was an attraction for some students especially those from Alaska or the northern states of Minnesota or Wisconsin.

After a year or so at the U of A someone asked Walt during a bull session why he chose agriculture when he had no experience in farming. He at first said for the adventure of it, but when pressed he tried to tell them he was willing to give it a try. Maybe he could help domesticate the musk oxen. That bought jeers and comments especially from the more robust of the other Ag students. "You are so skinny Walt you don't have the strength to make it on a farm and those musk oxen will never let you get close to them. Have you ever handled large animals before like a horse?" He had to admit his courses in agriculture seemed inadequate especially when the classes met with some local farmers. Also he was having some doubts about the value and work at the experimental station. It seemed like a regular farm that produced milk and eggs for the campus. He did not understand what their work was all about and got vague answers concerning the domestication of the musk oxen. When at one time George G happened to be hearing discussions on why some students chose the U of A, he calmly said he began to read a lot of poetry from Robert Service and read Jack London's books while he was in the army and just wanted to live that kind of life for a while. As an afterthought he said it was like running away from home. He came from Nebraska.

BEING PEGGED

Saturday—in the afternoon—after lunch, at the end of the first week of enrollment, several main-dormers decided to look over the town

133

after lunch and maybe see a movie. A mass of them took the bus into town including Walt. Although the theater was next to the bus stop and there was time before it opened, a sophomore who knew the town suggested they all go to the bar down the street for a beer. The place looked like a small restaurant outside and inside but there were very few people this early in the day. So without asking, someone pushed two tables together and everyone found a chair. Soon the bartender came over and began to ask what anyone wanted. He named off the kinds of beer he had available. Each one named "his poison" but when it came to Walt all he could say was, "Do you have chocolate milk?" The normal buzzing stopped and one of the guys said out loud, "Good-bye Walt." More "good-byes" were echoed by the others with laughter. All Walt could do was shrug his shoulders and say, "I will see you guys later," as he got up and walked out of the bar. Thus for his entire stay at the university everyone began to know Walt does not or did not drink. In a land where beer flowed freely, this was a mark of some kind, perhaps a quirk of character.

It was not the first time Walt had entered a bar with a bunch of others. At one time at A B Davis some of the guys decided to go bowling. At the end of one line several of the guys went to the bar and ordered a soda pop but "Wendy" (Wendell) wanted a beer. The attendant looked at him as he started to pour the beer and said, "Are you old enough? Do you have an ID?" Wendy took the beer with one hand and reached in his back pocket with his other hand, pulled out his wallet, and with one motion plopped it on the counter. The attendant took another look at Wendy and said, "That's OK," Wendy and the others went back to play another line. Later Wendy did not mind saying his bluff works every time. If he hesitated that would clue the attendant to actually open the wallet.

Walt was now known for not drinking beer but others too were pegged for their quirks or peculiarities. For example, "Moocher" was known for asking any other smoker for a cigarette during the weekend poker games. "Dr. Agony" was known for giving advice on some medical problems anyone else may be having; but also the way he played ping-pong. He never had any special skill in how to make the ball spin in any direction. He just seemed to put his paddle in the front of the ball no matter how fast or slow it approached him. He just let it bounce over the net. It always landed well on the table and frustrated any opponent. It was agony to play with him. He seldom lost but it was a challenge to some of the better players to keep up their skills. Usually on a Friday night right after supper Gary L always shouted out in the hall way, "Canasta!" and always accumulated a bunch of guys to play the night away; late players did not have Saturday morning classes. After a while Gary was nicknamed "Canasta." "Art" was known for his drawings of cartoons and caricatures. However most everyone was called by first or last name, it didn't matter.

Hey Gunther! Why Are You Here?

Walt Fluegel

CHAPTER TWENTY-SEVEN: GETTING TO KNOW A COUPLE OF PROFESSORS

Any formal education has its book learning, lecture learning, laboratory learning, and seminar type learning all centered on a given discipline. Facts, theories and ideas sometimes flow in and out of each other and a student hopefully grasps what that study meant to him. In one particular biology laboratory afternoon session from Mrs. Carr, students were asked to make drawings of the cross section of a stem. They could also use the textbook to compare the photos with the slide and what they saw under the microscope. They also had to find a way to label neatly the parts of the stem. Mrs. Carr told the students she could not stay the whole afternoon but the lab would be open until the janitor closed it for the night. When finished, the drawings had to be placed in a box on her desk.

A BETTER OBSERVER

The next day before her lecture Mrs. Carr said she did her homework and looked at all the drawings last evening. She was both pleased and disappointed at the same time with some of the drawings. She named no names. She used terms like sloppy, inaccurate, cheating, artistic, and other negative terms. In her first specific comment she asked in general if the students actually looked at the label of the slide and the label in the book. The book label was of one plant cross-section and the slide label was from another, a different plant's cross-section. She said a couple of students copied the book and did not make a drawing of the real thing. The stem structures had the same features but their proportions were different.

With chalk in hand she drew on the board what some students drew and next to it the way it should have been drawn. At that moment one of the students dared to exclaim, "We are not artists!" Without any show of anger or indicating the student should be chastised for being rude, Mrs. Carr said in a calm voice, "I am so glad you said that." And continued with, "This is a science class not an art class. In science we aim to be accurate in our reporting of what we see and measure." She went on and said that artists create, and imagine things or give impressions of things so as of now in drawings, students should record what they see and record accurately. If a cell is round, draw a round cell, but if it were square and had a thick cell wall draw a square cell with a thick wall. She went on to give other examples and indicated that the students could pick up their drawings later after lecture. There were no grades on the work, but when Walt saw his drawings there were several little notes or marks. These were valuable lessons on being a better observer, the beginnings of becoming a scientist, and from then on Walt intuitively knew he was being given a higher education. (This lesson stayed with him and was useful when he eventually became an academic.)

Lecture information in biology and chemistry classes such as vocabulary and nuance of examining details came at a fast clip compared to what Walt was used to in high school. He was pleased that he had a good beginning from A B Davis but realized constant daily study rather than wait a few days before the scheduled exams would pay off. Mrs. Carr for example gave a pop quiz before the third day of her lecture and graded the exam. Walt got one vocabulary term incorrect and did not expound clearly enough a certain process in an essay question. There was a low level of grumbling from some students but she indicated this was college, no longer high school. It did not take Mrs. Carr long to get to know each of the 20 or so individuals in her class. Walt also began to know Mrs. Carr.

Walt Fluegel

A BETTER WRITER

The first time around for English 101 in summary was a most difficult but interesting class. At high school it was not required to write anything in great detail, perhaps a paragraph, but at college here in the University, weekly writing assignments were routine. Walt had to find the time to absorb the requirements of good writing and apply that to putting his own thoughts down on paper. Although he did a good amount of reading of all sorts he slowly understood there were different grades and kinds of writing. His Eng.101 class pointed this out to him. Some things were easy to read, other things were difficult to understand. Class discussions and examples were another example beside biology of learning nuances in any given discipline of study at college. Even though he liked biology a lot, Walt thought that the ability to write well was the most important topic he could learn. If one could not express what he knows or learned how can he transmit that knowledge clearly to others? But alas, he flunked Eng. 101 and had to repeat it. The same for taking and repeating Eng. 102. In other words it took two years to pass the first year's English courses.

Walt did not feel discouraged in having to repeat these courses because he was convinced it would work for him. He needed to do more writing. As such there were two writing outlets for improving his skills. Those two outlets were two newspapers on campus. The university administration had an official newspaper called the "Farthest North Collegian" which was sent to a wide set of people all over Alaska and some of the lower states and of course to all students and alumni. The second newspaper was called the "Polar Star" which was published by the Student government representing views from the student point of view. The "Polar Star" may not have agreed on everything the administration was doing but Alaskans did show their independent thinking through the "Polar Star." For the Collegian Walt was given assignments that were edited by a faculty or an administrator editor and at one time a gifted student. Editors were patient with Walt by trying to help him "say it right" and write as a newsman would write. It was a struggle until both editor and student were pleased with the article. With the "Polar Star" any student could submit whatever they wanted but articles had to be in reasonable good taste but still could be critical, cynical, or spoofing the administration or students in the student government. But also good old fashioned reporting of events, or personalities, sports and other events or ideas needing airing were printed. The editor was a student who took his responsibilities seriously and he too struggled with Walt to "get it right."

EXPAND HERE

Although it was not required for acquiring the major in agriculture or in pre-med, Walt took a course in advanced writing. By just passing with a "C" in the freshman Eng. 101 & 102 he knew he needed more training. It was designed for students in their junior and senior years. It required students to write articles or themes in depth and explore a wider vocabulary. There was also a creative writing course where stories were explored but that did not interest him. In the beginning Mister Burns wrote a sentence on the board and asked students to elaborate on the sentence or to add to it. He encouraged students to think in depth or show analysis but not to entertain as one finds in stories. As the course progressed Mister Burns often wrote comments on returned papers, his favorite one being "expand here." Students began to understand what was required. Mister Burns had a different way of grading papers from the other English professor.

First of all there were regular classes for the handful of students. Secondarily as the class progressed Mister Burns required longer length themes but gave two weeks time between new themes. However, one lecture time was omitted as a lecture hour but there was a one-on-one session at that time for students who had a tight class schedule and an arranged time for those who had more flexible time. All students eventually got individual attention on each theme they wrote. Walt always started his writing the first day it was assigned, because he needed lots of time to make corrections. Walt never consulted other students on how they were graded or what the student talked about with Mister Burns. He concentrated only on his own progress. When the individual analysis began, most of his earlier shorter themes showed a 'D' or a 'C' or mostly an 'F' with many a

140

correction in spelling, and the other technical points. But now with the individual attentions there were two grade marks such an A/F or A/C or B/D. Mister Burns explained that the first letter represented the overall process of the work, the thoughts expressed, or the analysis. The second letter represented the mechanics of the writing, the tenses, the spelling, the word order, and so forth.

Fortunately Walt knew how to type and he thought that by handing in assignments in type form was better than handwritten material with lots of erasures. Walt used "onion skin" paper in his typewriter too because it erased with little or no smudging so the paper on first glance looked neat. (Mister Burns also wanted pages stapled not folded and crimped on the corner.) Yes, Mister Burns did appreciate type over script. However he began to notice a peculiar form of error in Walt's material. Whereas previous instructors or editors noticed the same thing, Mister Burns knew the reason. Previous admonitions to Walt from others were, "Be more careful." In spelling, "Don't be so sloppy." "You are not paying attention," and so on. Mister Burns exclaimed, "You seem to transpose your letters," and began to show Walt what he meant. He knew there was a technical name for this difficulty and then also asked if Walt had trouble in math classes. Yes, Walt did. It was sometime later in life that the technical term 'dyslexia' became known to Walt. It was not severe but annoying and frustrating. And when known it might happen, Walt did consult the dictionary more often just to make sure. But there were lapses. One other thing Mister Burns took time explaining was tense and person. It helped; but future, going to happen, did happen, could have happened, if it did happen, and who said what and when became a confusing set of rules. But he did improve. He still had lapses.

PERMAFROST WRITING

No doubt Mister Burns did like to see the improvement and certainly complimented Walt on his subject matter chosen or assigned. Walt enjoyed the investigating part of the assignment especially one assignment in particular. Walt wanted to know more about permafrost and searched the library on the topic. By the use of the card catalog he narrowed down many of the facts but the references seemed old. It seemed to be a new area of investigation for the military in Alaska, right after the Pearl Harbor attack. The construction industry who were building military bases were also interested. The indigenous people had their own way of understanding permafrost By chance Walt asked the librarian if there might be newer reference material. "I think someone in Geology or the Mining department may have something, try there." He tried Geology first with luck. He asked the department head for help. Yes, Walt could use the book but not take it out. He had to use it there. The book was no more than a year old and there were some photographs. One photo was from Fairbanks and it showed the effects of the thawing of permafrost. He found the address listed. After getting enough notes and eventually seeing the old tilted structure Walt wrote his theme. This exercise on permafrost was one more aspect of being in Alaska and knowing more details of his adventure in this land. What made this theme memorable was the compliments given to him by Mister Burns. Mister Burns said he too had a slight interest in permafrost but Walt's report stirred his thoughts too on the subject. He did not realize the geologists on campus had the latest research but he thought he would consult someone he knew at the military base at Ladd Field who might give him some answers.

RAISING STANDARDS

Walt's grade on this permafrost paper was A/C but with very few red marks or corrections. He had noticed for the last two reports he also got A/C but this one had fewer corrections, the best so far. When it appeared that the discussion was about to close. Walt asked Mister Burns if he thought he was improving in his writing. "Oh yes, you are improving but you have lapses."

Walt in frustration looked Mister Burns in the eye and asked, "How come I keep getting a C?" For the slightest moment Walt thought he saw a crinkle of a smile on Mister Burns face just before he said, "I keep raising my standards," and then smiled broadly. Mister Burns also saw Walt smile in response but in Walt's mind he was saying, "You clever S.O.B." His grade of A/C was a compliment toward Walt for his ability to find interesting subjects to write about. However, the

Walt Fluegel

C was an administrative need to report that Walt had average qualities in the mechanics of writing, especially his lapses. There were no permafrost problems between instructor and student.

Hey Gunther! Why Are You Here?

CHAPTER TWENTY-EIGHT: EARNING COLLEGE MONEY IN ALASKA ON CAMPUS AND IN SUMMER

GOPHER JOB

On the first official day at the University and while waiting in line at the registrar's office to pay some fee, Walt scanned a bulletin board and saw "Jobs on campus" notice. Under the large print there were two positions needing filling soon: cafeteria and various janitor jobs. The notice told who to see in what building. Walt thought he noticed a similar note in the cafeteria that morning also saying the cafeteria had an opening for some student help. After paying his fee he went back to the cafeteria, inquired, and got the job. It was the first time he heard the word for his job. He thought he heard Mrs. Wilkins say "gopher." She explained she meant go-for as in go for this and go-for that and other odd little chores that needed attention. Later on he also heard others call him a flunky. That did not matter what the job was called; it meant he earned a bit of cash or got some meals free, meaning he did not have to get his meal-ticket punched when he had time to have a meal. His class schedule that first semester did not compete with the time requirements for the cafeteria job. (It was different for the second semester where timing was not favorable.)

Although folks were supposed to buss their own dishes, occasionally some left in a hurry for class and it was Walt's job to remove these dishes and wipe the table clean. He had to wear a bib apron and push a cart with deep trays to accept the delinquent dishes and tableware. It was a chance to get to know other students and sort of swap chores to break up the routines of the job. No one minded if he (or anyone else) helped himself to an extra dessert morsel or donut, or the last small glass of orange juice or milk at the end of the job time. It would be wasted otherwise.

JANITOR

Each semester there were different arrangements for campus jobs few other students took advantage of but money was money and it gave Walt assurance he would make it through schooling at least the first year. (Most students had good summer jobs that gave them enough money to get them through the year.) One other job was being a janitor for his dorm. Keep it clean, was the overall demand of the job. That meant mop down the hallways on Saturday afternoons, make sure there was enough toilet paper daily in the stalls, and clean toilets, four sinks in each of the three bathrooms, and the showers on each floor. Everyone was responsible for his own room. Generally, doors were not locked but those few students who insisted on having a key, arrangements were made with the dorm counselor. (A member of the faculty who might have an office in one of the rooms but was not always present except on special meeting times.) Walt was allowed to open dorm doors and mop the first few feet into someone's room. Some rooms looked familiar inside because these rooms seemed to be the favorite places to have bull sessions or card games.

There were very few complaints about the janitorial upkeep when he had that job. One complaint however, was that Walt seemed to use too much bleach in the showers. The wooden floor board above the drain became slippery at times. Especially if the last person did not lift the wooden floor drain and allow the wood to drain and dry. By tackling this problem the first thing in the afternoon with rags soaked in bleach and letting that react while the mopping was being done was thought to take care of the situation. It helped to remove the slipperiness if the boards were allowed to drain without too much washing off the bleach. A shower or two later and the smell was gone. Another situation was in favor of Walt. Someone was working on his car and brought parts into the bathroom and attempted to clean them

146

free of grease. Big mistake for this person. Walt was notified. A thought came to him. He went into his room and wrote a note in big letters and taped it on the mirror above that sink. A GOOD EXAMPLE OF A BAD EXAMPLE. He went on to say he did not mind ordinary dirty sinks but this was not his job. Fortunately the dorm counselor was available and ask around who left the mess. Walt did not know who made the mess but later that day it was cleaned up.

The cafeteria and janitor jobs did ease the concern that Walt had enough money to survive the full year at the university. In fact there was a couple of hundred left in the bank by the end of the second semester just in case he wanted to go back home in Mount Vernon. But that was far from his mind. He was in Alaska and wanted to know more about the Territory. Somehow he heard about a possible summer job on a Yukon River boat. That riverboat job was in the hands of the Alaska Rail Road. The main job for him was to be a cooks helper on the boat. Arrangements to get hired occurred in Fairbanks.

YUKON RIVER BOAT FREIGHTER (FIRST SUMMER)

Walt hopped a train to the town of Nenana on the Tanana River to make introductions concerning his job. He noticed the sternwheeler Nenana docked along the shore not too far from the warehouse which was receiving goods from a freight train. From the warehouse he could see the boat being loaded with boxes or bags of goods. He mentally compared this boat with side paddle wheelers he had seen in various books about the Mississippi River but never got close to any kind of paddle wheelers before. He was shown where he would bunk out for the trips down the Yukon River. He then met his boss cook in the crew galley. "Call me Angelo or Andy" the cook said at the introductions. He was about 5 foot 7 and very stocky. After looking over Walt he sort of said something to the effect that Walt would have to do a lot of little work while he and one of the crew would do the heavy lifting jobs. Walt found out what that meant when Andy soon got a large chunk of meat from the cooler and began to cut it up to make a stew for the crew loading the boat. Walt's first chore was peeling potatoes and when that was done to start on the carrots. Little by little Walt became more and more efficient in the chores he had to do. Dishes, pots, pans, and tools also needed to be cleaned and the galley itself had to be neat. Someone else from the crew was also assigned to help in the galley when necessary. Those stevedores unloading boxcars into the warehouse were fed at the dormitory for railroad employees while those relating to the boat activity were fed on the boat. The officers (first mate, purser, pilot, chief engineer and others) were fed somewhat the same food as the non-officer crew but with more fancy presentation of dressings or gravy. They ate separately in the dining hall on the upper decks with a handful of passengers. Food was sent above via a dumb waiter system and served by a waiter.

Boxes of canned or dried goods, bags of flour or other merchandise were loaded into the boat or on a barge according to location down river. Marshall and Russian Mission being the last anticipated stops on the Yukon were stored deep into the middle of the load and separated by a canvas or other dividing indicator. When Walt arrived most of the loading was accomplished. In a day or so later the lines were cast and the Nenana was allowed to drift before the steam engaged the stern paddles to churn the water. The craft moved gently into deeper water in spite of the noise from the paddles.

Girl friends or wives were waving their goodbyes from shore, and when the dock was out of sight the crew drifted into various parts of the Nenana. Walt wanted to examine the paddle wheel but was directed by Angelo to head for the galley. While most of the crew could now laze around until the first new port down river, they needed to be fed, and that was part of Walt's job to do.

GALLEY

Angelo kept strict standards for the crew in the galley. No unnecessary conversation, only the usual 'pass this or that' type of talking. Food in large serving containers was placed (by Walt or another of the galley staff) on the table with a ladle or two or large fork and the crew helped themselves. There was always baked bread at all meals from the morning baking. Coffee or water never ran out. The crew somehow seemed to eat in unison and when done eating one batch of men left while another batch waiting outside took their place. Depending on the crew size for a particular trip, two or three rotations were accommodated. The crew seemed to be familiar with the operations and procedures of the boat from previous years. Because the Nenana operated only when the river was not frozen, the crew's permanent residents were scattered to other places in Alaska or the States. Some of the stevedores were Native Americans. Little by little in the three trips Walt made he absorbed the value and mission of the Nenana.

The mission was to deliver goods to towns along the Yukon River and if possible bring back other goods produced by the river such as salmon. However the first thing was to unload cargo at towns along the Yukon River. Many of the villages or encampments along the river were initially established for access to the river by local people. Also the height of the river depended upon the season and distant snowmelt in the Mountains. Hence, the Nenana being a shallow draft craft required a skilled captain or pilot to decide how to park the boat for unloading of cargo. Many times the boat had its paddles directed toward the center of the river while its bow headed toward shore. Just in case the boat's bow would get stuck in the mud or sand the paddles in reverse could pull it away from shore.

UNLOADING AT PORTS

Unloading was always done by the stevedores and their two wheel carts. At the bow, there was a long wide gangplank stored in an upright position and held in place by a spar and ropes. At unloading times it was lowered on to the shore and if more distance was needed, additional gangplanks were always available. If the landing site was too steep for the men to handle there was an ingenious mechanism Walt never saw before. A special cable was designed with at least three flat stout "J-shaped" hooks spaced a few feet apart. This cable was brought to shore and attached to a pulley which in turn was attached to a poSt embedded in the ground near to the place where the full carts were unloaded. On the gangplank the first man engaged his hook to the axel of his cart and waited for the others to engaged their hooks. On a signal, the operator of the winch tightened the cable slowly while the stevedores balanced their carts and in a smooth operation the carts were dragged up hill on the gangplank. On top of the hill the carts were disengaged one at a time from the cable. Others on shore, with the help of the store owner and his helpers, took charge of the merchandise. After the last hook was disengaged a crew member then gabbed the hook and the winch operator reverse the cable tension and the hooks were dragged down the gangplank. If the timing was right the emptied carts soon followed the cable down while three other carts were waiting to be hooked.

FISH WHEEL RESULTS

Every now and again Walt saw a man made raft-like object floating in the water near shore that resembled the stern wheel of the boat but only smaller and having four "paddles." The paddles rotated slowly because of the current of the river and in detail each paddle looked like a large square wire basket. The contraption was held in place by ropes or poles from the shore to keep it from being swept downstream. He asked one of the crew what it was. it was called a fish wheel, meant to catch a salmon as it swam upstream. The current would turn the basket in the water and if a fish were close by it would be caught and scooped out of the water as another basket in the water would keep the wheel moving. It was explained to Walt that once caught in the basket, the fish had to be removed, and that was done automatically by gravity. Once the basket holding the fish was in an almost upright position the wiggling fish would slide toward the axel of the wheel and be directed by a chute into a box with high sides. On a routine basis depending on the run of fish someone from a nearby encampment would harvest the fish. Scaling, cutting the fish body into strips and drying in the sun and/or smoking of the fish appeared to be a community enterprise. There was more than enough to satisfy the local population for winter food so surplus was prepared for shipment upstream for the Fairbanks market.

Walt Fluegel

SALMON FOR SUPPER

Marshall was the last town the Nenana visited with its cargo. That is the place where geological fanning out of the Yukon River into an alluvial plane makes navigation very difficult. At the second trip the Nenana arrived in late morning about noontime and the usual unloading procedures occurred without difficulty. About an hour after the lunch shift, Angelo beckoned the oldest crew member who was a native Alaskan to come with him on deck to discuss something. He then went to the purser, talked with him for a while and then went into town. Within a half hour later Angelo came back to the boat struggling with two freshly caught large salmon he was carrying by the gills with his bent arms close to his body and the fish heads pressed to his ears. Now, Angelo was a short but stocky man but the fish were awkward to handle because of their weight and length. One of the fish was so long that its tail curved as it was dragged on the ground. Someone shouted, "Here comes Angelo!" and pointed in his direction. As the men turned to look, cheer came from all the crew; they knew what to expect for supper. This cheer from the crew also alerted one of the passengers in particular. This passenger happened to be a serious amateur photographer. He insisted that Angelo stop on the gangplank so he could make some photos. The camera he had was indeed a fancy Lica camera, the 35 mm kind, the kind used to make Kodak color slides. Other passengers had black and white film cameras. Angelo felt pleased to be asked, but his arms were getting tired. The photographer used his light meter often during "one more please" requests. That night everyone, from the captain on down to the passengers and crew of the Nenana had a delicious salmon supper.

On Walt's last trip upstream one empty barge was used just to haul smoked salmon collected from various points along the Yukon. At Nenana different lots would be sent to various commercial markets. The salmon on the barge was covered with tarps against possible rains. Depending upon the wind conditions the smoke-fish aroma did cause some temporary discomfort to a few passengers but brought nostalgic memories from the native crew members. Walt found out later that a small operation in Fairbanks found a way to dry pack the smoked salmon for an upscale specialty market in major US cities.

What was considered a survival food for a native population became a delicacy for another distant population. Later on in the year Walt managed to buy a small packet of this delicacy to sample its qualities. He could not acquire a taste for the smoked sample but some years later his mother found she would enjoy more of it in the future.

CUTTING HAIR

During Walt's third and last trip up river he made sure he talked with the purser that this would be his last stint on the Nenana because of wanting to go back and enroll at the U of A. If he made one more trip, school would have been started before the trip ended and it would be too late to register. The purser would radio headquarters with the information. He found out that by coincidence there was a temporary vacancy at the dormitory for railroad workers back in port. Since the Alaska Railroad also managed the boat Nenana the paperwork was a small matter. Walt would be a helper in the kitchen and do janitorial chores in the dorm as necessary to fill his day. It would be one month before he would enroll, and when he counted up his bank account he knew he would have just enough cash. It would be nice to have a little more so he knew he would need a campus job again.

The Nenana dorm housed men who were stevedores on the dock and rail workers (gandy dancers, carpenters, painters, various mechanics etc.) who maintained the rails, cars, equipment and stations along the line between Fairbanks and other towns south toward Anchorage and Seward. Depending upon the work load for the regional maintenance of the line the dorm population fluctuated. The dormitory was managed by a husband-wife couple—the Runnings—who had radio contact with various crews. They had the assistants of another cook, Dilbert known as "Dill" and occasional other "flunkies" from the local population of town. Dill occasionally hit the bottle but when available made the best breakfast and box lunches for gandy dancers who worked up the line during noon time. Walt would be a flunky for a month until he enrolled at the university.

There was one modified complaint lodged against Walt during that time. Yes, he took good care of the bathrooms but could he not use too much chlorine bleach in the showers? It sounded familiar but he adjusted. After he got familiar with the routines required in the kitchen and dorm duties Walt was able to be with some of the residents and find out more about people of the Territory of Alaska.

After one supper, one of the men was looking into the mirror and running his hands through his hair. He looked at Walt and suddenly asked, "Hey Walt, where did you come from and did you ever cut someone's hair?" All that Walt could say was that he came from New York and no he never cut hair before. He had seen it done lots of times before. "Are you good with your hands?" was the next question. "Somewhat." Walt answered. He remembered his ability to handle the transplants of the greenhouse and his Jewelry business. "Stay here, Walt, you are going to cut my hair." And with that "Chuck" went to his room and came back with a scissor, a long comb and a hand barber clipper. That shear looked very familiar, it looked just like the one Miss Miller used when she cut hair once a month at half-B. "Don't worry too much if you make a mistake, in three or four days the mistake will grow back." Walt heard that joke before on some radio comedy program but it did ease the situation. With all the years of seeing haircuts at half-B and watching professional barbers do their work when Walt left the Wartburg it seemed a nervous repeat of the motions of using shear, scissor and comb. He was particularly nervous when his scissor cut around Chuck's ear. When he was finished he felt exhausted but had to mention and point on the back of Chucks head a funny looking place. "Don't worry about that, I wear a hat most of the time and besides in four days who would know?" Again that same joke and they both laughed.

"How much do you think that haircut would cost me in town or in Fairbanks?"

"I know in Fairbanks it is about a buck fifty or two bucks."

"I'll tell you what, I know other men up the line who were thinking of getting their hair cut. It has been a long time for them. Why don't you keep these tools for a few days and practice with them. I'll drum up business for you and see what they say. If they want to pay, take it and don't ask questions."

Hey Gunther! Why Are You Here?

And thus it was that a new adventure was literally thrust upon Walt that would ease his money need while attending college. Chuck took chances on other men to cut his hair and he in turn cut theirs. He related that his appearance varied in a few years from long then short, long and then very short or keep it long and also have a beard. Chuck realized he was becoming a drifter in many ways and wanted to settle down, perhaps get married. And Chuck did introduce other men to Walt and after several suppers he began to practice during the remaining weeks Walt stayed at the Tanana dormitory. One of the men suggested Walt should go to the Sears & Roebuck catalog store in Fairbanks and get an electric clipper. Each of the men gave Walt some money and he felt more comfortable in acquiring this barber skill. Once he got back to the U of A and registered for his second year he went to the Sears & Roebuck catalog store in Fairbanks and ordered the equipment he needed.

Walt Fluegel

CHAPTER TWENTY-NINE: YEAR TWO: NO MORE THAN A BUCK

In the men's dorm there was a basement closet cluttered with a couple of broken chairs, a desk needing a leg repair and some cardboard boxes and of all things a barber chair. Other odd things blocked most of the view of the chair. During all of the last school session he saw this closet while he was janitor but never paid much attention to it but occasionally he too stored some janitorial things there temporarily. It never occurred to him to wonder how that chair got there or whether someone in the past did cut hair in that closet. Walt asked the dorm counselor if he knew anything about that junk and all he got in response was a shrug. "If I clean out the junk and if the barber chair works can I set up a barber shop in that closet?" Walt asked, then added, "I learned how to cut hair this summer, maybe I can make a few bucks."

"On one condition, and that is if there any serious complaints from the others on that floor it's a no." Then the counselor asked, "How much will you charge?"

"No more than a buck."

"Just to be on the legal side I'll check with someone in the office."

Without waiting for legal permission it was easy enough to get rid of the boxes and broken chairs—and nobody asked him how he did it— and other junk but the desk with a broken leg was a problem for a while. Walt knew after his cleaning that the barber chair was easy to spin around, and when it was possible he was able to figure out if he could pump up the seat and lower it too. It did not pump very high

155

which meant it was short of oil but in a flash of understanding he realized he was short himself and did not need to have the chair rise to its mechanical limit.

Having had experience of living on campus for a year before, Walt sort of knew the lay of the land and some seldom visited crannies behind the power plant for example. When some minor construction occurred on campus some leftover material such as a concrete block or stone or a split board was casually dumped in a ditch. Some growing brush was allowed to hide the waste material. He had in mind to salvage the desk because only the back leg needed to be repaired, or removed and replaced or something. He talked with George G and borrowed a tape measure from his carpenter toolbox. George G always had this box because he thought that at some time in the future he was going to build his own cabin.

Walt's mind was racing in a way to solve problems of this kind and he began to feel his ears burning, the same feeling he had when he made the parachute and launching bow while in the Wartburg. He asked George to give him a hand in measuring the back leg. Then he asked George to come with him to the disposal ditch behind the power plant. He saw what he was looking for, a concrete block. When these thoughts of insight happen It was not in perfect shape with a knock out or two, but if the desk leg were sawed off just right and the rest of the desk rested on the block and because the block was really hidden from view in the back, and the desk, in the corner who would know there really was a block there anyway!! Walt's ears began to have a burning sensation, a comfortable familiar feeling. And so the idea happened. Walt's burning ears subsided, and it wasn't long after that that George was his first unofficial non-paying customer.

The closet was unusual because there was no electric switch by the door for the overhead light but there was an outlet toward the back where the desk resided. He could use this outlet for a radio and his clippers. The overhead light had to be turned on by hand by a chain or cord. By adjusting the length of the wire from the ceiling the lamp was high enough not to bother anyone sitting in the barber chair. Walt also managed to swap his room on the first floor for the room directly opposite the closet in the basement. By this time the dorm counselor called a meeting of dorm residents and asked if they minded having a barbershop in the basement. Someone objected about the possible in or out traffic in the hallway during the night, but he was hushed down by others who noted the traffic would not be as bad as now especially on weekends and how many customers were possible from the campus? Some doubted it was worth the effort, so why didn't Walt get a campus job instead? How much would he charge? When he said "No more than a buck," there seemed to be a quite acceptance to let Walt give it a try. The cheapest haircut in town was a buck fifty.

The administration was consulted and decided on a rental of $10 a month for the time being. This inspired Walt to get some artists paint. On the eye level panel of the door he filled the panel field with a light color and painted CAMPUS BARBERSHOP in red and blue letters on that field. Word spread. Customers ranging from faculty children with a parent, to male students, to maintenance personnel trickled in. In the meantime he used the desk for his homework assignments. Outside he taped a 3 x 5 card on the door with his class schedule and possible shop hours mostly on some afternoons and after supper. He also blocked off an hour for lunch and supper. He attempted to close at 9:00 pm so he could finish homework before his 10:30 bedtime.

A FEW BARBER SHOP STORIES:

BILL C'S DILEMMA

For Walt, he did not expect anything more than a shop just for cutting hair. Occasionally someone would come in and sit in the chair with the light right above them but just wanting to talk about something. At one time Bill C was in a dilemma about his mother. She lived in the States somewhere and she was very ill. She might die. Should he go see her before she did die or wait, or do something else? Major exams were coming soon and he went through all possibilities and implications of doing this or doing that and occasionally he did shed a tear. He also related that he was at odds with his family about something. In a sense he actually ran away from home and that compounded his problem and loyalty towards being home. When he had nothing more to say he just left the shop. All this time Walt just listened never making even a neutral statement. At other times two or three guys would be in the shop and talk to the one getting "clipped." A few days later Bill C poked his head into the shop and told Walt he just got a letter from home and said that the day he was there talking was the day his mother died and he was going to fly home. He also contacted the dorm counselor to notify all his professors that he would be back as soon as possible.

FLAT TOP CUT

At another time in spring, the big ROTC gala and dance was being planned and arranged. Warren C was the student captain (or the highest brass) of the class. He always got a haircut, the student flat top kind, at least on a regular schedule or when he thought his hair was bending over too much. Many of the ROTC guys also got the flat top style so Walt had lots of practice. They used the mirror quite often to make sure, even those who had a slight natural wave. It was two days before the big event and Warren came for his usual style. The sides were neatly trimmed, neckline well blended, and soon Walt began to ease on doing the flat top. Now if you asked someone with a flat top to bend down so you could see where the skull makes its natural curvature one would see more skin through the hair in the middle and a blending of more hair towards the sides and back. Whenever Walt was in this part of the process he never engaged in conversation. Walt was almost finished. But just when he had the clipper going right in the middle of his last pass, Warren made a hiccup, enough to raise his body enough to give the clipper more hair to cut than anyone wanted. Result, an almost bare spot nick right in the middle of the top of his skull. A couple of mirrors convinced Warren and Walt to work something out. The hair could not grow back in that short of time, and, at the ball after the ceremonies Warren would have to remove his cap. If he lowered his head in the slightest way when greeting guests etc., the nicked spot would show. "Even it up!" Warren commanded when he looked once more in the mirrors. Walt was nervous but steady, so was Warren. Result: a military style haircut not a student style flat top. The ROTC gala and dance went on as planned. Warren came back in four weeks for his usual.

158

Walt Fluegel
A PROBLEM TO BE SOLVED

Walt had just turned off the radio when it said it was twenty below. Roger M came into the shop, took off his parka, sat in the barber chair and just said, "Someday someone will kill me with my own gun!" Walt hardly knew Roger because he lived in the Club Dorm, but did know Roger had a hobby shared with one of the faculty men and a couple of other students from the Main dorm. They liked to target practice with pistols not necessarily rifles. Only Roger and the faculty person had the extended part of the hobby, that of making the bullets. They got the supplies from somewhere Stateside, loaded up the casings with powder, put in the slugs and somehow assembled everything. They used non-ferrous material so no spark would happen. This they did in the faculty person's basement of the campus housing for faculty families.

Rather than get the haircut this time, all Roger wanted to do was talk about his "problem." He said he had the strong desire to have a woman every day, and he was able to do so in one way or another most of the time. He did not elaborate but he said he had been going to the faculty man's house regularly and that the man's wife was eager to help him. She helped daily during the week because it was convenient for her or both of them that Roger and her husband knew each other's afternoon class schedules. Also they had a small boy in school in Fairbanks and at a given time each day after the help session his mother would go into town and bring the boy home. In the late afternoon the man would walk home from classes knowing his wife would be gone to pick up the boy. He also knew that his wife would let Roger into the house earlier before she left. Roger would be in the basement loading the bullets. When he came into the house the man would smell a roast or something cooking slowly in the oven. He then went to the basement. In unison each said, "Hi," to each other. The two of them would continue making bullets until they heard the boy and his mother come home. Rodger did not stay for supper preferring to let the family be by themselves. The faculty man did not realize his wife seemed (more) at ease with herself without the cabin fever of winter.

159

Hey Gunther! Why Are You Here?

Only on rare occasions did Roger come to the barbershop and mention his problem. At one time during a barber session he did ask if Walt knew this one woman student or another one but Walt didn't ask why the questioning. He could only guess. At the last haircut time at the end of the spring semester Roger wondered how he would manage this coming summer during construction season where he could earn college money as a heavy machine operator or cat-skinner.

TAKE ABOUT AN INCH OFF

It was about a quarter to five one afternoon when J-N opened the door wider and asked if Walt would give her a haircut. He had seen her several times in the cafeteria at noon but never in the evening. She lived in town. She looked older than other girls. They never had classes in common so he did not know her name but he knew she smoked when he saw her in the cafeteria or in the Cub. She introduced herself and said she would give Walt a try. Her hair was dark, very straight with no wave and just short enough to cup against her neck but not beyond. He never cut a girl's hair he said to her. That didn't mind, "hair was hair," she said. He was afraid he might make a mistake and make the hair jagged on the ends but with the men that part of the haircut could be close and mistakes were very rare he blubbered out. "If it happens I can wear a hat or my parka or a tall scarf," she answered.

She sat in the chair and this forced Walt to sweep the wrap around her and tie the strings behind her neck. She said in a quiet voice, "Take about an inch off." He combed her hair from top to bottom, then in the reverse from her neck upward and outward to slowly get an idea of what his initial cuts should be. He knew he was nervous but he began to sculpt the hair shorter than it was when she came into the shop. The bottom back edge became the right length above her shoulders but did not look like a square cut. It was wedge shape with a slight cupping. Her bangs seemed easy to do. When seen in the mirror by J-N face on, the bangs were nice and square across, just above her eyebrows. It took about an hour but he felt he did a good job and his nervousness dwindled as he used his soft brush to sweep

160

off excess hair. J-N looked in the hand mirrors to examine the back of her head.

"How much do you charge?" saying nothing else.

"There is a dollar's worth of hair on the floor."

"Don't you charge more for women, the shop in town does."

"As you said in the beginning, 'hair is hair'. Just a buck is all I charge." Over an hour passed since J-N came into the shop, almost twice as long as with regular male customers. While Walt looked at a clock on the wall he said he wanted to go to supper. J-N grabbed her parka and reached into her pocket. She did not have a purse. She took out a silver dollar and plunked it on the seat of the barber chair and also looked at the clock. At the same time she left the room saying, "I hope I don't miss the bus."

Within the next minute or so, Walt too grabbed his parka and headed for the cafeteria. The bus was just making its turn-around and he thought he saw J-N sit down just as the internal bus lights blinked off. The bus was heading downhill and on to Fairbanks.

IT IS NOT A DATE WITH J-N

As the weeks moved on, Walt did not register or remember the last time he cut J-N's hair. But he was just about to go to supper about a month later when she showed up and asked, "Can you squeeze me in?"

"I want to go to supper but it ought to be easier this time. Sit down."

Nervousness began to take hold of Walt's reflexes after he tied the strings. J-N never said a word; they were both quiet. One or two of the dormers poked their head in and asked Walt when he was going to supper. They did not bother to find out who was in the chair and the chair because it was faced away from the door could not reveal this time who the customer was. "Soon I hope but it may be a while." He didn't want to rush and said so quietly to J-N. He hadn't looked at the clock until he began soft brushing excess hair from her face and around her neck. He had an idea and asked J-N, "How about me taking you for supper in town? I need something different from the cafeteria food."

"This is not a date I suppose, I'm willing to pay my own way."

After a moments thought he said, "Okay, by me. I hardly know the town and its restaurants so if you have a favorite place, are you willing to let me tag along?"

It was not a date. It was an outing for the evening. On the bus into town there was little talk but in the restaurants the talking was not about other students maybe a little about student politics or even the food being served. It was on a mixture or salad of ideas of life, philosophy, political thought, some history or famous personage each heard about in their reading or college experience. At this first outing J-N asked Walt if it was alright if she ordered a glass of wine for herself (because she knew he did not drink spirits of any kind.) It was okay by him. On another outing, J-N once asked Walt a bit of the Wartburg when he mentioned it one previous time. He in turn asked her about being in a family and leaving home to come to Alaska. But there was no dwelling on any one topic. He also noticed she did not smoke but never said a word about it. If she had lit up he was used to having the others in the dorm do it. For Walt it was a far different atmosphere from conversations he had had on dates when he was in high school, or with a girl from campus. It was refreshing in a very pleasant way. He was also aware she was older than he and a bit taller which in a sense made the outing not a date after all. After the first meal and others that followed he walked her home to her small rental cabin. When she indicated that was her place he said he enjoyed her company and please stop again for a haircut. She just nodded and turned to go into her house as he turned around and headed into town to catch the next bus to campus. On other occasions toward spring-time when it was warmer he decided to walk the tracks back to the College flats.

Before the last semester ended for J-N, she must have visited the barbershop while Walt was having supper in the cafeteria. When he came back and turned the light on, he noticed a large square envelope resting on the barber chair seat. A note scribbled on the envelope said, "I thought you might like this," it was signed J-N. Walt recognized the envelope as one from a Fairbanks music store. It was a long-playing record, its title: "The Well-Tempered Clavier" by J.S. Bach and played on a harpsichord by Wanda Landowska. Walt had a few long playing records, some from Tchaikovsky, Brahms, Beethoven and excerpts from others but none from Bach. He was apprehensive at first but when he played the music he was convinced it would seldom be played again if ever. All he could do now was to shrug his shoulders and see how much homework that needed to be done. Later in life while listening to the classical music station, and someone played the harpsichord, the title of, "The Well -Tempered Clavier" came to the fore. Also the cupped dark hair from J-N.

EMERGENCY CASH ON HAND: A CAMERA

It was the week of spring final exams of Walt's second year in college. "What have you got lined up for the summer?" was of equal importance concerning summer jobs by many. So at the end of the first year of Walt having the barber shop, the shortage of cash by Erich Stevenson turned out to have unforeseen future pleasure for Walt. Erich lived in Seattle, Washington and he was short of cash and he needed money for plane fare. He wondered if he could borrow money from Walt. Walt said, "No," because Erich may not come back for the fall semester. "I can loan you money if you pawn something, fair enough?" Walt then added, "When you come back what ever you pawned will be returned." He also assured Erich that he was coming back too but Erich in turn did not indicate one way or the other if he would be readmitted even though he was a sophomore. Erich indicated he would be right back and left the barbershop.

When he returned, Erich had a camera with him, a Kodak 35. Walt had seen these cameras before but all he had was a box camera. Walt knew these cameras were expensive and used a different kind of film but he took out his wallet and opened it. When he looked inside he said all he had were three tens. In the meantime he remembered a chance meeting with Peters while he was using one of those 35 mm cameras. He also flashed into his experience on the Nenana riverboat where this one passenger was photographing Angelo and the salmon.

When Erich saw the tens he said, "I can sure use that money." Walt took a chance and the exchange was made. (It turned out that Erich did not reenroll so the camera 'officially' became his when the fall semester began.) As soon as it was possible Walt had a conversation with Peters on some basic principles of photography, color photography. One of the first places he used his new camera was at Mount McKinley Park hotel.

SECOND SUMMER JOB : THE MOUNT MCKINLEY PARK HOTEL

Campus jobs did help a few other students but most students acquired summer jobs in their hometowns at the canneries or other businesses. Mining students could work for Fairbanks Exploration Company, the dredging company that extracted gold not too far from Fairbanks. Construction jobs in and around Fairbanks could always be had, but Walt's second serious work off campus was at the Mount McKinley Park Hotel run by the Alaska Railroad. Because it was run by the Alaska Railroad and hence the Territory, in turn it was thought to be a civil service job. The busiest time at the hotel occurred when the train bought tourists to the Park a few times per week either from Fairbanks or Anchorage. (There was no road from either of these cities.) Walt understood that the Hotel was largely abandoned during the winter. In season, it was not too busy on Monday or Tuesday. Therefore there were many temporary jobs usually filled by students from the U of Alaska or from Washington or Oregon. He learned to be a desk clerk checking people in or out and operating the hotel telephone system. Because there were three other desk clerks there was a rotation system so others could become familiar with other various hotel chores. Walt also became involved at times with being a helper with janitorial chores or at the laundry, and of all places as a part time bartender.

Walt Fluegel

MAGIC TRICK

An unexpected assignment for Walt was to be a substitute bartender on Monday and/or Tuesday nights when it was the day off for the regular bartender. To gain practice he learned from the book of recipes and got tips from the regular tender for several nights in a row before being on his own. However there was not much to be concerned about because Monday and Tuesday nights were nights that had few or no tourists present. Walt served some of the hotel staff (waitresses/maid (W/M), power plant crew, grounds keeper, janitor, etc.) and in knowing Walt was new to bartending (and actually a non-drinker), the staff people told him how to mix the drinks they wanted. They also knew the price of the drinks, so he rang that up as well. However, there was one exception about one special Monday night time.

There happened to be a teacher's convention at the hotel and it was quite busy. Several of the teacher conventioneers asked Walt, "Aren't you too young to be a bartender?" Walt in a way was prepared for this kind of question. He told them his age; he was learning the trade; this was an unusual time because the regular tender was off for the night; and above all he said with a frown on his face, "Most of the girls in high school turned him down for dates because he was shorter than they and they never dated a boy younger than they were.

"I never did look my age, but you wait until I get to look like John Atlas!" It produced a positive response. Drinks flowed.

A little ways into that Monday evening Walt had a "magic trick" to demonstrate to the customers. Of course in magic tricks one uses deception as well as preparation. In summary a piece or two of hotel stationery is placed on the bar. A Manhattan glass is also placed rim side down on the stationary. A new bar towel is shown to a customer and asked to examine it. While doing so the customer is asked if they have a dime or quarter, maybe a half dollar to place next to the glass. They oblige. The towel is placed over the glass and a few magic words are said. After that, the glass and towel are picked up swiftly and brought down and placed over where the coin is placed, and as swiftly as possible the towel is removed. People look through the glass and do not see the coin. The towel is again given to a costumer to examine. Where did the coin go? A minute or so of this perplexing situation the glass is again covered with the bar towel, a magic word is chanted, and the glass with the towel covering it is removed from the area and the money reappears. "How did you do that?" and other questions followed. Walt tried it a few times again for others entering the bar, but Walt had to serve drinks eventually. At the last time he tried the trick on a tipsy customer also examined the money to make sure it was hers, but in desperation she also reached for the towel and managed to knock over the Manhattan glass. The secret was suddenly revealed to the onlookers with an almost collective expression, "That was so simple!" The solution of the disappearing coin? Preparation in advance.

THE MAGIC SECRET

A day or so before, Walt managed to get a glass, and the barest amount of glue or paste was put on the rim. The rim was placed on a piece of hotel stationery and allowed to dry. When dried, the excess paper was carefully trimmed from the glass and kept that way on the back counter with other glasses all with their rims down on bar towels. In other words if one put a coin down on a surface and covered it with the same kind of paper one cannot see the coin. The deception was twofold; firstly, the use of the hotel stationery placed on the bar was the same kind of paper attached to the glass; secondarily drawing attention to the bar towel covering the glass was also deceptive to make people believe the trick was in the towel not the glass. After all, by looking through the glass and one does not see the coin, it must "go" somewhere, why not direct attention to the towel. Walt made a few good tips that night even though his bartending needed help.

It was about this time Walt decided to keep his mother informed of his hotel job and wrote about the scenery, the people and how he felt about being in Alaska for a year. It was all so new and he hoped his summer job would allow him to go one more year to college. He calculated his salary would permit it and hoped his barbershop would help here too. He made no mention of wanting to go back to Mount Vernon but he was pleased with himself that his freshman chemistry and biology classes were easier because he had a good background at A.B. Davis. He only mentioned in passing that the English classes were something he would have to work harder at. He included some postcards into the letter too.

WHAT TO SEE IN THE PARK

In the rotation of jobs at the hotel several employees were free for a day or two during the week or at slack times. It was then possible for someone to round up a few others to go hiking up the hill (or was it a small mountain?) behind the hotel. However, everyone was cautioned by the management within the first week of assigning jobs that no one should go hiking alone anywhere. There were grizzlies roaming the park. Everyone understood because no one was experienced in being in raw nature before, that is why they all signed up to work at a hotel in the wilderness. The hotel did in a sense give everyone a sense of safety.

Two main notes of advice were given. "Make lots of noise, if you migrate away from the hotel and above all if you see a cub bear alone LOOK FOR THE MOTHER! Find out where she is and make noise. Mothers are very protective but they don't care much for people." Even those who wanted to go fishing in the nearby lake near the railroad tracks should not go alone. If they caught a fish the cook would gladly cook it for them. The advice also applied to anyone who wanted to take photographs. Never alone, always go with someone else.

On these occasional outings with five or six others, the employees began to know each other better. This time those who had cameras snapped a few pictures, including Walt. It was at one of these outings that Dick Z began to notice or had a distant interest in Sheila M. Now Dick was not handsome on first observation, but when he grinned his face was totally different and one had the impression 'here is a nice fellow'. His interest in Sheila eventually blossomed much later when Dick enrolled at the University to get an engineering degree. Walt

167

knew Sheila as one of the other student workers in the cafeteria at the University. When Dick took up residence in the Main dorm in fall he asked Walt what he knew about Sheila. Dick knew they knew each other from the chit-chat conversations at Mount McKinley hotel. "She is easy to talk with and friendly with everybody. I never had a date with her but she seems okay. (She was taller than Walt) Why don't you give her a try?" Although Dick did seem shy in several ways, it did not take long before they were seen together quite frequently.

FOOD REBELLION

Hotel food made quite an impression on the entire staff. The food served to the hotel guests was excellent and no one complained but it was limited to a small variety menu. However, the exact food was offered to the staff, day after day, after day, after day for weeks. Many of the staff people could not rotate this menu for very long and a small 'rebellion' occurred between them and the master chef. A simple ham sandwich or fried egg or boiled potato seemed beneath him to prepare but he was persuaded by the manager to allow the head waitress to fix different food for those wanting something different now and then. Extra box lunches for hotel guests who went on excursions were also used to satisfy the rebellious group. It did disrupt the kitchen routine somewhat but the rebellion subsided. To Walt, this rebellion seemed strange, because he remembered that a few years before at the Wartburg there was no thought of a food rebellion. You ate what was in front of you and that was that. At the hotel there were no alternative eating-places.

At the University there was variety but if one did not like the cafeteria-style food there was always The Cub, another dining facility on campus. The Cub was privately operated and the seating was limited. However it was open most of the day to nine or ten at night. By today's standards it would be known as a snack bar but when the cafeteria served lunch or dinner so did The Cub. There were different kinds of ice cream for example whereas the cafeteria maybe served just vanilla or just chocolate for the one meal. Of course anyone who did not have a meal ticket to punch dined at The Cub.

168

Walt Fluegel

EXCURSION

But back at the hotel, there were box lunches prepared for hotel guests who signed up for a half-day bus excursion into the park. Also, there were several pairs of binoculars that could be rented. The bus driver was Mister Rothmans. He was big, perhaps in his 50s, and had a pronounced low, gravelly voice. On the trip into the park on the gravel road he would stop here and there and point out some interesting geological features or some wildlife. Sometimes if there were a serious photographer on board he would give them time to set up their camera on a tripod and snap away. Most of the time the road was above or at the tree line where scrub type willow grew in patches. It gave everyone a chance to see great distances to the far mountain range where Mount McKinley might be seen. On one trip Walt and two of the W/M, Sheila, and Francis D were allowed to board the bus. About half way into the trip Mister Rothmans announced that there will be an outdoor shelter ahead with a men's and women's restrooms and a place to have the box lunches. When they arrived he also announced that absolutely no food was to be left on the tables and all garbage was to be taken back. "We do not want to encourage the bears to visit us. So while you folks eat I will be on the lookout." With that he showed his own binoculars to all the passengers, and when he said "bears" there was a noticeable change in conversation by the passengers.

THE CAMERA SNAPS MORE THAN SCENERY

Not far into having the box lunch Sheila noticed a ground squirrel sniffing around nearby. She managed to throw a small piece of bread in his direction and he promptly began to nibble on it. Mister Rothmans noticed this too but said if the critter doesn't eat it all, "You girl, will have to clean it up." At about the same time Francis got close to the ground and holding a piece of bread began to offer another squirrel a treat. Walt saw an opportunity to take a picture with his 'new' 35 mm camera of this feeding. He had been taking scenic snaps near the hotel but this type of photo seemed different to him. Yes, he could focus closely compared to his box camera but his viewfinder was small. He thought he saw one of Francis fingers rub the belly of the squirrel while he cupped his paws around her other fingers holding on to the bread. When Walt finally got his slides back from the processor he knew there was more than scenery to snap. This one incident in a small way directed him to become more observant in finding other interesting details of life.

CARIBOU MIGRATION

At boarding time at the hotel Mister Rothmans announced that even though it was clear weather, Mount McKinley might be hidden from view because it makes its own weather. So now at the rest area the mountain was not fully in view. Only a part of the peak would show its whiteness against the blue sky or maybe a side of the mountain became visible and then became clouded. The passenger with a long lens on his camera was happy enough. Everybody was concentrating on the mountain. A bit later the photographer gave an exclamation of, "Holy Cow, What is that?" and pointed to a mass of animals moving in the valley below. Mister Rothmans directed his binoculars into the valley. He passed his binoculars around and said "caribou migration." The others who had binoculars also saw the animals in detail and from their comments were pleased to have rented the glasses. The animals' antlers were still in velvet.

Someone said the animals look like reindeer. Mister Rothmans had to tell the people the difference between reindeer and caribou. If they wanted to see reindeer he could sell them tickets "real cheap" to Norway or Sweden. It was his sense of humor that put the people in a better mood. But the mountain was never fully revealed at any time. A lady who was often seen with a sketchpad asked, "When is the best time to see the mountain at its full beauty?"

In his gravelly voice he said, "You really don't want to be here at that time. I am told the best time is in the middle of winter when it is 20 below or colder." An audible groan came from the passengers. But then he also said, "If you have the money you can go to the end of the road outside of the park and stay at a place and wait and wait and have your camera ready. It is a rare sight to see the mountain completely free of clouds. If you can sell your photo to the National Geographic magazine you will make up your expenses. At this time Walt whispered to Mister Rothmans that he could see the mountain from the U of Alaska 200 miles away in the middle of winter. But it was just a small white peak on the southern horizon. This he related to nearby people.

OTHER ANIMALS AND ANIMAL LOVE MAKING

Finally the driver said it was about time they headed back but could stop for more pictures or scenery if the lighting were right. They did stop to gaze at a cluster of about 15 Dahl sheep about a mile away and an occasional grizzly who seemed to be eyeing the sheep. Someone saw a fox and the bus stopped. The sun was somewhat behind the fox and the way the sunlight shown on its ears it looked like two flames coming from his head. As Mister Rothmans was driving someone asked him, "Does Alaska have porcupines?"

"No ma'am, but I know how they make love." A few snickers and giggles came from some of the passengers.

The voice that asked the question then said, "How?" More snickers.

Mister Rothmans answered slowly in a loud gravelly whisper, "Verrrry carefully." Those who did not hear him asked their seat partner what was going on and in this case the whole bus was involved in the joke. It was an old joke Mister Rothmans said to a nearby passenger that he heard when he was in high school many years ago. As a result of this and other jokes told to each other, the ride back to the hotel seemed not so long. Also Mister Rothmans received a few generous tips as folks left the bus.

ARTIST AND CAMERA

When the passengers disembarked the artist lady with the sketchpad asked Walt if he was the temporary bartender at the hotel. "Yes," he answered with a surprised voice.

Hey Gunther! Why Are You Here?

"My sister was here this spring on a convention of teachers and she told me about your magic trick in the bar."

"That's the only trick I know."

"She played that trick on me and began to learn other tricks for family fun."

While the artist was talking, Walt momentarily looked down at the artist's sketchpad. He just pointed at it. She showed a rough sketch of a bus steering wheel and Mister Rothmans from the back as if he was looking toward the right. "I wish I had your talent," he said almost in a whisper.

She replied as she pointed to Walt's camera dangling from his neck, "Thanks, work with that as often as you can." Then she turned around and joined the others as all went into the hotel.

GOSSIP?

There were perhaps more possible stories or incidents that Walt could relate to directly. Other things could be gossip. One in retrospect involved but not proven to be true was that the assistant manager was a foreigner learning the hotel business in America and having an affair with one of the W/M staff. Another tale told but not known directly was that one of the engineers of the power plant had his way with one of these W/M employees or was it one of the hotel guests who stayed almost a week? Another story perhaps true was that one of the engineers in the power plant fell asleep on the job and was awakened by someone only because the lights were flickering in a strange way. He had to shovel more coal into the fire to boost the steam for the generator. But the summer was coming to a close. Less tourists were visiting McKinley and Walt and other students from the U of Alaska and elsewhere had to make plans to return.

CHAPTER THIRTY: IN THE SOPHOMORE YEAR

Aside from the barbershop and classes, other events and routine activities made up the life of Walt and other students. Some very personal, others which involved other students like sports, dances and choral practice all continued semester after semester.

Back at the University for his second year, Walt found the campus did not seem to change much. He managed to go through the procedures of registration, paying fees, getting a meal ticket, establishing himself in the Men's dorm and meeting old class mates from the year before. He also went down to the College flats to say 'hello' to Nick and his wife Zelda. Nick was one of those adult or irregular students, parents of two boys ages 9 and 11. Walt never really knew what Nicks occupation was but as a student in the Meats class Nick seemed to know more than the instructor knew. Zelda was a sometime nurse assistant before they both came to Alaska several years ago. At that time Walt did not realize how important Nick and Zelda's friendship would progress within three years.

DRAINO

In a reminiscence of his first year first week, a bunch of guys at night gathered in a three-bed dorm room to have a beer or two. A few freshmen mingled with upperclassmen who related how the previous summer jobs went and to renew friendships, and to impress on freshmen they were no longer living at home with their parents. So

Hey Gunther! Why Are You Here?

drink up. One of the seniors off handedly said something about "Draino."

And almost immediately someone else said, "It's too early for that, they are just going to have to wait." This wetted the interest in a few newcomers.

A naive guy not knowing the culture around Draino said something about, "Isn't that the stuff to clean out pipes?"

"Oh, it sure will clean out your pipes!" someone called out and to those in the know all laughed, making the topic of Draino something more to learn about.

In his first year, Walt and a few others were invited to a house party on the College flats for some fun with a few girls. Of course there was something to eat and drink and tell stories and have a few laughs. It was sort of crowded but cozy. It was in the middle of the winter at about twenty below outside but plenty warm inside. After a while someone asked, "Do you think it is ready?"

"I'll check. It is about time." And everyone noticed Jim getting up and putting on his gloves and headed for the door. Those not in the know wondered why should Jim leave the house without a parka. Before that thought could be answered he came back carrying a gallon jug. The host who asked the "ready" question was just coming out of the kitchen area with several shot glasses.

The gallon jug held some kind of foggy liquid and ice and no cover on the opening. Still with his gloves on, Jim gingerly tilted the jug over the first shot glass and poured a little of the liquid into it. "Looks good!" he exclaimed.

Everyone noticed that the shot glasses were accumulating condensation but soon warmed up. "Give it a try," Jim said to the host.

He raised the glass and made a sweep motion across the room and said, "The first of the winter, cheers to all." He then took a small sip and swallowed it."

It is no exaggeration to say that the host demonstrated with harsh loud whispers trying to force out his voice to say, "Boy, this is good!" but

174

his audience did not have to hear the exact words, they just had to see his face pucker up, his tightly closed eyes, the shaking of his head back and forth, the exhalation of his breath and finally hear one more word, "Wow!" He also reached for his beer, took a sip and finally said "Draino, not for the faint of heart." Two older guys and a girl gave it a try. They too went into the same antics as their host. The host recommended to the new comers who wanted to try drinking Draino to mix it first into some water. Jokingly he asked a rhetorical question: "Now do you know why it is called Draino?"

It was about time to explain to the new onlookers what Draino was all about. It was very simple to make. All one had to do was get a gallon jug. Add a handful or two or three of raisins, some bakers yeast, and add water. Then let it ferment near a warm radiator. When the fermentation stopped in a few days AND if it were at least 20 below outside, the jug now containing raisin jack should be placed on the snow outside. For how long? Experienced Draino makers have a feel for the length of time for the water to freeze. They say it is an art form. But in essence what does not freeze is poured off and this is imbibed. Draino wasn't made often because some impatient student was just as happy to have only the raisin jack now and then.

BULL SESSIONS?

Sometimes no matter in mid week or weekend or even on a Monday night there was bound to be an open discussion in someone's room on any topic being discussed. It may have been started on a subject in math or geology or English. But whatever the topic, if the door was open and guests other than the resident were present, anyone could add or detract from the topic. Sometimes the topic would degrade to girls or religion. Quite often some older guys would tell of "conquests" back home and encourage others to tell of their adventures with their girlfriends in the home town. Walt listened in quiet but often he found a way to leave the discussion with a "nature calls" explanation or, "I got to make sure my English assignment is done," or just not say anything or answer a request to tell about his recent date with so-and-so.

Hey Gunther! Why Are You Here?

At one time George G and he left at the same time but this time the topic ended for them both on religion. Previous to that, girls were discussed. On the way toward their rooms that were close, George said, "Most of what you hear about girls there," as he pointed over his shoulder, "is wishful thinking. They must not realize their mothers were once girls."

Walt's answer was, "I learned long ago not to kiss and tell." And just as George was about to open the door to his room he also said, "I have something you might like to read, wait a second." He went into his room and shortly later came out with a well-used paper back book, called something about "How The Great Religions Began." As he handed it to Walt he implied that it should be read but that he wanted it back.

FLAVORS

The bull sessions about religion seemed to be on the finer points of Christianity and the different churches each person attended. In very rare cases did anyone mention or want to discuss another religion in different parts of the world. But this was a vague something Walt had been thinking about ever since he was confirmed right after he left the Wartburg. Since being at the orphanage everyone he knew had a religion of some kind, as he remembered Miss Roget saying "flavor." He also knew not everybody went to church or a synagogue on a regular basis, he didn't either. But when he began to read about the Mormon Church and visited Mormon places in Salt Lake City before coming to Alaska, certain aspects became interesting. In Fairbanks the Sunday Mormon meeting place was in the upstairs lobby of the movie theater. He became conflicted with what he knew of the Lutheran doctrine and the Mormon teachings. He often wondered if he really needed a religion to being a good person. Many around him, other guys and many adults were not conflicted but neither were they strict adherents to their faiths or seemed concerned about being a good person or not.

In a sense it was an on-again, off-again thinking for ten years or so about religion since Walt left the Wartburg when he came to the

176

realization that people all over the world had a religion of some kind. Creative things like music, art, architecture and other activities happened in the name of the religion and bad things too, such as wars, enslavement or subjugation, and destruction. It was not only the large religions depicted in the book given Walt to read by George G; but the smaller religions even the ones which worship stones, trees, mountains, and other objects seen on earth that interested him. In all this time Walt never contacted or asked an adult or a religious figure about religion except in anthropology class during regular question and answer sessions about the topic at hand. Nothing about his doubts or questions on a personal level. In letters home his mother did not know whether he went to church or not, and she never inquired one way or other. He wanted it that way. The question that slowly came to mind was, why did humanity in all its forms develop over thousands of years the concept of religion or what is now better known as spirituality? He never found that answer in Alaska or thereafter. It became a mystery, something that inspired a certain awe. Much like the awe Einstein felt about the cosmos. But Walt knew he could not mention any religion in the bull session or ask unanswerable questions without some sort of changing of the topic. "Who has a church key?" (A beer bottle opener.) was fair game to start talking about something else.

Hey Gunther! Why Are You Here?

CHAPTER THIRTY-ONE: VARIOUS STUDENT ACTIVITIES

SOURDOUGH CLUB

"Are you going to go to the Sourdough Club tonight, Walt?" Howard asked Walt as they both left the cafeteria that night.

"What is the Sourdough Club?"

"Oh, that is a folk dance group that meets in the gym on occasion. Good place to meet girls!"

"I have a hard time with dancing, mostly left feet…but girls? What time?" Howard told him the time but said he would be late because he had to go into town to pick up his date.

It was Walt's first week on campus, and it seemed like a pleasant way to be introduced to the social life at the university. Mention dance and there were remembrances of the first time he entered the Wilson Junior High back in Mount Vernon after he left the Wartburg. It was a cultural shock then but this time he was prepared for anything new. But he knew he had a difficult time with dancing. He also remembered his recent "steady" from A.B. Davis high school who he had lost before the graduation prom a few months ago.

The Sourdough Club always met in the gym. He thought, if it were supposed to be a social event he at least dressed for the occasion with a "Sunday" jacket, white shirt, tie and pressed pants. When he entered the gym there were some students and some other folks from town gathered around a table toward the rear of the gym. First of all Walt

179

felt he was overdressed because the others were less formal in dress than he. So he took off his tie and put it in his jacket pocket. He saw people at the table and some one picking up records and placing them near a phonograph machine so he walked in that direction. He was noticed, "Are you a new student to the university?"

"Yes I am."

The person who asked, introduced himself to Walt and Walt said his name in return.

"Do you like old-fashioned folk dancing?" Paul K. asked. Paul was a senior student and president of the club.

"I don't know. All left feet and my rhythm goes off. I have a hard time but I want to give it a try."

"Then you are in the right place, this is a good time for you to start." With a short hesitation and glancing at the people around the table Paul directed a question toward Ruth, "Hey Ruth, do you want to be a teacher for Walt tonight?"

Ruth answered, "OK, if he is all left feet maybe we should start with the schottische."

And this was Walt's introduction to the Sourdough Club. Ruth was a senior, a bit tall, a bit bulky but very pleasant in her manner. She took Walt off to the side and tried to explain more about the club. Within a few minutes there was a loud voice saying, "Welcome to the Sourdough Club; let's start with the familiar schottische." And with that, couples drifted into a line on the gym floor as the record began to play an introduction to a melody over the loudspeaker system.

Ruth turned toward the dancers and asked Walt to look at the dancers for a moment and at the same time she took his hand and began to move it up and down forcefully in time with the music and saying "One, two, three, hop, one, two, three, hop, one hop, two hop, three hop four." She then repeated the hand movement to the music. He noticed all the couples were going in the same direction and eventually they all danced in a circle. A moment later she told Walt to look at her feet as she let go of his hand and began to move her feet in rhythm with the beat of the music. "The music tells you what to do, now follow me." And with the beat and hearing the "one" from Ruth he proceeded to begin the dancing. They repeated the routine several times. Soon the record stopped and Ruth asked Walt to stay where he was and almost ran to where the phonograph was being prepared for another record. She asked for another schottische.

It was a different melody but Ruth kept saying quietly the one, two, three, hop cadence as she picked up Walt's hand and brought him closer to the other dancers. Then on the "one" she began to dance forward with Walt in tow. Ruth soon did not call out the "one" but kept pumping Walt's hand gently in time with the music. Even her hand pumping slowly diminished and it was just his feet keeping in time with the music but all the time he kept saying in his mind 'one, two, three, hop' and on and on repeating, repeating, the cadence. Past halfway through the music Ruth stopped their dancing and pointed to various couples and telling about their styles. Pointing to a couple coming in their direction, "That couple likes to run rather than step." A bit later, "See that couple over there—they like to twirl!" "These are variations you can do once you get used to the beat of the music." "Some girls like to twirl." Just then the music stopped and Ruth excused herself saying that she was needed at the phonograph. Walt looked around and spotted Howard with his date.

After a brief introduction to his date they drifted toward the side of the gym where they found chairs. Just then the music started and Howard's date said, "Oh good a waltz!" and they joined other couples on the dance floor. All Walt could do was to sit down and watch the dancing. He saw a couple of girls off under the right balcony but since he did not know how to dance the waltz he just enjoyed himself watching. At one time during the waltz he saw a couple who did a lot of swirling. It reminded him of seeing movies of dancing in an elegant place with chandeliers and where the dance floor was made of black and white squares. The ladies were in flowing gowns and the men in tuxedos but here the couple was in regular clothing and the gym lights did nothing to enhance the gala atmosphere. But he did find it interesting to realize there were variations to the dance.

When the waltz was over there was a moment where folks were busy talking with each other. He then saw Ruth with one of the girls and by taking her by the hand brought her in front of Walt. In politeness he stood up while she said, "This is Mary she knows the schottische, that is the next dance. I hope you did not forget what I taught you." And with that, Ruth turned around and went toward the crowd around the phonograph. All that Mary and he said to each other was, "Hello." The music started; the melody was different from the previous records but Mary took Walt by the hand and said "Remember, one, two, three, hop."

"OK."

He managed to go through the dance routine with only a few mishaps but got his rhythm back every time Mary repeated the ONE, two, three, hop mantra. It seemed like a conspiracy Ruth had with some other members of the Sourdough Club. Every time a schottische was going to be played, someone, man or woman, would introduce themself to Walt while he was watching other dances. They noted that the next dance or two after a polka for example was going to be a schottische. The man would give his partner to Walt and Walt was always given the ONE, two, three, hop routine. In this way by the end of the evening of dancing, Walt had the routine down without any missteps. Even though there was a punchbowl, after the last traditional waltz, Howard and his date said they were going to go to the Cub. Would Walt like to join them.

This being the first social event for Walt at the university it was also the beginning of being a member of the Club. He willingly paid his dues over the years and in time became a reliable member. He had to admit however, that he was not the best dancer. Unless he knew the record music and strong rhythm it was difficult to know what steps to start with. There were other "left footers" guys in the club and in one case the guy took advantage of this to "meet girls" who were tolerant of his so called lack of talent. His better talents were in getting a variety of movie dates.

It was not clear who really owned the phonograph machine but it was always available for other dances held in the gym so the Sourdough Club took responsibility for the equipment. As such, different organizations sometimes held dances on campus. For example there was the annual Miner's dance in which the Fairbanks Exploration

182

Walt Fluegel

Company (FE), the local dredging company, which extracted gold from the ground, and student miners had an annual dance. All kinds of music from the Lindy to swing, to jitterbug and fox trot was played so there were a mixture of dances for all couples; college or towns folks. There were also different mixtures from the "Pump House" from the miners competing with the usual punch bowl provided by the Sourdough Club. By the end of the evening it seemed that vodka somehow mysterious appeared in the punch bowl and equaled that from the Pump House. Those who knew what was happening kept quiet while everyone had a good time.

During wintertime when daylight was in scarce supply any source of entertainment eased the onset of cabin fever. The Sourdough Club tried to do its part. There was a Halloween dance too with the usual ghostly or pumpkin, or farm costume requirements and gym decorations. And on April Fools Day or near it, anything was possible. The gym was decorated with decorations seen at Christmas time, Halloween, Easter even left over material from the ROTC dance. Any type of costume was permissible so long as it added to the good time everyone wanted to have. At one time Walt came as a robot. He managed to cobble some boxes together and painted them a lime green with black dots to resemble bolts holding things together. Walking around in a spasmodic way on the dance floor as a robot, had its limits, so he had to abandon the pretense very quickly because everyone knew anyway that Walt was in the boxes.

LATIN DANCING

The Sourdough Club dances were largely of Scandinavian folk origin. One day Walt was given a notice that someone from Fairbanks was starting a class in Latin American dancing. At the next meeting he asked the members if he should contact these folks to see if they would come to campus and talk about the class. The idea appealed to many. Perhaps it would be possible to have a few lessons if it did not cost so much. Walt made the contact first by phone then in person. The husband-wife couple were new to Alaska and so their conversation with Walt about prospects of a good business was somewhat limited. But the campus would be a first good try for them

183

to advertise their talents. Walt made plans with them to come to the Club at the next meeting.

The Latin couple arrived a little early with a few of their records and checked out the phonograph equipment. When they took off their parkas and handed them to Walt to hang up, he had to quickly shift his glance from the lady to the man. She was in her early thirties and wore her bright sunny clothing as if they were painted on. A record of Latin music was played in low volume as Club members and others began to assemble in the gym. Some people began to talk with the couple. Attendance was good that night and when the time came Walt had to tell the folks there what the Club was trying to do.

There was a small demonstration of the various dances that most beginners could learn easily. When the man asked for volunteers there was a little reluctance from the women or girls but a marked difference when the lady asked for a volunteer partner to teach. Except from the married men, they were naturally restrained. The Latin couple then asked if anyone actually knew the various dances they named. A few folks mostly married couples from town knew and were invited to join the Latin couple in a further demonstration. It seemed to go well, but if Walt was an example of the average college age male it was not the usual couples they saw at previous meetings but the dance experts, specifically the lady in her bight clothing.

At a quiet interval someone called out to the couple and asked if they knew how to do the polka or waltz or the schottische or other folk dances. The lady said she knew the polka and the waltz but never heard about the schottische. "I can teach you if you let me," said Peterson from the far right of the gym.

"Will your girl friend let you?" the Latin lady rejoined.

There was a relief laughter from everyone but Peterson responded by saying; "Helen taught me so I volunteer her to teach your husband."

In one way one can say that music and dance is universal to human-kind so this spontaneous gesture helped this couple understand Alaskans better and the Sourdough Club was known for its social inclinations. The Latin lady picked up the rhythm quickly from Peterson and soon began to improvise her steps to where Peterson

184

began to learn from her what to do. In the dorm for those who were at the Club that night, this dancing lesson put him in seventh heaven for quite a while.

THE CHORUS

To gather about 15 to 20 people who like to sing from a total of 250 enrolled students amounts to about 10% of the student body. It really was a half credit course but most singers thought of it as an outlet for fun. The chorus met twice a week or more for about an hour or more practice shortly after supper. Campus and non-campus students were enrolled. Miss Don was the music instructor but most of her students had limited talent. Many, including Walt, could not read music directly. Everyone needed a note from the piano or her little mouth organ to get started and learned the music from memory not from the notes on the page. If he saw the notes go up Walt knew to make a higher pitch and if notes went down his voice also went down. How long to hold a note also was a memory thing as well as watching Miss Don lead the chorus with traditional gestures. The students were clustered into bass, tenor, sopranos, altos, etc. Walt considered himself a low tenor or a high base depending upon the music being sung. Baritone somehow needed a mellow sound, something one had to be born with.

It was practice, practice, and more practice for various programs such as the Christmas show, Easter time, and other occasions such as a comedy variety show or two. (One snippet of a scene had the woman singer sing that she needs to cultivate her voice, but her opposite boomed out that it needed plowing under!) Sometimes the chorus sung in town for an organization. A subgroup of students who had previous voice training in the States or other schools sang with the A cappella. Their music was more technical to perform and they did it without any accompanying piano. There was an initial problem with one student, Uri, which Miss Don accepted once she understood his reason. Uri was a devout Jewish person and a very good baritone singer but if the music to be sung glorified the Christian faith he would not participate in that music.

Hey Gunther! Why Are You Here?

At one time to the surprise of every one, a new woman in her 30's and from town entered the chorus rehearsal room. She had met Miss Don previously that day and was accepted immediately. Ellen was a contralto voice. Miss Don announced that Ellen would sing a solo piece at the next show being rehearsed and asked Ellen if she was ready to sing a few bars for the rest of the class.

"Gladly" she said. A few preliminary notes from Miss Don's piano and Ellen began to sing something from a Wagner opera. Everyone was surprised. After the first few notes that this "Brunnhilde" type singer performed, everyone knew there was talent close by. What intrigued Walt the most was the clearness of the vibrato. None of the chorus singers, men or women, had that kind of vibrato in their voice. Back in Mount Vernon while he was making his Jewelry he would be tuned to the WQXR radio station for the Saturday afternoon Metropolitan Opera. To hear someone here in Alaska, of this quality so close was a gift for everyone. Ellen told everyone that her husband was on temporary assignment at the Airbase and she just had to keep practicing as often as possible and sing for anyone who wanted to listen. She also said it was a good experience for her to sing with whatever group she met except the barbershop quartet types because of her vibrato. When she sang with the chorus whenever she could, she kept her voice on low volume. Within four months her husband was transferred again, but the students felt pleased to have known Ellen.

SNOW AND ICE

For a university that had roughly 250 total students enrolled, outdoor winter sports were not a prominent winter activity. Yes, some students happened to get a ski lift built on a hill about a half-mile from campus, but how many could assemble at any one time to keep the ski lift machine going. Walt heard that an old car engine, a rope to hang on to, and pulleys were all scrounged or loaned from somewhere. Without the machine if anyone wanted to do downhill skiing, it was the climbing up the hill that was the big discouragement. However, some students, both men and women were regulars in cross country skiing.. When Walt tried cross country he

186

injured one knee early in his attempt, so his outdoor winter sports activity was limited to the 'walk into town type' via the rail road tracks. It was a three-mile adventure if bundled up and wearing a good pair of mukluks. (At the end of the tracks by the railroad station there was a small SpudNut store which served hot chocolate and donuts made of potato flour. Walt understood at the time this store was owned by a local Mormon family. They did not serve coffee but they served Postum as a substitute.) Sometimes he borrowed snow shoes for exploration into nearby woods on a occasional Saturday afternoon. Skating or hockey on campus was difficult especially in mid winter at way below zero temperatures when flooding for a smooth surface outdoors was impossible. There was one attempt during a warm spell in spring when a rink was built and players from the military base were challenged by some campus players.

BASKETBALL

The biggest sport in winter for the university and all of the Fairbanks area was basketball. Name a bar or organization in town and there were a few players willing to have a game somewhere at different gyms or at the university. In the middle of winter when cabin fever was evident this social event took the edge off the fever and boosted spirits for everyone. The university gym was not very large. Spectator seating was provided in two balconies, one on the left of the entrance and one on the right of the playing area. There was very little standing room under the balconies. Anyone who thought he could keep up with the team was eligible to play but Walt knowing his high school experience did not have the stamina. He was an occasional spectator. In those days (mid '40s) the coaches were of the opinion that the lower the score you kept against the opponent the better the game. A defensive game or the thought to keep the opponent from even approaching the hoop was the important strategy. The referee made sure the ball was always in motion either by constant dribbling or passing. That meant most of the activity was in mid court to prevent the opponent from getting close to the hoop. This tactic encouraged shorter players who seemed more nimble and swifter, to weave their way between other players to steal the ball from the opponent. But their lack of height or arm strength made for fewer baskets to score. So it was up to the taller players in the team to be ready near the basket. But the opponent players knew about this tactic and they too had to be ready to block the attempt to score. This meant that the entire court had players in it. Very seldom were players bunched near the basket. So all teams had short and tall players all in good physical shape and for the most part the university players were always ready to play the game.

Occasionally the local radio station (KFAR?) broadcast a game and if the reporter thought a student knew the players on a team that student was recruited to help the reporter. T-shirts for the U of A players were of a uniform color with no numbers or names so the reporter did need help. At one time Walt was "volunteered" to sit beside the reporter who had a list of U of A players in large type. Whoever had the ball at any moment, Walt pointed with a pencil at the name and the reporter did what his vocabulary allowed to describe the action. Also, on the opposite side of the reporter someone from the opponents side also did the same thing. One has to visualize from radio descriptions three people with eyes on the ball, a list of players and one voice from the radio describing the action. Depending upon the verbal and excitement skill of the reporter and the correct identity of the players, the radio audience got a play by play account of the game. Walt never listened to the radio reporting, preferring to see the game from the mid balcony area.

THE 22 RIFLE

ROTC (Reserve Officers Training Corp) was required of all incoming male students who were not previously in the military during the WW2. Because of numerous marching drills, these drills substituted for physical education classes because there were no phys-ed instructors on the university staff. As such, the ROTC drill sergeant wanted to establish a rifle team and make it a sport of some sort. Target practice occurred in the gym and the rifles were single shot 22's that had to be loaded one bullet at a time. The bullseye targets were mounted on to a soft upright board which in turn was backed by a slanted sheet of thick steel. This target assembly was on a dolly that could be moved out of the way under the balcony at the far side of the gym. There were three of these dollies. The slant of the steel assured that once the lead slug that easily penetrated the board, and hit the steel, its fragments would be projected down into the cart. Only members of the team and the sergeant were allowed in the gym during these practices.

Walt decided to give it a try. And was disqualified almost immediately after the first day. Why? He had never fired a rifle before, maybe a B-B gun, but nothing as serious as something with live ammunition. After preliminary instructions five students (one for each target on display) were instructed to lie on the floor and given a rifle and a bullet. They were then instructed on how to load the bullet and cock it ready to fire. All students, except Walt, put his rifle tight against their right shoulder and sight down the barrel and aim at the targets. Walt put his rifle on his left shoulder and aimed with his left eye. The sergeant was disturbed at what he saw and wanted Walt to switch back to sighting with his right eye. "After all, these rifles were designed for right handed shooters." But the sergeant allowed Walt his way when he explained his right eye was weak. Everyone then knew they would fire upon command when Walt was settled in position. Then on the, "ready, aim…fire, " command the rifles cracked, the paper targets flickered and the shell casings discharged from their chambers to the right. The discharged casing from Walt's rife nicked his glasses. This was another one of those "good bye" moments for Walt, not verbally but in reality. The sergeant used Walt's experience as one of those safety measures, and Walt realized he could not be in the rifle team. However he continued to use his left eye for all microscopic work far into the future.

POKER AND OTHER GAMES

During the week after supper the dorm was relatively quiet except for the occasional clicking of a typewriter or maybe a radio was on a little too loud if doors were left open. However, somewhere in the dorm or in the lobby, a canasta or a poker game of four to six players was probably in progress on weekends. Early poker games were a penny to nickel to a nickel-dime affair but as the evening progressed beyond

Hey Gunther! Why Are You Here?

ten or eleven or one in the morning the ante would rise until silver dollars were tossed on the table with a dull thump. There was always an audience contributing to the blue cigarette smoke haze accumulating from some players too. Different kinds of poker were played and everyone knew the rules. Walt was sometimes drawn into the game early at the nickel-dime level if he had no date that weekend. As usual most guys had a pocket full of coins they soon stacked on the table.

There was a slight chatter as cards were dealt or bids were made and pots were collected and coins stacked. It was obvious that some players were better at bluffing than others or someone was very lucky that evening at least for a while. Every now and then at winning a pot, Walt would "squirrel away" a few dimes or nickels into his shirt. Because his shirt was tucked into his pants and his belt was tight, any coins slipped into the front of his shirt would be trapped or caught. During the game anyone who wanted to borrow money to cover his "winning hand" was gently told to fold or go back to their room and rob their piggy bank. While he was there he should come back with a beer or two and some glasses, and don't forget the church key. As the night wore on and the bidding got a bit steeper the usual beginner players quit the game and sometimes "congratulated" the one guy who seemed to have the most coins remaining. There was always a spectator willing to take his place. Walt had his limit too and begged off by saying he had to pee or he needed to go for a walk. In his room he managed to collect the squirrels buried coins. Most of the time he broke even for the night, but if he lost some, it wasn't much. Within a minute or so after going to his room and the bathroom he had his parka and mukluks on. He went for a short walk and saw the northern lights.

Sometimes these lights were brilliant, other times just so-so. But he seemed to need that night walk now and then. Sometimes on a Friday night he would call on Flo in Hess hall and asked her if it was OK if he could walk with her. He knew she wanted to see her sister over the weekend. Her sister was Walt's chemistry lab partner and she lived with her husband in a small house on Farmers Loop Road about a mile from campus. The Hess Hall housemother knew of the arrangement of Flo with her sister and knew Flo would not be back

190

until Sunday night. Thus curfew demerits were avoided. Sometimes the aurora were more brilliant than on other nights, and this seemed to encourage some smooching along the Farmers Loop Road. These delights seemed more important than other smooches in the dimly lit hallway near the campus post office mail box area when checking for mail after supper. Other couples too found their ways to play natures games.

Hey Gunther! Why Are You Here?

Walt Fluegel

CHAPTER THIRTY-TWO: CHANGE OF PLANS, ANOTHER HERE

In review of the early chapters we know that Walt read a few books about arctic adventurers. He finally decided to enter the University of Alaska to study agriculture because of its potential adventure for himself. He remembers the jeers from some high school class mates and later on there were jeers from some of the University campus ag students. But we all realize that at this age, tell a young man he can't do something and it becomes a challenge to give it a try. Also the adults who knew his college dreams when less than ten percent of graduates ever went to college, admired his 'grit' but were quiet on the subject that interested him. So he went to Alaska with a fortified dream. Later he slowly realized in his second year he was not going to be a farmer. But, what was he going to be? The official method at college was to go to someone in the administration and change to a different major. Could courses and credits he already accumulated be applied to a new major? In the 40's the major coursework for most University of Alaska students was clustered on mining and agriculture with a smattering of pre-professional outlets and anthropology. What Walt accumulated so far could fit with the pre med cluster of courses. But he knew he was not going be a doctor but perhaps his new advisor, Mrs. Carr could help him further in the next couple of years.

Mister Sterner talked with Walt about the change of major. He looked over the courses and asked many questions starting back to Walt's orphanage experience and his little Jewelry business and his reason to become a farmer. The thing Walt remembers mostly was a comment best described as, "You should think of leaving this place, you will find more opportunities if you went to a larger university." Walt remembers the words but his desire to stay in Alaska subdued all logic from Mister Sterner's talk with him. His advice made sense but Walt continued at the University for two more years. It was the time of year, springtime and he needed to find a summer job that would sustain him for another year of enrollment.

In the meantime he wrote a letter to Miss Lewis of A B Davis high school about his change of plans and in due time she responded by telling him she sort of knew what might happen. She expected there will be a "bubble bursting" time and said that what happened to him usually happened to many students in their second year. This especially occurred if their parents insisted their children take up a certain profession like being a lawyer or doctor when they had no inclination in that direction. She did indicate he should think of something in biology or perhaps in business because she thought he had talents in these two different areas. Walt also wrote to his mother about the change but she did not know how to help him, and she did seem to worry when or if he would come back to Mount Vernon.

After the talk with Mister Sterner, Walt contacted Mrs. Carr concerning his third year at the university, and shortly after that he went into town. He entered the bank building, which also housed the Federal Government Offices. He knew from a campus bulletin board notice that there were several USA and Territorial government jobs available. One job in particular interested him because he could be working on the improvement of the ALCAN (Alaska-Canada) highway made famous right after the Pearl Harbor attack. Both the US government and Canada built this road as a military road to assure the military the capabilities of delivering supplies to Alaska in case of a Japanese attack. The job he applied for amounted to another flunky job of just following instructions from a surveyor and do other chores necessary.

Walt Fluegel

THIRD SUMMER JOB ON THE ALCAN HIGHWAY

He was given a standard application form. He filled out the required blanks such as name, date of birth, where born, citizenship, school level etc. When Walt handed the form to one of the clerks he specifically asked a question the clerk could not answer. "It asked me where I was born and I say Germany, and then it asked my citizenship and I say right here, USA." as he pointed to the filled in blanks. "I have my citizenship paper in a safe deposit box right here in this bank downstairs. Do you want to see it?" The clerk took the application and looked it over on the front and back and all he said was, "Since there is no blank for you to fill out about that, all you need do now is sign it that you are telling the truth. So just sign it and you will be notified one way or other."

Within a couple of days he was notified by mail that now he would be an employee of the Bureau of Public Roads. Walt knew this was a federal job not a Territorial job with the Alaska Railroad. Included in the mail was the location where he had to report but if he had no transportation he would have to meet on such and such a date and time at the bank building. It also gave details of the location of a camp and what in general to accept in terms of living away from any town.

Fortunately the spring semester with final exams was coming to an end and everyone was busy packing up to leave or getting summer jobs lined up. Dorm rooms had to be emptied but Walt had little possessions to worry about. He had a box or two that Nick and Zelda were willing to store for him and he had his duffel bag crammed for taking to his summer job out in the boonies about a hundred miles south of Fairbanks. The road leading out of Fairbanks as most roads out of town were gravel and dusty and at places like washboards. Mister Marvin Tesky his boss, drove the van or was it a small bus holding four other passengers. Introductions were soon made and little life stories were exchanged so each would get to know one another. Marvin informed all riders of what to expect and they would meet more of the crew at the camp.

Hey Gunther! Why Are You Here?

When the van arrived it parked near a long low, log cabin and frame construction house (the mess hall) and several tent like canvas topped structures.These would be the sleeping quarters for not only the survey crews but some truck drivers and others of the contractor responsible for improving the road. In a large parking lot there were quite a few small trailers and cars owned by more of the workers. By looking at the license plates they were all from the states, people looking for jobs in Alaska. Each of the tents had one hang down light but with the constant daylight of the season it was seldom needed. Inside the long low building there was a kitchen and a hall of sorts and some office rooms. One of the rooms had a radio, which made contact with headquarters in Fairbanks and with walkie-talkies in the field.

Along the ALCAN several miles down there were other camps similar to this one but from what Walt was able to understand this was the main headquarters. It was the middle of the afternoon by the time he arrived so all he could do was to take a vacant bed in one of the assigned tents and dump his duffel bag into a small foot locker. He was also informed he could rent a combination padlock for the foot locker or else make arrangements to put anything really valuable in the safe in the office. He walked around to inspect the camp after more instructions of what he was supposed to do on the job. There was a small breeze at the time he arrived but when it subsided the mosquitoes came out in full force.

At around five o'clock the parking lot was beginning to fill further with some trucks and cars and the tents were beginning to hum with activity. There was a temporary shower being used: water draining slowly from a barrel supported on tall legs that was warmed by the sun. First come first served until the pumped water was too cold except for the hardy users. Other showers were in the main place. He decided to go back to his bunk tent and meet his tent mates. There were six to eight beds per tent. HIs tent held six and he learned that most of them also worked for the Bureau. All of them came from the States wanting to know more about the Territory. As one of them was telling Walt about his home town, he slapped a mosquito and with a few colorful words added, said where he came form in Idaho they were not a bother. Walt also related that on the riverboat it was no

196

problem, likewise at the McKinley hotel. He told others around him that he came from New York. "No wonder you sound funny." someone called out from the back bed.

Within an hour of the crew's arrival at camp the dinner bell (triangle) sounded. The long low cabin mess hall began to fill up and Walt found a place to sit and was immediately told to, "move on down, new guy, " by a burley truck driver. Walt didn't argue, he moved. And as usual with a large gathering of working men wanting to eat at one time the cook had complete control of the situation. He allowed no talking while food was on the table. Only gestures indicating to pass something was permitted. A snap of the fingers and pointing or a jab in the ribs drew attention. Within 15 to 20 minutes of eating the exodus started with two or three men departing at a time. Walt always felt rushed but after a few days he adjusted enough to not be the last man to leave no matter what was being served, breakfast or dinner. On Saturday or Sundays there was a lunch served for those who stayed in camp.

During a working day near noon there was food on the job for the survey crew and presumably the truck drivers and machine operators too. Somehow the kitchen staff found a way to deliver the food to the proper place thanks to the radio.

By asking around the night before on his first day Walt knew what clothing and boots to wear on the job. Either wear two shirts to keep mosquitoes from biting your back or a light version of an Eisenhower jacket capable of withstanding walking into brush now and then. He did not have that kind of jacket so either a different jacket or two shirts would have to do. Others said they have citronella to ward off mosquitos he could use and pay back later while others said it did not work for them. Walt said he would take his chances. He had a bill cap ever since his river journeys. He was as ready as he could be the next day when he climbed into the van with other members of the crew including Benson the surveyor and Marvin Tesky. Tesky drove and let some of the men out about five miles from base. Benson unloaded his own survey equipment except he asked someone to carry his tripod. Martin drove the rest of the crew further along the road.

Hey Gunther! Why Are You Here?

On the first day Walt's job seemed simple enough. All he had to do was to watch and follow Drake as he carried the surveyors rod into the brush looking for new wooden stakes pounded into the ground just before heavy frost came last fall. Many of these stakes had numbers inked on their flat sides. Sometimes another stub of a stake was pounded deep into ground level next to the numbered stake and often colored with a blue marking. Drake pointed out these stubs because they were very important ones to find. Then they looked toward the road and saw that Benson was looking in their direction with his transit. After an arm signal Drake placed the surveyors rod on the blue stub in the ground. "Watch this, Gunther, " Drake instructed as he slowly moved the rod forward and back slowly several times. "What this does is to give Benson a more accurate measure of the true height between him and this peg below. The rod must be perfectly straight up and he can tell that when he sees it in his transit. Benson's tripod was directly above another stub next to the road. In this way with doing 'levels' all morning and afternoon the day ended. (Mosquitos were not too bad if one could find a breeze.) On other days the chain was used to confirm distance and Walt was assigned to wind up the steel tape. By just observing and asking a few questions he could see the importance of his job and the overall project. But within two weeks of doing this work all could be in trouble when Marvin Tesky came to Walt's tent after supper.

CITIZENSHIP PAPER

"Are you an American citizen?"

"Sure am."

"I got a radio call today saying I have to ask you for proof."

Walt then told Marvin about his application for the job and the clerk who did not want to see the paper even though it was in the safe deposit box at the bank. He also made a soft grumbling remark about that stupid clerk.

198

Walt Fluegel

"As of now you don't have a job until I can see your papers." But then Marvin said he and a few others had to go to Fairbanks anyway tomorrow. They will leave right after breakfast. Be ready.

On the way to Fairbanks, Marvin explained to all that the ALCAN was still considered a military road, Gunther's job was a government job and America just finished WW2 with Nazi Germany. Gunther was born in Germany and who knows where his loyalty really lies and all sorts of things. Marvin trusted Gunther's story just so. But he had to obey his orders too. He also said directly to Walt, "I'm giving you the benefit of the doubt otherwise I would have had you pack your duffel and dump you off at the Fairbanks office.

Things were going fine but this still being spring thaw melt time Marvin had to stop and assess one part of the road. It had fast flowing water flowing over it. It looked mired up from a previous truck travel. Will the van-bus make it too? Someone said 'Let's stretch our legs while Marvin looks over the road.' The three others and Walt got out and walked around but two guys and Walt who were on the side of the road found themselves sinking quickly into ankle deep ice cold water. In reality the side of the road seemed to be a temporary fix to a floating road which was fine if frozen completely in winter. Spring thaw claimed three victims. With wet boots and all, every one was on board when Marvin took a chance and backed up a ways. Then in first gear he gunned the engine, released the clutch, and skillfully managed to cross the flowing water. With a relief to his voice Marvin asked out loud if the walkie-talkie was in the back somewhere. It was. He finally stopped and tried to make contact with someone up the line or back in camp. Contact was made to report the problem, maybe someone could put a load or two of gravel on the low spot. After that there were no memorable problems. All wet boots were taken off, socks were rung out and attempts to dry out were only partially successful by the time they reached Fairbanks.

"I know you others have something to do in town. Once I take care of Gunther here meet me in this parking lot at three. We have to get back, but let's hope there are left -overs in the kitchen." Marvin said to the other passengers as he parked the van-bus in a space for government vehicles. Marvin and Walt entered the bank by the front entrance and did not appear out of place with muddy boots on Walt or the unkempt hair from Marvin. Walt went right to one of the tellers and asked to see someone concerning safe deposit boxes. He gave his name and university status and showed his social security card. He also had to fill out a small form before being allowed to follow the lady into the vault. With a stern voice she said to Marvin, "I am sorry you can't come into the vault with him."

"That's all right ma'am, he is my boss and he has to see my citizenship paper."

"I have to insist, he can wait right here, and you Mister Gunther come with me."

Marvin seemed annoyed but complied. In a couple of minutes or so he calmed down as he saw Walt coming with the paper in hand, followed by the bank lady. Marvin looked over the paper, read a few lines out loud and said, "This is the first time I have ever seen a citizenship paper, congratulations Walter Gunther you have your job back." And then shook Walt's hand. The lady was also relieved at the change in demeanor of Marvin.

But Marvin said, "Let me write those certificate numbers in my note book and send them off to headquarters upstairs, that should clear up everything." They saw him take a small spiral notepad from his shirt pocket that had a small pencil imbedded in the spring like binding. The lady and Walt watched Marvin write, then return the document to Walt. Walt then turned around and asked the lady if he were allowed to return the paper to the deposit box.

"You are good for two more years of rental." Marvin looked toward Walt and indicated he had business to attend to upstairs in the government offices so come back at three and we can all get back to work.

Before leaving town Marvin stopped at the grocery store, but told the others he would be right back but could Iverson come in with him. Prior to three that afternoon Marvin called the grocery manager by phone and made certain arrangements. When Iverson and he came out, each carried a large box filled with fruits and other perishable items, items not seen often in camp. On the way down the highway, everyone seemed relaxed, little businesses were taken care of and the others seemed more at ease talking chit-chat with Walt and each other. Soon one or two including Walt were so relaxed they must have snoozed sometime in spite of the occasional washboard road. They did arrive in camp late, the cook was upset to have to fix something for Marvin and his bunch but was mollified to have the special boxes.

MIDNIGHT SUN

That night at about 4 in the morning Walt had to visit the latrine. He met someone he had not seen before in camp. He was a new arrival the day before for the Bureau from North Carolina and he seemed bewildered. "Doesn't the sun ever set around here?" he asked Walt. The man had never left his state to be this far north before. Oh yes, he knew intellectually there was such a thing as long daylight in summer but he was amazed he actually was a part of it now. Walt suggested he wait for December and January for the opposite effect of darkness and cold. The man did not want to know and both did what they had to do and get more sleep as best as they can.

Taking care of natural needs required adapting to the overall situation in camp or out on the job. Away from camp any tree that was available to urinate against was a common procedure, but the BM function required a slight request or signal from whoever was in charger that you just had to go into the bush. Everyone adapted. In camp Walt decided to shave about every other day after supper rather than compete for a mirror before breakfast. Some of the men had electric shavers others had a straight razor, Walt had a simple double edge Gillette blade. (at 4 for 10 cents). As far s haircuts went, he did not tell anyone he could cut hair because for the most part he was on his feet all day. Besides, most everyone kept their hair long to help prevent mosquito bites on the head and neck even though all had hats of one kind or other. One guy had the simple hand clipper Walt was familiar with when he started, and from the results seen, the guy did a reasonable job.

Hey Gunther! Why Are You Here?

PAPER WORK

There were more survey chores, more mosquitoes and the burning of birch bark torches to keep the buzzers at bay and more brush to wade through for another week until Walt was given a different assignment. This time there was a bit of paperwork, lots of bits of paper, one page with carbon paper per dump truck filled with gravel. In order to pay the contractor for every yard of gravel dumped on the road there had to be a record of each truck load, and the station or place it was dumped at. Walt was given a squarish booklet each morning. Each page was numbered in sequence and there were several loose carbon pages to use if needed. The page required the date, the truck number, yardage if known, the nearest station (survey marker) and his own name. At the end of the day this booklet was handed in for use in the office to calculate the progress of work. A new booklet was issued the next morning. The contractor's trucks were all the same make and model and held the same yardage, and all had wooden extensions on the sides to increase the yardage. However there were other trucks owned by their drivers who were their own subcontractors. These trucks came in all sizes but with numbers painted on the doors Walt did not have to know the yardage. It was the governments way of keeping tabs on the contractor. Once the loads were dumped or spread on the road the trucks went back for more gravel. Road graders and other equipment spread the gravel as needed. After suitable intervals a surveyor ran levels and noted this in his log book. Sometimes he would take out his slide rule, make some calculations and talk with someone on the crew of operators, then head down the road with his crew.

When the trucks filled with gravel arrived it was obvious the trucks were filled to capacity because Walt could see a mound of gravel above the boards. At about the second week on this job he noticed that he could not always see the mounds of gravel in several of the trucks belonging to the company. It appeared to be the same trucks during the day, and appeared delayed in arrival. He noted this on one of the pages and thought no more about it. About three days later in the late morning a small pickup truck stopped along the side of the

202

road away from the dump and work area. A man came out of the truck and asked one of the grader operators who this Gunther guy was. Gunther was pointed out. The man came toward Gunther, "Are you Gunther?" the man asked in a demanding voice.

"Sure am."

The man who looked like a boss in a clean work jacket did not introduce himself to Gunther but asked him how long he was doing this job. "A couple of weeks I suppose."

"Just a minute sir, I have to record this truck." And he did that for three trucks that came in succession.

He then gave his attention to the boss like man. "Your office tells me some of my trucks are not quite full. Is that true?"

"I noticed that this morning again. Just a minute, sir, I have to make another page."

He almost forgot the carbon paper. But after that he flipped through and noted two other entries that morning and gave the boss man the numbers of the truck. After a few moments the boss man gave a quiet thanks to Gunther then said. "I know your memory can be good but this time you don't remember seeing me or know who I am. Understand!" All Walt could do was to nod his head and then began to make another entry. (He never knew who the boss man was until a week later.) By late that afternoon all the trucks were filled to capacity with all showing the mound of gravel expected.

SUPER CARLSON

About a week later Walt found out who the boss man was. He was called Super (for superintendent) Carlson because he oversaw a large section of the road building. One of his often dictums was, "be sober from Monday to Saturday." He did not mind someone taking a drink off the job but he did not tolerate drunkenness while his men were on the job and operating machinery. In spite of the union, Super Carlson fired anyone found drunk on the job. Super Carlson, after seeing for himself why a truck or two was not quite full of gravel on delivery, drove to the gravel pit where the gravel was being mined. The gravel pit was along a river but a small stream emptied into the river. Super Carlson saw the shovel operator and a truck driver doing something in that little stream. They were panning for gold. After a short while they realized they should get a move on and get the truck loaded and "get the hell out" before the next truck arrives for a load. Too late, Super Carlson did see them and drew their attention. When he introduced himself to them he said one thing for them to remember: "You either pan for gold and make breakfast or work for the company and make enough money for dinner and your kids back home. Your choice, gentlemen!" Without saying more, he turned around and went to his pick up truck and drove off.

Different versions of the story drifted into Walt's hearing over the next few evenings in the tent after supper. No one ever asked how Super Carlson knew of the gold panning. But just in case someone suggested the connection between himself and Super Carlson, Walt thought up a story. (He saw my name in the office and wondered if I knew another Gunther in New Jersey, some shirt-tail relative of his wife he knows. I told him I came as a babe in arms.)

A couple of weeks later on one Sunday after lunch Walt was asked if he ever panned for gold. Not really, but he did see a demonstration at the university when he first arrived a couple of years ago. If he wanted to see more gold panning he better get into a car waiting for another passenger. He took the opportunity and within a half hour's drive the car stopped along a side road and everyone got out. There were three other cars off the road too and to reconstruct the scene Walt was told that this is the place where some of the gravel he recorded each day came from, "over there by the river." The side road led to where the shovel was seen a short distance away but it being Sunday it was not operating. As the car passengers were walking down the road it was obvious other men near a small stream were excited about something. They saw flecks of gold in the pan being swished around by someone up to his knees in water. A cheer went up as the last bit was drained into a cup someone found in his car. After several more attempts at swishing the pan and removing the gravel, they saw a few more flecks. At one time a very small nugget generated a big cheer and congratulations. Others who did not mind the stream water gave panning a try. Finally a voice from the onlookers said, "Didn't Super Carlson say something about breakfast but not dinner in the pan?" Walt recognized the Super Carlson words to this story but it was modified since he first heard it weeks ago.

Whoever said the word 'dinner' sparked the suggestion of getting back to the mess hall. On the way back Walt asked the question, "How much is gold worth?" He knew the answer but was surprised by an answer blared out, "That socialist Roosevelt made it 35 dollars an ounce but those other bastards might take it away."

There was a rush of protests, one saying, "Let's not talk politics now, it's Sunday."

"Amen, " and laughter. It was dinnertime not breakfast.

WHAT YOU DON'T WRITE HOME ABOUT

This Sundays adventure was something to write home about, more about the panning of gold rather than telling about what led to finding the stream where the gold was found. He also mentioned his citizenship paper story and tried to describe the different characters he met. On a return letter two weeks later his mother wanted to know how he felt about being in the Territory, how was his overall life going? He thought he wrote her previously about his change of plans and not wanting to be a farmer after all. Walt reminded himself he would make his plans more clear in his next letter.

Walt was somewhat conflicted in reporting to his mother on the lesser desired behavior of people mostly other men he met and what he thought of them. Ever since high school and into college he was aware of the erosion or differences in his 'polite' vocabulary he knew from the orphanage and perhaps what others called 'street language' in a negative way. But now being a mixture of men from college age to later 50 years or more on this road job no one seemed to care what vocabulary anyone used, polite or not. It all seemed natural, Walt adapted to his new environment but felt uneasy in the process. Part of that process was to make choices of doing in Rome what Romans do or just be an observer, perhaps a tourist.

Hey Gunther! Why Are You Here?

In college he did play nickel-dime ante poker but in camp the stakes were higher, sometimes with poker but more often by playing craps. Walt never played it in the camp but he saw many a game and was a constant onlooker. One lesson he learned early from another non-player was that, "The house always wins in the long run." It was not like poker where bluffing and intelligent guessing are essentials of the game, whereas craps is a game of chance, betting on the throw of dice. (As an aside, no one in camp played poker unless a new deck of cards was used and a new deck could be asked for at anytime.) Whereas many men had a portion of their paycheck sent directly home in the States there were some men who had no family in the S67tates and kept their checks and cash with them. Temptations to bet recklessly were prevalent but a few of the younger players learned a lesson from "Mother" Carlson, the wife of Super Carlson.

MOTHER CARLSON

Walt never met the lady but there were consistent stories about her and her playing craps with some of the older company men who followed the company to different projects in the states and overseas. She and Super Carlson had a mid sized trailer as their primary home on distant jobs. They were very compatible with each other, with grown kids off in their own lives in the States. Craps was a form of entertainment for her and anyone working for the Super could play. A game could start right after their supper but had to quit by nine so everyone could get some sleep. That was her rule. She was the 'house' at the game. She did not mind cleaning out the pockets of the older men who were unlucky that night. However, if any of the young men were reckless in their betting she would warn them in her "motherly" way to take it easy. If they continued and ignored her warnings and 'lost their shirts' so to speak she had a technique to impress the reckless player. Before the quitting time at nine, Mother Carlson would go to a closet and bring out a new medium sized red-white-blue flannel shirt.

Stories from here on vary quite a bit. The flannel shirt probably had a symbolic meaning of motherhood warnings, or forgiveness, but a reminder not given by anyone else who was looking to the players

Walt Fluegel

best interest. When Walt saw anyone wearing a red, white, and blue flannel shirt he was reminded of Mother Carlson and was tempted to ask especially if it was warn by a young worker.

STRESS RELIEF

During summer time the road construction for many miles in either direction from camp was going well. There were times when the civilian traffic had to be stopped for a while to allow the heavy equipment to complete a section. The flagman was given a signal and he in turn allowed the civilian traffic to flow. During one release of traffic, Walt noticed one car veered off enough to let other cars behind it pass and go on. Only the civilian car remained as the traffic moved on. It appeared to be stalled with the engine making various strange noises. A woman got out of the car and raised the hood. This of course attracted some of the heavy machine operators. They wanted to help a lady in distress and gathered around the car. There were three other women in the car and the windows were rolled down. A conversation started. There were some giggles and laughter and before the men realized it, or maybe they did realize it, they were invited to visit with the passengers after supper on down the road at a certain milepost. At that milepost they would find a good-sized trailer waiting for them. They were told the men would be relieved of their stresses and feel better about working all day. After the hood was lowered and the engine restarted, the car had no difficulty going down the newly compacted gravel road. This type of incident occurred about three more times during the summer and into the beginning of fall right on pay day.

Fall did come with its chill and leaf change. Everyone knew the work would slow down. Walt and other college bound students in the different base camps received their last paycheck. Walt made sure his duffel bag was ready for his last trip to Fairbanks with Marvin and others. The road was a lot smoother, no more washboard vibrations that rattled many a truck. However, come winter it would need grading eventually. Many a tourists families too were heading south in the opposite direction. At Fairbanks there was a final handshake with Marvin remembering regretfully he had to treat Walt with

207

suspicion in springtime. "I didn't like the Nazi either," Walt said in an off-hand manner. He then lifted his duffel to his shoulder and headed for the bus station next to the theater.

Walt got off the bus at College rather than at the University because he knew that offices would be closed this late in the day. He knew intuitively that if he carried his duffel bag to Nick and Zelda's house they would perhaps let him stay overnight. Zelda was home with the two boys getting supper ready and welcomed him inside with the usual hello's and how have you been greetings. Zelda added, "We got your letter just yesterday that you would be back soon. Nick will be home from work any moment now." When Nick came into the house there were more greetings. Right after supper, a home made supper far different from the camp suppers, Nick made a suggestion. Because he had to go to work early the next morning why not load into the trunk of his car Walt's two boxes he left in spring and the duffel bag. In that way it would not take time away from the morning. After that there was good review of the summers activity at College and on the ALCAN highway. While Walt answered questions about the ALCAN Nick gave Walt a summary of his attempt to extend electric power to homesteaders out in the boonies Finally, Walt slept on the couch.

Walt's stuff was unloaded at the back door of the Main dorm and from there he transferred everything to the barbershop. He met and greeted fellow dormers who also were early. When it was time to go to the office, it was a low-key grand homecoming event with others he knew but tempered by the realization that summer was over.

Walt Fluegel

CHAPTER THIRTY-THREE: OTHER SUMMER JOBS

THE GREEN CHEVY

Every springtime if it wasn't preparations for final exams it was the urge to line up a summer job for those students wanting to stay in Alaska. Stanley a graduating senior, however, wanted to go back home to California having satisfied his longing to know more about this 'strange land.'

With snow melting, he was attempting to repair his Chevy pick up truck. It was parked behind the power plant all winter near the site where odd bits and pieces of construction material were dumped after a small project. One afternoon after a lab class, Walt visited Stanley who was leaning into the opened hood of his truck. After the usual chatting about the weather there was a silence. In that talking silence there were noises of wrench on metal and one sudden clanging as the wrench slipped from Stanley's grip. Stanley's language did not prevent the wrench from landing in the melting snow. He said to Walt, "Hey, can you see it from there?"

"Yeah, I suppose you want me to get it." As Walt bent down to retrieve the tool in the melting snow he heard Stanley say something about selling this truck because he was going to leave Alaska for good. A chief reason given was his girlfriend in northern California he wanted to marry, would probably not want to live here in the winter. With that last statement the conversation shifted to the possibility of Walt wanting to buy the Chevy.

Hey Gunther! Why Are You Here?

After each year of summer work and the barbershop (and other campus jobs) his bank account was growing. Expenses were mostly for college things needed not wanted. Also, by not smoking or buying booze he needed very little and wanted less than other students wanted. He did not consider dating girls a frivolous want but a need for his soul. For someone a few years ago who had hardly anything in the bank to now accumulating funds to buy an expensive thing such as a truck was a serious matter. He gave assurances to Stanley that he would look into buying the truck from him long before the end of the college term. Most students too were getting low on their own finances while Walt kept quiet about his own bank account.

Stanley had been quietly spreading word he was willing to sell his truck but he also knew, like himself, most student pockets were becoming empty. It was a surprise to him that Walt pursued the possibilities. If he could sell the truck, plane fare to California was assured.

But little by little with getting the paperwork in order and making sure the truck was in sound mechanical shape the truck became the property of Walt Gunther—but with one small problem. Walt never drove a car or a truck in his life. He needed to learn how.

It was during this time of negotiations with Stanley that George G needed a haircut. During the clipping, the truck was mentioned. The details seem so long ago that all Walt remembers was being in the truck with George who gave him instructions on what to do and what not to do. George drove the Chevy towards the Experimentation station. Walt took over and was surprised that in a very short time he was able to ease into taking off without jerking and shifting into the different gears. He learned by sound which gear was the best at any one time. There were two more lessons, one about backing up and parking between other cars, another on making emergency stops and other maneuvers. At the last time just before he went solo without George, all George said was practice every time you can and remember the guy ahead of you is an idiot who does not know how to drive.

Farmers Loop Road in late spring in the later morning was somewhat difficult for a novice driver but little by little practice paid off. The

210

best time to practice was before breakfast before the sun thawed low muddy spots. An occasional trip into town in the afternoons after some lab classes gave Walt confidence in getting a driver's license. There was no problem here. At the same time he felt he needed to attend to the barbershop to make up for buying gas.

JOBS THROUGH THE UNION

Fairbanks was growing now that WW2 was over the Territory of Alaska was getting more attention because of the improvements in the ALCAN highway and construction of military bases. There was then a need to house the influx of people and becoming permanent residents. In Walt's years he decided to try a different approach to earning college money, a bit more risky but more lucrative than previous summers if all went well. George G suggested he contact one of the unions and see what they had to offer. In the final choice he joined the common labor union rather than the carpenters union because the pay per hour as a laborer was better than the pay as an apprentice carpenter. Since he had just bought a used Chevy pickup truck he had confidence he could get around the Fairbanks area.

Union dues in the Labor Union for the first month were paid in advance and thereafter subtracted from the wages paycheck from each job. It seemed reasonable to him after consulting George G who happened to be in a different union. In essence what did a laborer have to do? The simple answer always was anything the boss wanted done; except a laborer could not do anything which a union cement worker or finishers did, could not do carpentry of any kind that union outlined, could not handle or drive equipment, could not do any union electric work, in other words any flunky work the other trades did not feel they should do.

If you wanted a job the usual procedure was to go to the union hall, sign in and wait for the morning announcements. A company was named and the kind of jobs were read out and perhaps 10 laborers hands were raised. "OK you and you over here." guys were directed to a table to sign up. Other companies were announced. A laborer worked for a contractor until that contractor did not need the laborer.

211

Hey Gunther! Why Are You Here?

A work day may be 8 to10 hours (because of the summer light) and anything over 40 hours in that week was at time and a half for pay. A job may last maybe a week or a month depending on many factors. At that time (middle '40's) in Fairbanks the hourly pay for laborers was $3.09 per hour, a reasonable wage for summer work in the '40's. Cost of living differences between Alaska and the States determined the pay scale.

MEETING UP WITH WOODY

When Walt contacted his first job assignment he was ready with tough leather palms work gloves. The overall construction site was on a road that led to the airport. He was assigned to a small crew whose job was to remove nails from used lumber. Three apartment complexes were being built and at times the boss also managed to salvage used lumber from elsewhere. Rather than burn it up he salvaged this wood and discarded the nails where they fell. There were claw hammers and pry bars on a rough table and a couple of saw horses to work on. Not a bad work for the morning with some conversation during the pounding, prying and cursing reluctant nails, Erick kept asking about the need to do what they were doing. He asked in different ways about the use of paying so much per hour to salvage the wood and the comparison of buying new wood. Somehow he also let Woody and Walt know that his father in the States was some sort of accountant and interested in something called economics. "How much does anything cost and why?" he asked. "A pile of damaged and now nail-less wood compared with a bundle of new 2 x 4's must truly cost more. Our labor must cost him something." Walt and Woody kept insisting that Erick keep his complaining down and besides the pay will be good for all.

Right after the half hour lunch break from his lunch bucket the foreman called to Woody and Walt. "I got another job for you guys." He had two number 2 shovels with him, and led them to a new concrete slab encased in its wooden forms.

"These have to be removed and piled over there and then back filled with the rows of gravel you see." He assumed that all one needed was

212

to put the square end of the shovel under the form and leverage it out of the ground. He showed Walt and Woody what to do then started to walk away.

He had gone no more than five feet away when there was a loud shout from a cement finisher. "Hey you bastard that's our job!" There followed the middle finger gesture from the foreman as the cement finisher came closer, still shouting obscenities. He asked Woody if he knew union rules, "Don't answer me, look to your foreman, he should know our rules." And thus on the first day on the job Woody and Walt began to know of the division of labor rules. They had to wait only a minute or so before the cement finisher pounded the form free from the cured concrete. Only then could a laborer pick up the pieces and pile them up in one place and backfill with handy gravel. Nails would soon be pulled from the forms by their economist friend over at the used lumber pile.

SHEET ROCK GETS HEAVY

For the next few days there were other number 2 shovel jobs over the complex of three apartment buildings being built. One of the three story buildings seemed to already be built and enclosed except for some windows. The middle building needed one more floor to complete inside. "Do you see that crane over there? Do you see that pile of sheetrock next to the crane?" the foreman pointing to what he had just said. "The machine broke down and we need to get the sheetrock up to the second and third floor. The crane was supposed to lift the pallet of sheetrock to the opening for the picture window. Guess what you guys have to do?" Woody and Walt looked at each other and nodded at their foreman and began to slide one bundle off the pile. Each 4 x 8 panel was actually two panels paper glued along the edges so the good paintable side would be inside the bundle.

Woody was a bit more muscular in the shoulders than Walt so he initiated the sliding of one bundle off the pile to where they could carry the sheetrock into the building. However, a problem occurred inside. It was awkward as hell to make the turn around of the stairs because they were still in a rough construction stage. The sheet rock installers being paid a bonus by the rooms completed wanted Woody and Walt to be quicker. They demanded of the labor foreman to get more help. He and another laborer compounded the problem at the turn of the stairs too. Fortunately the labor foreman and the sheet rock installer foreman solved the problem. The sheetrock was just delivered to the landing. The installer foreman had one of his apprentices make the larger cut of the sheetrock called down to him from his journeyman. With his large T-square, a tape measure, a good utility knife and a snap, the cut board was easily carried to the next level. However the design of each room was such that many 4 x 8 foot sheets need not be cut but were cut to speed up the job. Later, the finishers would have to contend with the extra cut. The crane was repaired overnight to the relief of the sheetrock crew and the two laborers.

TEEN AGE ARTIST

The foreman seemed to keep Walt and Woody together on jobs, the latest one being to go from floor to floor of each building with a push broom and keep the place clean of sawdust, bent nails, bits of electrical wiring and scraps of sheetrock and insulation. As more and more rooms in the apartments were being attended to by the other trades, the more different debris was accumulating. One day a teenage boy perhaps 16 years old came into one of the buildings, saw Walt with his push broom and put his finger to his mouth as if to signal not to say anything. He had a paper bag in one hand and whispered to Walt. He wanted to pick up scrap electrical wire the electricians discarded. Walt pointed to the room he was going to go into and also pointed to a big plastic bucket in the middle of the room. When the kid came back Walt whispered, "What are you going to do with this wire?" He told Walt he had a hobby in which he heated the wire and pounded it sort of flat to make jewelry, and treat it so it does not turn green on the skin. He also made wire sculpture. This little conversation reminded Walt of a few years ago and the sea shell jewelry business he once had. But by going through the building being assembled and asking a question or two of the other workers he intuitively understood what an architect must do to make blue prints in his mind before putting it all on paper. When that thought came to him he was glancing at a newly installed door with a more modern lock system than the one he drew at the Edison school.

KEEPING CARPENTERS HAPPY

On another job where Woody an Walt worked together, one hundred crawl space basements or foundations were already in place from the previous fall construction season in a development project. The streets were all installed in rough form with hints of where the driveways would be made. These preliminary foundations would eventually support one-story pre-fab houses. When finished the housing project would have a mixture of one, two and three bedroom houses. Every house would have a garage but that garage would be on a slab of concrete. Speculators bought in advance some of the lots and houses not yet finished. If they wanted a two-car garage, a double slab would be included. Some of the houses were already in place and many others needed rough sub-flooring before the houses were assembled on these foundation basements. A saw-mill was located at one end of the project to assist in cutting odd angles of lumber at the request of any carpenter.

Woody and Walt's job was in a sense to keep the carpenters happy by keeping their work space clean; no accumulated sawdust, no loose nails, no scraps of splintered wood and so on. Because the houses were pre-fab that did not mean they always fit neatly into place all the time. Sometimes the carpenters complained that it was the foundation and at other times it was the factory stateside that made the structures. The pre-fabs were already insulated, wired and in some cases with plumbing in the walls. Many of these houses were still in their wrapping next to the foundation prepared for them. After the wrapping was removed, a crane did all the lifting and placing wall sections in their proper place. A crew of carpenters braced the walls. Another crew secured the roof panels After about a fourth of the houses were assembled the city inspector insisted the floors be insulated. The original design concept did not take into account the constant below zero temperatures of Fairbanks winters. It took a while to get this sorted out with the contractor. A few men did not like to be under the floor in a crawl space with itchy rock wool insulation allowing only four feet working space. For the other houses not yet put into place the insulation was easier to do.

HAMMER

"Hey, Walt and Woody you got to see this!" Mister Metzger a master carpenter who knew them both came out of the house he was working on and pointed to another carpenter on the roof of a future two-car garage. Two car garages had to be built separately because they were not in the original plan. Up on the rafters or peak of the roof "Hammer" was nailing the wood together. He was a hefty man, broad in shoulders and arms to match his proportions. "Now watch this," Metzger said as he pointed to Hammer. Hammer tapped a nail in place and for the second strike he raised his hammer as high as he could and swiftly, forcefully struck the nail head one powerful blow. That's all. One hard precision smack and the nail was driven home. Other carpenters had to make several strikes to pound the nail in all the way. And for some strange reason for the rest of the day the John Henry railroad work song about that 'steel driving man' popped into Walt's mind. Strange.

OFF ANGLE

Occasionally a carpenter called out loud from an open window space for Walt. Walt may have been in a nearby house cleaning up something but in the cluster of houses where the carpenters worked, word spread that Walt was wanted by so & so. When he came to see who needed him, the carpenter handed him a piece of note pad with dimensions written on it. "Something's wrong with this pre-fab, it's not square." was the reason in most cases for this request of the sawmill to cut a stick of lumber. It was a long thin triangle to fit into a space resulting from the lack of being square. Walt was quick of step and nimble in jumping over odd stuff in the way between the house and the sawmill. He waited for the wood flooring to be cut into a long thin triangle. With the wood balanced on his shoulder he returned

216

with no mishaps. This sometimes happened two or three times a day until all the floors were finished.

DITCH WORK; GREYHOUND AND JEWISH BOY

There were five or so laborers in a wide ditch making sure the ditch had a slight slope. A long carpenters level was sufficient in this case and the conversation had mixed topics to keep a social vacuum from developing. No one seemed to care what the ditch was for but the curiosity of 'why are you working here' proved interesting and memorable to Walt. When Voletz was asked, he had an unusual answer. He said he came from Florida and often bet on the greyhound racing's. Just before he left to work in Alaska he figured a way he and a pal could make a killing on the dogs. He had a way of betting on the dogs without doping the animals that others do to horses. He needed a bankroll to get started. There were all kinds questions about the betting process, and the honesty of his pal but all Voletz said was he had plan and that was that. Walt asked him what he knew about the pedigree of each dog. Voletz said that did not matter, he knew this guy who was using high class mathematics. Laughs came out until someone asked Al Steel why he was in this ditch.

He said that now that the WW2 was over he wanted to travel to the countries we fought and wanted most of all to meet the ordinary people who let Hitler come to power. He was a history major at the University of Washington and needed the money for travel. That seemed reasonable to almost all except Rudd. "That Hitler guy may have had his faults but he did stop the Jews of taking over Europe." Before he could say more there was an immediate collective condemnation directed against Rudd. "What about this guy Gunther here, he is a German and Gunther is a Jewish name and he asks too many questions, just like a Jew." There were more protests again and fortunately Rudd was at the other end of the workers in the ditch. Walt called out and said, "That is okay guys. It seems that Rudd knows something about Jews." He then directed his next question directly at Rudd. "Hey Rudd, tell me what happens to a baby Jewish boy within an hour after it is born?"

"We all know they cut a bit of his dick off."

"Good. Now, tell me Rudd can you prove to us that YOU are not Jewish?" There was a silence and anticipation of what or how Rudd would respond. In the meantime Walt slowly and deliberately reached for his belt and pretended to open his fly. Walt gambled on the knowledge that it is traditional for all boy babies born in the U.S. to be circumcised early too. It took a moment before the rest of the workers understood the meaning and gesture and began to jeer at Rudd and ask in various ways for him to respond. All he did was to grumble, "You bastard!" and drifted up the ditch away from the others. Someone asked Walt if he was bluffing or what? With a smile on his face he said, "You will see when I pee on a tree," Byron Hendrickson of the Wartburg came to mind; and he was the cause of the smile. Byron was a fellow orphanage inmate friend and one of his pet phrases told in Hey Gunther! You Don't Belong Here Anymore! was 'pee on a tree.'

The rest of the crew laughed and Pete Merritt also broke the tension by giving his reason. He was in the defense industry during the war and now that the war was over he had to do something else. "I have an answer that never fails." He began to change his tone of voice. "I am employed by this company but I work for my wife and two kids." That changed the direction of conversation to sports, mostly the current baseball season.

HOMEWORK ASSIGNMENT

At most of the construction jobs there was usually a small "office" somewhere on the job but at this one situation it seemed not to be the case. However, with three foremen on the job everything seemed to go well. This particular job had no walkie-talkie either. It was their habit to call into the office by public phone or take time off and go into town. The office wasn't far away. At one time Walt's foreman, Swanson, said casually during a mid morning break he had to check on whether some of the other workers were actually doing their

218

Walt Fluegel

"homework." Walt being new on the job let the expression go. Within the hour Swanson was back and continued to make his rounds. Laborers with number two shovels were doing as expected and carpenters seemed on schedule.

Swanson often bragged of his masculine attributes. A week or so later Swanson said something about the "right" or was it Wright "homework?" Walt put two and two together after he saw Swanson take off in his car. Should he "squeal" or keep it to himself. But to deliberately take unfair advantage of a man at work or his wife at home did not seem right. He quietly went to Kolstaad, the oldest of the foremen and asked if he knew a worker named Wright. He did. Walt may be wrong he said but he did ask Kolstaad what he thought of the Swanson's expression "homework" as applied to this one worker in his crew. Kolstaad said he suspected Swanson was up to no good earlier. "Now go back to your own job and it's a good thing I have a bad memory," he also winked at Walt.

By the nature of the job it was not always possible to see the employees parking places but he got the impression that a carpenter was instructed to go over some plans in the office. After a while that same carpenter came back feeling agitated but with a set of blueprints and was talking with Kolstaad as they examined the new plans. Swanson was finally back to see how things were going with his own crew. He looked in terrible shape with a black eye and bruises on his face and his shirt was torn along the back. When someone else of the crew asked him what happened all Swanson could say was that he was jumped by some bastard who demanded his wallet just as he got out of his car. They had a fight, the car window was smashed, and he must have been knocked out. He found his empty wallet next to him when he revived. Swanson showed somebody his empty wallet. He didn't want to talk anymore but stayed away from Kolstaad's crew. Later that evening after work several workers surrounded a car with a smashed windshield. Walt didn't think about this for quite a while.

A couple of weeks later on a different construction job Walt happened to recognize then meet another laborer, Jim Andrews, who also worked on the same job and one of Kolstaad's crew a couple of weeks before. During their lunch break they discussed both their former bosses.

Stories never come in a direct line of events but Walt rearranged the pieces according to what he knew and what Jim did not know. Jim began to talk or remember seeing at the end of a work day a car in the parking lot with a smashed windshield. It belonged to Swanson. Earlier in the day he noticed that Swanson was in bad shape. Jim wondered if Swanson was in an accident that also gave him the black eye? All Walt answered by saying Swanson told his crew that someone jumped him as he got out of his car and demanded money. They had a fight and this guy took his money. His car windscreen was smashed too. He did the best he could to drive back to work. During their munching on sandwiches Walt and Jim swapped a half an orange for a half an apple.

In the next day lunch break conversation with Jim, Walt asked Jim what he thought about Kolstaad. Jim liked his foreman: Kolstaad because he seemed to care about his crew and their families. Jim mentioned Wright the carpenter for example. "On that same day your Swanson's car got smashed I overheard Kolstaad tell Wright he should go into town to get a new blueprint and maybe check up on his wife who might be in trouble." Jim thought Wright's wife was ill or something. He added, "When Wright got back he said something to Kolstaad about that SOB and his homework assignments, and his wife was glad to see him."

Jim wondered what Wright meant about an SOB but was cut off from further query with Walt asking, "Do you put ketchup or mayo on your chicken sandwiches?"

RIBBONS OF GRAVEL

"Hey what's the hurry? Take it easy! Slow down. The slower we go the longer the job lasts." These words and other expressions were directed towards Walt by his work mate Dennis Wilmots. It was a small job of getting driveways ready for the concrete to be poured in a day or so. Walt had a certain cadence of pushing the shovel into a new soft pile of pit-run gravel, lifting it and in a sweeping motion spread it

220

into a neat long arched ribbon which needed very little smoothing out. His work mate had a cruder technique and averaged just half of what Walt was doing. Walt tried to slow down but that made his work seem harder to do, so he adapted to what he felt was just right.

No one noticed Mister Rankin, the owner of this small construction company, arrive in his car. He honked his horn three times and the foreman busy at a different part of the house went to see his boss. Everybody kept working as usual. A few minutes later the foreman called Dennis to the car. Gravel sliding off Walt's shovel in long arched fabric of stone, silt and sand slowly came up to grade. Maybe five minutes passed as Dennis, the foreman and the boss were talking with each other. At one sweep of gravel Walt heard his name being called by the foreman and looked up just in time to see a shovel coming in his direction. Fortunately it skidded to a halt just at his feet. No harm done. But he did see Wilmot give the middle finger salute as he walked away from the boss's car.

Hey Gunther! Why Are You Here?

CHAPTER THIRTY-FOUR: ANOTHER DIRECTION

The third year was well into late fall-early winter when Walt realized that letters from his mother in Mount Vernon hinted that she may want to come to Alaska, not for a visit but to live there. He did not know if his letters sparked his mother's interest but they sounded serious enough. Also she said she wanted to change her clientele to something different or look for some other employment. She began to work part time for a hat manufacturer. Soon she was complimented on her dexterity in sewing on the feathers, ribbons and other embellishments to where her hats were used by the traveling salesmen as a typical well made hat and stylish too. But the company folded because the other workers hats appeared to be inferior in construction and design.

But just in case her plans were serious, Walt consulted Nick and Zelda on getting established in Alaska other than being a student where it was easy to get housing and meals and spend money that accumulated over the summer. Where will she live and what should she do for a living and would mother and son live together? This was also the time he changed his major from agriculture to pre-med. But he knew he wouldn't want to be a doctor. It was just a convenient administrative adjustment.

It just so happened that Nick knew of someone who had a few lots for sale about a mile and a half from the University just off the main road into town. It was platted but no real road led to the property except the usual car tracks showing in the weeds, which led to a trailer with an attached shed a small ways further down. Walt was not ready for

223

anything like this because it was all new. Nick said he would contact the guy he knew that there may be a buyer, but it depended. Walt also knew now that Nick worked for the lumber company so he knew a lot about costs of material and building a new house. And he also talked about getting electric power to places because he got himself involved with a cooperative organization. So getting started brand-new was going to be something serious to think about, all while going to college. More and frequent letters were exchanged between Walt and his mother during these times.

His new advisor, Mrs. Carr, was helpful to Walt in navigating through university requirements, rules and procedures. When it was obvious to Walt that his mother was definitely wanting to come to Alaska, Mrs. Carr was helpful too in one major way. In conversation with Walt she found out about his mothers occupation, the good, the bad and one irritant. He told her that his mother did not mind the work, the dirt, the food preparation and so on but the way she seemed to be treated by others, mostly the women in the household. The men were more polite but the women treated her as a lowly worker and always called her Emelie, on and off the job.

Mrs. Carr intimated that there seemed to be a need in Fairbanks for someone like his mother but she made one suggestion. She suggested he write that there may be good prospects for her here, but by all means she should not introduce herself as Emelie but at all times as Mrs. Gunther. She gestured with one hand in her lap when she said Emelie and with the other hand raised to eye level when she said Mrs. Gunther. The meaning to Walt was clear and when she was in Alaska, Mrs. Gunther understood the value of her title.

ELECTION TIME

Aside from the academic studies there was the barbershop to attend to, the Sourdough Club to participate in, go to basket ball games, have a date or two with a girl in town, and there was a stint about the student government. There were spring elections to get things in order for the next academic year. Walt did not represent the Main dorm but he did attend the regular meetings and from time to time make

224

suggestions for consideration for the campus as a whole, not just representing the dorm's view. Someone else did that.

One night he and Howard Bowman were talking things over about the coming election. Howard was skeptical that Walt would come close and gave his opinion. By this time George G was listening at the door. Howard thought Walt was too idealistic, yes the ideas were good but impractical for the campus and the administration at this time etc, etc. Then George G made one other comment. "Walt, you don't drink around with others and that puts you aside from the rest of us." He said to the effect that if anyone who is different in certain ways, not the usual..." His voice became soft and then after a deep breath he also said, "It's a good thing you date girls otherwise..." his voice drifted off. Howard then added, "Aside from all that Walt, you are a short guy, you need lead in your boots to weigh much." That seemed to be a standard joke on campus, which triggered Walt to laugh. He rejoined with his usual that the lead was to keep him on the ground in case the wind blew a bit too hard. Then Howard became serious and said, "Walt, everything about you...you don't look like the presidential type, and a lot of folks go by looks." Walt admitted to himself that Howard may be right. And sure enough, after the election of the three candidates, Howard was right, Walt didn't come close.

MOTHER COMES TO ALASKA

The election time was not as important in Walt's adventure at the end of the third academic year as a letter from his mother stating she made plans to actually come to Fairbanks. At that same time after a usual visiting with Nick and Zelda, Nick wanted to show Walt something about the lot he inquired about last fall. When they arrived, Nick said he did not know who did it but there was a rough road graded from the main road way past the trailer and shed. When they were looking over the site Rosemary who lived in the trailer with her husband Ed came out of the trailer and asked Nick if he knew who did the grading. Nick didn't know but said he would look into the matter. (Later on the newly "graded" road was recorded as Caribou Way and a companion road about a block closer to town, graded at the same time was called Alaska Way.) He also asked Walt if he still had an

Hey Gunther! Why Are You Here?

interest in buying the lot. Walt thought so and mentioned that his mother was definitely coming to Alaska. It turns out that the guy who graded the road did so as a way to encourage the sale of other lots. Nick said something to the effect that this would also help in getting more electric power to the general area.

Events had to move swiftly. Construction workers, either single men who arrived by plane or families in trailers from the ALCAN all needed a place to stay for the summer season. Trailer parks were going to be filled and spare rooms in town were getting ready to accept the workers. After half a morning with the most recent paper in hand opened to the classified section, Walt went from 'room rental' to 'room rental' and finally found a suitable place he thought his mother would accept for that summer. And that he too could live in during that time while he worked on a construction job. It was a large room with a small alcove that could be divided off with a blanket for privacy. A two burner hot plate was available on one corner counter and a closed off toilet in another corner. Entrance to this place was at the back of the house and it seemed this was a most recent modification from an old house built many years ago before WW2. To make assurance that it would be for his mother he willingly paid one month in advance and in return got a written promise it would be held for that long. Henceforth all rent was in advance. For the college time later Walt would resume living in the dorm on campus.

In due time Walt's mother arrived by plane and he took her to the room he rented for her. She met the landlady and later her husband. Mrs. Gunther understood the primitive situation, and adapted quickly. So many things were now going on in rapid succession. By the end of the spring semester Walt could keep his duffel bag at his mother room and go to his first construction job where his first assignment was to pull nails. There he would meet Woody who lived in town. Nick and Zelda were introduced, and the potential buying of the lot was finalized. Mrs. Gunther managed to get three day jobs in a short time, one which proved to be important within the coming months. Other day jobs filled the week before the summer came to a close. At the end of the construction day work job, Walt would in the beginning, just have a supper with his mother and fall asleep on the fold out bed until early morning. Being a student all winter long required a person

226

to have some adjustment from brain power to brawn power. It took a week or so to adjust.

Mrs. Gunther's first client, Mister Rasmussen was an owner of a small business which repaired typewriters and other business machines. The whole Fairbanks area and the military were growing now that the WW2 was over. Therefore he began to sell new business equipment and added stationary supplies. His repair shop and storage place was getting too small and he needed to expand. Should he move to a new place or should he remove his work shop and expand on his own property? It was one of those fortunate circumstances that he talked with Walt's mother and he knew she also was planning to start a new home for herself. He made a suggestion that she buy his repair shop, move it to her property and convert it into a home. It was already well insulated and had several electric outlets and a chimney. It also had a small but adequate picture window and two small windows towards the back that could be opened. It had no plumbing but that could be taken care of once the shop was moved.

BUILDING A BASEMENT

Walt consulted Nick. Nick made calculations on various costs of bulldozing a hole for a basement, pouring concrete for footings, buying concrete blocks to build the basement, moving the shop to put on top of the basement, and then backfilling. That was all preliminary. There was additional thinking about getting the basement wall built, who would build it, who would move the shop. Walt did not know nor ever consulted with his mother on whether she had the money saved and could afford any of the expenses. But he showed her the estimates and possible overruns. She said it would be tight but she could manage. She had saved money all these years so now she thought would be the time to spend it.

Walt also suggested he could help with building the concrete block walls on the weekends. In the meantime he had his daytime construction job. It was here that he met Woody on at least three different construction labor jobs doing flunky work together. Woody was just about as tall as Walt but was more stocky and had better shoulder strength. He lived in town with his folks but they thought it best to send him to the University of Washington in Seattle. He came home to take advantage of the summer construction season. Walt was willing to pay him the going labor rate for each time he helped lay the block on weekends and some evenings when the day work load was not so heavy. So by mid summer all arrangements were made. The hole was scooped out with a contracted bulldozer operator. There were no permafrost problems in the silty soil. The footings were going to be poured. But prior to that the measurements of the shop to be moved were double checked before the forms were built. Walt added extra floor space inside the room to be for the coal furnace and water heater to rest on. In a sense Nick thought this wise, better to do it now rather than later just before winter when other things may need attention too. There was also a projection to build a coal bin on a slab of its own that could be knitted with the wall. By not installing a block on the initial line of blocks a shovel for coal was easily inserted through the wall into the coal bin. Nick was helpful on giving hints to how to make sure the walls were strengthened, plumb and level.

Both Walt and Woody had built up strength earlier in the summer and after the footings were poured and cured the block laying could start. The block wall had to accommodate a small house of about 20 feet by 10 feet. Many a cabin or house around Fairbanks were of this size to start with. When people could afford it there were add-ons of equal size or larger. It was thought best to do that part now while there was the excavation so another wing of footings of 9 foot square was part of the footings for the wall. That future room would be on the east side of the house where one could see Rosemary and Ed's trailer and shed. In Alaska it is common to have a small structure or room protecting the main doors. One enters this room and then closes the door before entering the front door of the house. It was sort of an air lock, to keep as little of the warm air leaving the house or the cold air coming inside. This too had to be considered and was solved as soon as the house was transported to the foundation.

Walt was on a construction job when the house was transported and placed on the foundation. Mister Rasmussen had seen the foundation earlier and made arrangements to have his former shop transported from town to the lot. Either the house or the foundation was a little off because one corner protruded about an inch over one corner block. Nick suggested it was a cosmetic thing and besides it was a back corner not at the front of the house. Mister Rasmussen also thought the house was too high maybe one block too high, but that was no longer his problem. Mrs. Gunther and Walt would have to solve that problem themselves. Temporary stairs had to be built for the front entry and the east wing had to be covered in some manner to protect the insides from the winter snows and cold soon to come.

In brief what followed was that Rosemary and Ed had a carpenter son, not living with them, who built an entry and temporary stairs both into the house and down into the basement. He did this while winter was just getting started. While Walt attended college for his senior year his mother still resided at her room in town for the winter. Walt also put his pickup truck up on blocks for the winter, brought the battery indoors so it would not get stolen and got assurance from Rosemary and Ed they would look after the place.

SEARCHING FOR SOMETHING HIGHER

In this now senior year university academic life seemed just a continuation of the previous years only different subjects to study and debate with other students in bull sessions or occasionally the professor in class. Mrs. Carr his advisor guided Walt on the final requirements for graduation. She wondered what he would do once he got his bachelors degree. He did not have a clear understanding of any talent he could excel in but seemed to have a desire to keep going to school and learn things. He always did like biology especially the use of the microscope. Would it help to go for a Masters degree? What would that entail? Maybe narrow it all down to bacteriology of some kind? The final thought of course lie in his desire to learn something entirely new and Mrs. Carr was there to advise but not discourage. Did he have the basic smarts to succeed in acquiring that degree?

The University of Alaska did not have any Masters degree in bacteriology but the University of Wisconsin at Madison and their legume project might be the place to ask. He wrote to them earlier explaining that he might be interested in studying the effects of cold soils on the rhizobium bacteria invasion of the legume roots. He also wrote to the North Dakota College of Agriculture (NDAC) in Fargo wondering if there was a place to study cold soils on bacterial activity. With his mixed background in the various subjects studied he got a more favorable response from NDAC than from Madison. He applied to NDAC and was accepted.

LEARNING MORE ABOUT MOTHER

It was also at these times that Walt visited his mother at her room on weekends when possible. It was here too that she was able to tell him a lot of her childhood, her sisters and their "belly full" experiences. She related the times they went to Germany in 1937 before WW2 and Hitler. Also what happened to her mother at the hands of the Nazis. It all came out in dribbles over the winter, a bit here and a bit there, with a more detailed remembrance each time. It was also the time when his mother told him the two different versions of his father's death. However, she never told Walt anything about his father as a man other than he got impatient with customers and sometimes he would get into a mood. His father was a blank before Walt went to Alaska and now that he was older his father was still a blank and he did not know what questions he should ask. But his mother did seem happy to be in Alaska and soon living in a home all her own, the first home she would ever own. She had steady jobs with other prospects if regular clients no longer needed her services.

Walt Fluegel

CHAPTER THIRTY-FIVE: A THREATENING LETTER AND GRADUATION

As spring approached it was possible to visit the house, rejuvenate the pickup truck and do things that were necessary. But first the electric power had to be connected. It seemed a chore at first.

"Why not tap from the pole that feeds Rosemary and Ed's house," seemed like a reasonable request to the power company by Walt. He talked to Nick about that knowing he had an interest in getting electric power to people. There was a difference between the power company and the cooperative getting started in that area. The cooperative did not have their lines in that place and it seemed only if there were more houses near by would the power company feel it worth their effort. After talking with Nick, somehow power was connected to the existing system in place from the former shop. Walt made other connections internally from what he gleaned from watching electricians on construction jobs and also having information on wiring from Sears and Roebuck. But before the main switch was engaged he did hire a professional to examine his wiring and make corrections. No problem here.

While on the electric story it might be interesting to relate something else about Nick. Somehow Walt wrote a letter to the editor, or responded to an article in the local paper concerning the TVA (Tennessee Valley Authority) in the States and the concept of electrifying America. Somehow he must have mentioned Nick and his attempt to do the same in the Tanana valley in which all the farms and

231

Hey Gunther! Why Are You Here?

homesteads around Fairbanks needed affordable electric power. Shortly after the article appeared someone wrote an unsigned typewritten letter to Walt castigating Nick. In the last sentence or two they threatened Walt with bodily harm if he continued to tout Nick's efforts in his project. "Holy Cow, this guy is serious!" Walt thought. Walt was still in the mode of academic discussion and did not think that electric power to the people was this serious to threaten anyone who thought well of Nick, who seemed like an idealist. After supper Walt walked down to the College flats and visited Nick and Zelda. Nick quietly read the letter and asked if he could keep it. He also quietly asked how his mother's house was coming along.

He assured Nick that he soon will connect the pump to the sand point already in the ground placed there before the basement was built. The need for water to make mortar while building the basement wall came from using a hose from Rosemary and Ed's house. Walt's house needed plumbing inside and a septic system outside. Also, a small coal furnace and water heater had to be installed. He wasn't sure how soon he would get to build a room on the east wing or a greenhouse his mother thought she would like. He would make a good effort to get these jobs done on weekends and some evenings once summer was finally here. He knew he needed some money for this kind of activity and graduate school too so he contacted the union offices and renewed his dues for the season. Walt had to make sure his grades would be acceptable too, to graduate soon with a BS degree. He did keep his grades up to at least Bs and Cs.

The graduation ceremony was performed in the gymnasium, a familiar place where many different campus functions occurred. People were dressed in their "Sunday best" even some of the onlooking students. Graduates had the mortar-board hat and black robes. Speeches were made but who remembers what was said? When the ceremonies were over and people gathered outside, Walt's mother recognized some of the people from town she knew. Introductions were made and congratulations given all around, many with the expression, "You must be very proud and pleased that..." Mrs. Gunther was very proud and pleased. After the visits and folks began to disperse it was time to have lunch at home on Caribou Way and resume the chores necessary to start summer. On the day before the barbershop was closed, duffel bags were filled with clothing and radio and phonograph were boxed and transported to the house. From now on Walt had no access or need to be in contact with the U of A campus. Graduation was not just getting a piece of paper but also to sever ties and ready to make new ties.

Once the electric and plumbing and septic system was installed the house was livable enough for Walt's mother to give up her room in town so she could live in her own home. By not having rent to pay that helped her with other expenses. Also some of her clients came to her house on Caribou Way to pick her up for the day. That saved bus fare and was very convenient especially in the middle of the winter. The same day Walt's mother gave the keys back to the landlady for the room she rented she went to the Sears & Roebuck store and ordered a small refrigerator and a four burner stove with oven. The household amenities were the barest essentials but it was a home for both to come home to after work.

Hey Gunther! Why Are You Here?

Walt Fluegel

CHAPTER THIRTY-SIX: (JOBS BEFORE MASTERS DEGREE)

On the first construction job after graduation there was no equal because it appeared to be couched in secrecy. All workers of this particular job had to assemble in a certain parking lot at a given time. "Grab your lunch buckets and follow me," was a general order given to all. All men no matter what trade followed an executive type, maybe a military officer, and were directed into one of two camouflage painted buses. Names in alphabetical order were called from a list and when called, men entered the bus. The windows were boarded up. Workers looked at each other wondering what was going on. Once the bus was on a roll the name reader got up and began to tell why all the procedure.

They were on a secret project for the military. The boarded windows were necessary so no one could memorize anything seen outside. And from now on they should not tell anyone the time or distance it would take to get to the work place. And in fact each day it may take longer or shorter to get to work. "Never mind gentlemen, you get paid from the time you got on the bus." Of course the laughter eased the tension. The bus finally came to a halt and everyone disembarked. "Laborers come with me," was shouted over the din of other machinery in the background. A few men including Walt followed. Names were called off again from a shorter list, and cautioned not to tell anyone about where they were or the type of work going on. That is all Walt could talk about to this day. His name was called off each day and his pay was normal for the two week hours worked and traveled.

Hey Gunther! Why Are You Here?

PEA SIZED GRAVEL

During the summer there were small and large contractors to work for. Some jobs lasted one week others three or more weeks. Most of the jobs involved a number two shovel with gravel having to be moved around in one way or other. Much of it pit-run gravel with occasional crushed gravel with very little sand.

At one time the gravel was crushed and sifted until it was pea sized and no silt or sand in the product. Its purpose was to cover recently sprayed hot asphalt applied to a recently constructed air force runway. The spray was applied by a tanker, which followed the edge of the runway until its tank got empty. The next part could be tricky and only truck drivers experienced in the procedure were hired to lay down the gravel over the asphalt. They had to back up their truck and open the back gate but control the opening with a chain. They also had to have skill that as they backed up at a steady slow speed the gravel would dribble out at a constant rate as they raised their load. And stay in a straight line down the runway. The dribbling gavel would be sufficient to cover the spray so the tires would not enter the asphalt and mess things up. Also in the process it helped to have someone walk on the side of the dribbling truck ahead of the travel and constantly look into the bin as it was being raised. The gravel had to be coming out at a steady rate and if there seemed to be any hesitation in the flow, the bin watcher made a whistle signal to alert the driver. The driver may then nudge the break pedal to jolt the load to slide. As the bin was near being empty another double loud whistle signaled the driver to stop. An experienced driver who knew his load could often stop just before the whistle. A quick stop, a last dribble of gravel, then a shift into forward gear. As the bin lowered and the truck left, a new truck load of pea-sized gravel was ready to apply.

One can imagine what a laborer had to do. There were uneven streaks of gravel in the beginning and at the end of each run. Perhaps some unevenness about two thirds along each run depending how the gravel flowed out the bin. These had to be smoothed out with a number two shovel enough so the roller to follow would not have to go over "bumps."

236

Walt Fluegel

Before the procedure was well on it way a jeep with an air force officer came by, stopped and asked for the crew to assemble. He began to talk about the importance of the work being done to the runways because of the jet plane. At that time (early 1950s) the jet plane was relatively new to the American public, maybe being seen only on news reels in movie houses. He told of their speed and military importance but stressed how all this was connected to the work now being done. He explained as best he could that the plane sucked up a lot of air and compressed it inside the body and spit the hot gasses out the tail. That is what made it go and go faster than a propeller plane. He thought this would be the future. But, he emphasized if a small stone was sucked up and got caught inside in the wrong place the plane could explode and we would lose a pilot and an expensive piece of machinery. So in the final work necessary there should be no loose pea sized gravel. It all should be imbedded into the surface of the asphalt. He was not sure of what would happen during the Alaska winter. "All this was an experiment," he finished. Then in parting he added that the day being hot already everyone should drink lots of water and make sure they took a salt tablet. "Good bye gentlemen."

Near noon time it was convenient to take a half hour lunch break. Everybody gathered around in the shade of a truck. By this time Walt was use to wolfing down his lunch and within 10 to 15 minutes he was done. He went over to a small gravel pile, lay down on his back and snuggled in the loose material. He put his cap over his face to protect it from the sun, and took a snooze. He was soon aware of a voice, "Hey, Walt we have work to do, you can sleep when you go home. Better take a salt tablet now, it mixes better with your lunch. Com'on let's go."

ERIK LASSEN AND JACK B

After work for the day and if Walt wasn't too tired or weary there was always something on the house that needed attention but he could now rely upon having a good supper and conversation with his mother. Rosemary, the next door neighbor, and his mother would be seen talking with each when Walt came home. Ed was seldom around preferring to be with the 'boys' in town but he was glad for Rosemary that she had a good neighbor as a friend. Also by this time Walt met Erik Lassen who lived in a house some distance away. The roof of his house was somewhat visible from the picture window. A few spruce trees blocked most of that view. From College Road it was easy to miss Erik's house because it was tucked into the trees with only a hint of a curved driveway revealing there was a house amongst the trees.

Erik was a carpenter by trade. He had a Guild card in Danish testifying to his expertise. Erik was a recent immigrant from Denmark who wanted some adventure in America, he and his wife chose Alaska. It appears he was in the resistance against the Nazi during WW2 back home doing what he had to do. He didn't go into details, but he said some German soldiers did die and also some of his neighbors died in retaliation. He was young at that time and learning how to be a finished carpenter doing all indoor work. But here in Alaska it was mostly all outdoor and rough construction he was doing now. When indoor finish work was called for he said he would talk his way into those jobs.

He told Walt that in the beginning when he applied to the union for work he was ignored several times until the late morning roll calls. It wasn't his accent but wearing carpenters work clothing that set himself apart from being chosen. Finish carpenters in the Netherlands worked indoors in homes and new indoor construction and seldom if ever got their overalls or jump suits dirty. It made a good impression to be clean. Also he noticed other men who in the beginning of the season had brand new overalls were not in the first pick either. Erik realized he had to change into something suitable, giving the appearance he could handle rough work. He went to a used clothing store and picked out what he needed. He also made sure his toolbox looked well used and had well used tools within, keeping his more refined implements at home until needed.

What Erik was doing to his house was typical of many a person who bought an old house. Erik's house was somewhat bigger than Walt's house. The house was practically sitting on the ground perhaps up on some rocks that would prevent rotting. Some of these old houses had a kitchen trap door that led to a small dug out hole, enough for cold

238

storage of hardy food items such as potatoes, turnips and some canned goods. The soil was often cold and if permafrost was nearby so much the better. What Erik wanted to do was enlarge the hole to make a full basement, and put up a permanent wall if possible to fit the existing house. That meant digging under the house and removing the soil while the house was still standing or dig a hole away from the house, put up a wall and move the house over on top of the new construction. He decided to dig one deep trench at a time for one wall at a time, lay footings and use concrete blocks for that one wall. By the end of his first season and with the help of some friends he was able to secure his house at least one block showing above ground level. By the time Walt saw his work it was obvious that Erik had considerable skill in solving these house problems. His next problem to solve was getting rid of a big pile of soil in the middle of this new basement. He had all winter to remove one bucket at a time in between finish carpentry work in warm surroundings.

In that same summer as Erik was working on his basement wall, Walt's mother had a new next door neighbor, Jack B. He worked in the office for Standard Oil in Fairbanks. Right after Jack bought the property next door in late spring he had a hole dug for a basement, but nothing came of it for the summer. Instead he let it go and as the soil dried, its silt sides slowly settled, and then collapsed and what remained for years was a shallow cone being filled with debris, leaves and branches. Instead of building a basement he changed his mind and brought in a trailer and built a long shed in front as an air lock, similar to what could be seen at Rosemary's place.

Walt always entered his property on the corner never disturbing the surveyors stake pounded in at that time. He had previously parked his pickup near the house but left enough room for delivery of coal and room for guests. Jack B decided he too would use that same corner of his lot as his entrance. In effect, from Caribou Way there was a truncated Y entrance; to the left was JackB's place and to the right Walt and his mothers house. From the picture window through some alder and willow brush, could be seen the tarpapered shed of Jack's residence. When Walt was in Fargo getting his masters degree, Jack sometimes visited Walt's mother. She wrote to Walt that Jack was a member of a dance club and he said he was the "cats meow" with the ladies on the dance floor. But from side remarks of people who knew that her neighbor was Jack, they had a different opinion. And of course she did not like that he smoked those very thin cigars in her house.

The summer had to come to an end eventually but all summer ever since NDAC accepted him to enter the masters program neither his mother or he discussed the coming winter. There was coal in the bin, the furnace was working properly and his mother knew how to keep the fire going. Also, the hot water system had no problems. Some times one of his mother's clients would probably help her with delivering of groceries. Walt assumed that what funds he saved in the bank would carry him through the school year. This time too as in four years before he would leave home to a new place in pursuit of more learning. But for what learning? Learning to obtain a job in the subject of his latest interest? But what was that? Bacteriology applied to understanding cold soils for agriculture? He decided not to ask himself too many questions but to see what this new adventure would bring.

Walt Fluegel

CHAPTER THIRTY-SEVEN: AT THE NDAC

Compared with the University of Alaska, the campus of the North Dakota Agriculture College (NDAC) was well established with brick buildings, lawns and tall elm trees. Walt was assigned to one of the three-bed capacity rooms but there were many more other rooms holding two beds. His roommates on that first year of residency were brothers from a town near Bismarck. The older brother just returned from military service and on the GI Bill but it was his younger brother Norman who he often went to the cafeteria with at meal times. The whole atmosphere of the campus was different from the U of A; the undergraduate student body was larger including more girls. As an added benefit it was easy to get into town by walking or taking a frequent bus.

CAFETERIA FOOD

There were also two different eating places right off campus across the street so to speak if you did not like the AC menu being served. The menu was predictable in many ways. Breakfast was the usual bacon and eggs, pancakes, juice, or various cereals, hot or cold. Every Monday for dinner or supper there were two or three choices this week, next week, the week after, and so on. However, on Tuesday the menu was different but every Tuesday for weeks on end it was the same menu. Wednesday was entirely different from Tuesday, but why change Wednesday menus, so, let's keep all Wednesday the same too. Of course on these days there were three different ways to fix potatoes so one did have a three day rotation if so desired. Choices for meats were also varied except for Friday, when fish was the meat choice. What kind of fish? Come Friday to find out. Only the fussy eaters drifted now and then to the off campus diners. But the cafeteria was always full; there were no food rebellions while Walt was there.

STUDIES

The academic standards seemed rigorous enough and challenging. The bacteriology lab was fully stocked and had its own stock room attendant who prepared growth media and sterile equipment. But as Walt progressed in his studies he had become more responsible for having to sterilize his own material. It was expected that on the graduate level he would become more independent while working on his thesis. As fall drifted into winter he spent less and less time in the dorm in bull sessions and more and more time in the prep room or at his own desk in the lab of Dr. Sleeper, his advisor. Part of Walt's understanding for himself was also to study soils. Soil lectures and labs were entirely different from anything he had ever known. He was not sure he would get used to knowing the finer points of this important study. There was the chemistry, the physics too and the dynamics of wetting and drying, clay formation, settlement of soil particles and overall geology of soil formation. Walt had lots of study to do.

WHAT WAS IMPORTANT?

In the normal dorm chit-chat of getting to know each other Walt told about some of his experiences in Alaska and Norman in turn told of farm life or life in the small town of Valley City. He told of his parents and his ancestors who were pioneers in suppressing the Indian population and making a living from farm life. Why was Norm at the AC? He was going be a high school math teacher. He loved math and all the tricks one can do with the numbers and the manipulations to get answers all in numbers that had meaning—to him. Was he ever going on to become a serious mathematician and solve some problems yet to be solved from the old masters long gone? He wasn't

242

sure and besides how do you make a living stuck in an attic trying to solve these old problems...and who would care? A high school teacher salary would be fine for him. Later when Walt was deep into his soils and bacteriology studies and Norm would discuss his high school teachers; Walt too began to think of Mister Stokes his high school chemistry teacher and Miss Landis and her biology teaching. Walt remembered how enthused Mister Stokes was about the subject of chemistry. Always suggesting there was more to study and maybe work for DuPont for example. So after he acquired his Masters degree what would Walt do? Work for the state on soil problems or maybe teach biology in high school? It was a thought, another thought that may change his life's path.

ABOUT GIRLS

Sometimes after coming back from the cafeteria at noon and relaxing, several other guys would congregate in one of their rooms until it was time for the afternoon classes. They tried to exchange some not really important topic, maybe the latest scheduled sport event, or a dance, or some important VIP visiting the campus or maybe a new gal or two they all noticed at a distant table that day. Jerry started making comments about the geology class this morning on mountain formation. He said he saw some mountains just recently and wanted to explore them as soon as possible. "So I had mountains on my mind when I saw those Cindy Mountains at that corner table!"

"Her name is Mount," said Chet. "Mount," and quickly added, "She is spoken for, so you better be careful or else that line backer—what's his name?"

"Saunders," Norm interrupted, and Chet finished by saying, "will grind you to a pulp." It seemed fair game at these noon talks to mention about a girl not "spoken for" by any of the guys present, little realizing in a different part of the dorm their girlfriend either on campus or at home may be mentioned in the same manner. Walt always listened, never making any comment until he had to leave earlier for a lab prep.

Hey Gunther! Why Are You Here?

But one day Jerry always having girl desires on his mind asked Walt if he had a girl friend in Alaska. Others buzzed in with, "Tell us, Walt."

"Yes, I did have a girl friend, not steady, just a date now and then."

"Is she an Eskimo?" There was much laughter.

"No just like any other girl we see around here."

"Are you serious about her?"

"No, just a nice girl but not serious."

"You have been so quiet about girls. Don't you like them?"

"Well gentlemen, you know I must be a few years older than you. I had enough years experience and learned long ago not to kiss and tell. Until I can prove to myself I can get a job to support someone at home I will not get serious about any gal. I understand Jerry there will be a time when some sweet thing will come along and hit you square in the eyes. You will fall for her like a ton of bricks and before you know it wedding bells will ring." And then looking straight at Jerry and in a quiet voice said, "It will probably happen to most college guys like you and me. It will be your brains rather than your brawn that attract them."

Jerry said in a rather dejected voice, "You sound a lot like my father!"

Someone exclaimed, "Hey guys, we had better hurry, it's almost time for classes."

BRING YOUR LAUNDRY

It was the second Thursday night on the NDAC campus when Walt came from the lab late and he thought he was watching Norm just throwing clothes into a small suit case, not really packing, just throwing. "Fancy way of packing," Walt chuckled.

"I'm saving laundry money. Going home for the weekend to see my parents. Mom wrote that she wants to do my washing." And so it was; about twice a month Norm and other guys who came from distant places further west went home for the weekend, usually taking their

244

laundry with them. Mom would do the laundry, son would see his girl friend, or visit dad and his cronies, and have meals that did not compare with cafeteria food, and everyone was pleased to see this young scholar. Walt also saw a cardboard sign saying VALLEY CITY in big black letters; Norm could not afford to have a car, neither could most other students. It seemed to be a Friday afternoon tradition that on a certain well-traveled street near campus if students showed their sign most of them would have no trouble hitching a ride home. A few decided to take the train westward toward Bismarck and beyond. The result was a campus mostly deserted on weekends except for home games, big dances or other events. Girls never hitched a ride because dad took off from work early to go to Fargo to retrieve his daughter for the weekend. After picking up his daughter she might ask him to go past the traditional hitching area. In this way she had the pick of which boy and his sign would accompany her on the way home. Sometimes her father picked up two or three others wanting to go in the same direction. "Oh Dad, I don't know the other two." Dad apparently ignored his daughter saying, "We have room for three in the back." However, a ton of bricks were being prepared ever so slowly.

INTRODUCTIONS

As in all campuses across the country in the fall there is always a system of enrolling, which included paperwork, fee payment, dorm assignment, meal ticket purchase and contacting an assigned advisor. When Walt found where the Bacteriology Department office was located it served as a locus for everything else. The hallways were filled with inspirational messages printed on the walls, mostly that agriculture was a noble venture. The department was located on the third floor. The office door was closed but its glass panel was highly beaded and frosted, revealing a window for that room. Mrs. Beverly Baldwin was the secretary for the department. When Walt introduced himself she indicated that Walt was expected soon and glad to have him come before the big rush of classes.

He was introduced to Dr. Schultz, who was an expert on soil organisms and the head of the department. He was a tall spindly man with graying hair and never got out of his desk chair. He told Walt this would be his last year because he is retiring so many decisions were being shared by Doctor Dubbly and Doctor Sleeper. He asked Walt all sorts of questions about his youth and schooling and about his family back home. When Walt summarized his story, he asked Walt if he ever heard about the orphan trains of the '20's and earlier. Abandoned or disadvantaged children were boarded on to trains and at each station local people, on looks alone, just adopted a child and took them home. Some were used as cheap labor, others were well-cared for. Doctor Schultz told Walt that his mother told him of the orphan train. After knowing Walt's background at the Wartburg he assured Walt that he was on the right path; getting a good education. He then called Mrs. Baldwin and had her introduce Walt to his advisor Doctor Sleeper and then Doctor Dubbly.

The first thing one noticed about Dr. Sleeper was thick-rimmed glasses and a patch over his right eye. His eye was lost as the result of a WW2 injury. He never spoke of it but did let people know he was trying to quit smoking, which he acquired during service in the army. After introductions and a type of interview, Walt was taken to the lab used by Dr. Sleeper for his research. Next to a laboratory bench Walt found a small desk assigned to him knowing he would arrive. Because Walt was Dr. Sleeper's first and only graduate student it was all a new experience for professor and student. While being shown around the lab, Annette, Dr. Sleeper's research lab technician had to interrupt for a moment. They took a few moments to discuss a procedure but also to introduce Walt. It was her job now to help Walt learn how to use all the equipment and do procedures but not to do any of that for him. Dr. Sleeper emphasized that Walt was here to learn to be a scientist and learn about the tools of the trade. After this Walt was introduced to Dr. Dubbly. He taught a course in immunology and medical bacteriology, an area Walt was not familiar with so he thought it would be interesting. In a low and gruff voice he said to Walt, "I am a tough task master, so study to please me. " Walt wasn't quite sure that he saw Dr. Dubbly give Dr. Sleeper a wink, but later in his course he realized Dr. Dubbly had his unusual method to guide any one student to learn new material.

246

Walt Fluegel

Once classes started all over campus certain routines were established. Classes in the morning, lunch around noon, more classes in the afternoon and finally supper. In between a certain lecture time there may be a break time at the Student Union and then back to class or laboratory. It was customary in the department for the bacteriology staff to have their own coffee break in mid afternoon. This occurred in one of the back rooms entered either from the student lab or internally from another office on that side of the building. Mrs. Baldwin usually kept the coffee fresh and all the staff and sometimes Walt met there informally. It was a method of introducing any grad student into the upper level of this intellectual enterprise. Sometimes Mrs. Baldwin was also included because she too had a masters degree in bacteriology. But she also had her ear alert to the phone in her office.

For Walt he knew there would be extra time to dig deeper into the project of his research with Dr. Sleeper. He did things with Annette to learn procedures, make his own mistakes and learn from them. He also spent a bit of time with Mister Lemke the man who prepared all lab materials for all bacteriology classes. He was supreme boss of his prep room. But after making sure Walt knew how to handle the sterilizer and other equipment he allowed Walt to use his room without supervision. Dr. Dubbly too had an influence on having Walt learning things not necessarily given in class. During regular class he willingly answered students questions but answering a question by Walt out of class was a different matter. If Walt came to his office and asked a question not related to lectures Dr. Dubbly would get up from his desk, go to his book shelf, remove a book and hand it to Walt and say, "Look it up!" Sometimes it would be a recent monthly Journal of Bacteriology. When not in class during the day Walt occupied his desk in the lab. The lab atmosphere was becoming his air to breathe. Most often too he would be at his desk or the prep room after supper until the janitor hinted he will lock up for the night pretty soon.

PASSING GRADES AND LETTERS

Fall studies blended into winter and then into spring. Yes, there was a Christmas break, a big dance or two and a play or two and other activities to give variety to anyone's college life. Walt spent those

Hey Gunther! Why Are You Here?

longer breaks either in the lab or at the library "looking it up." Letters with his mother were exchanged with optimistic results on both ends. His mother was surviving well at home and it was very warm, and she was making quite a few friends especially now that she began to go to church. She would visit with Rosemary and Ed and be visited on rare occasions by Jack B. She also got information about installing a greenhouse for the east wing. Because it was a kind of double layered plastic windows it would be light and easy to assemble. His mother assured him that the measurements made by Nick or someone from the lumber company did the right thing. It would be shipped from the States as soon as possible through the lumber company. He wrote back to give it a try. All Walt could say about his studies was that he enjoyed some classes and had a tougher time with others but he was passing them all. But when spring finally came the Department knew that Mrs. Baldwin was going back to Canada with her husband and raise a family. Also during the summer to come the Department would have their new chairman, a Dr. Paul Adams. By the time final exams were over Walt had made travel plans to get back home. He assured Dr. Sleeper he just had to get back to earn college money and he would return. He made sure to go over his potential course work for the next school year with Dr. Sleeper and gave Mrs. Baldwin the form he filled in. He had learned a lot and understood procedures and well on the way of understanding what kind of advanced learning meant.

Walt Fluegel

CHAPTER THIRTY-EIGHT: A FEW MORE SUMMER JOBS

When Walt arrived in Fairbanks the construction season was well on its way with the advancing light hours of the day. He and his mother were glad to see each other but soon they had to decide on little things about the house. He had previously made contact with the labor union through letters by paying his dues in advance. To get used to the strenuous work ahead he began to dig a garden for flowers and some vegetables—some cabbage, carrots, peas, and cauliflower. He needed to get into shape. He also rejuvenated his truck, trickle charged the battery and with Jacks help filled up his gas tank. When his truck was mobile he visited Nick and Zelda and caught up on local happenings. Nick also related his activities with the Golden Valley Electric cooperative. He also checked on the progress of Erick and his basement. It was quite an achievement to see a full basement under the house with all the dirt removed one bucket at a time during the winter. All he had to do now if he wanted to was get a floor slab poured so he could put in a work shop. He was serious about doing wood working.

TEN HOURS NOT EIGHT

Summer jobs ranged from working on the Ladd airbase for large national contractors to working for small local contractors who were doing driveways, footings, landscaping, and individual houses with garages. The first summer job involved getting things ready for installing a driveway at several nearby sites. Because other houses were close by it was generally difficult to bring machinery to any work area. Therefore, the number 2 shovel was the tool for moving gravel around before the pouring of cement and after curing. Once the forms were removed added gravel had to be tamped down along the edge by someone using the square tamping tool. A couple of laborers switched as someone spread new gravel close to the concrete before it was tamped down. It wasn't so bad, but this one contractor had a ten hour day rather than an eight hour day to take advantage of the summer light. It was grueling especially when at the end of the day everyone was famished and used to having supper soon after a normal eight hour work day. On this one job, Walter would have supper, talk a little with his mother and fall asleep on the couch until morning. Consequently he needed the weekend to recover and did nothing on the house. At the end of two weeks everyone who remained 'till the job was finished' was given their pay check. There was a small bonus but Walt wondered if he should ever take on another ten hour day.

PLANTING TIME

At this time there was a small window of opportunity to get native tree and shrubbery plantings started. The job would be varied and the local landscaper had hurry up jobs to do more than his own workers could handle. Laborers were needed all over town at sites almost finished with everything except for the landscaping amenities. After Walt and two other laborers were introduced, one of the landscape workers asked out loud, "Hey Walt, can you handle something like this?" pointing to a large spruce whose roots were wrapped in burlap and rope. It was already loaded on the truck along with smaller evergreens in buckets or burlap bags.

"That's a three or four man job, but I can handle things like those buckets."

"OK you asked for it! Com'on guys let's climb aboard, we got planting to do!" said their foreman. Amongst the compost, various sized plants, digging shovels and bags of plant food, workers and laborers managed to squeeze together. At each job site, the truck stopped and some of the bushes or trees were unloaded and a worker

250

and a laborer remained. The landscaper worker knew what to do and consulted written instructions and the stakes in the ground as to which plant went where. It was an interesting and varied morning learning what to do, and by the time all vegetation was planted and consulting with the home-owner or whoever was around, verbal instructions on the care of the bushes was given. Often no one was home and fortunately, the worker used the outside water faucet to water the plant. If there were no hose available Walt had to carry buckets full of water. Fortunately there was a good time before the truck came back so this small crew could relax. The larger trees such as maturing birch were handled by the more robust workers, but Walt and another laborer had to dig a very wide shallow hole for the tree roots. These trees were treated differently. When they were dug up, because of their shallow root system much of the root structure was saved and bundled up. At the planting site the wide hole accepted the splayed out roots. The trees were anchored to the ground. Also some concrete blocks were placed about a third of the way inside the root zone to make sure the contact with the soil was secure. After a year or so the blocks were removed.

GREEN HOUSE

There were other jobs not as demanding which allowed Walt to attempt to assemble his mother's greenhouse by himself when it was delivered. At one small job he met Woody again. Woody was glad to have the extra work on the weekend and meet Walt's mother. They talked over the times when both were constructing the basement. The greenhouse was a two man job to assemble but took more than the estimated time to get it built, after all Woody and Walt were not carpenters. Rosemary's son who was a carpenter fashioned a doorway from the house into the greenhouse. In time, attachments were made weather-tight against the coming cold winter. However, there was a door to the greenhouse from outside. When she saw the progress, Walt's mother always remarked happily how wonderful it would be to have new plants by next spring season.

Hey Gunther! Why Are You Here?

UTILIDORES

A military base is like a small city with housing, barracks, machine shops, a clinic, offices, and food centers sprawled in a wide area. At twenty or more than thirty below winter weather the military needed to keep these facilities warm and functioning. A power plant kept all distant structures warm thanks to underground tunnel like structures called Utilidores. Someone had to build them, and the sooner the better. They were of different sizes depending on location. Some were as tall inside as a standing man, others were short so a man had to crouch. They carried all sorts of pipes and wires and tubes. Some were constructed on site others were assembled from pre-cast concrete slabs. In some places the excavation necessary was a simple matter of making a long very wide ditch and in other places the ditch seemed just wide enough to pour concrete into forms. It all depended upon what other structures were nearby. Consequently, there were all sorts of work needed of laborers. At the end of construction and of pouring the concrete, the forms had to be removed and someone had to remove them and stack them for transporting them down the line. That grunt work was largely left to laborers.

Some of the forms were just two feet by four or eight feet being the smallest and others as large as four by eight feet. All were oiled and strengthened by 2 x 4 inch framing. They were also very messy and if one were not careful protruding nails could give a good puncture. Sometimes these nails were pounded down with a stone or someone carrying a hammer. The smaller forms were easily a one man job to stack up but the larger ones took at least three men some effort.

MEETING ROGER AGAIN

In the middle of the afternoon everyone heard a loud whistle from on top of the embankment. They looked up and heard a voice yell that a cable was going to be lowered down, so be careful. Walt thought he recognized the caller but he disappeared for a moment to let a cable descend. Someone had to wrap the cable and its hook over some of the forms and give a signal all was ready to hoist. The machine that

252

hauled the forms up resembled a large crane winch that removed trucks or busses that got stuck in ditches. When a good batch of the forms were hauled up Walt managed to climb up the embankment and meet the operator of the crane. "Hey, Roger is that you?"

"Hey, you the U of A barber? Walt?" Just then Walt heard his name being called and saw that the foreman was giving hand signals for him to come back. Walt told Roger that he owned a green Chevy pickup in the parking lot over there, see you in half an hour—and ran off toward his foreman.

At the end of the working day, Walt talked with his foreman and signed a paper stating that this was his last day on the job. His check would be mailed to the bank as in past weeks. Walt waited in the parking lot for about 15 minutes when he saw Roger coming by. They greeted each other again asking, how are things going and what are you doing here questions. Walt explained he was going for his Masters degree and one more year to go, and he built a house for his mother, and you? Roger explained he had construction jobs and decided he might begin to buy equipment and start a small construction company on his own. "But you know what? The guy I was dealing with suddenly got some kind of kidney failure or something like that and died." He explained that after the funeral his widow needed all sorts of consolation and he was there to help her over her lingering grief. Walt listened just like in the old barbershop days at the University. He asked Roger if he still wants to be doing contracting on his own? He is thinking about that but he thinks because the widow knows something about that kind of business he may have a business partner. After a bit more chit-chat they wished each other good luck and maybe they will see each other again.

MOTHER TELLS SON MORE OF EARLY LIFE

It was a week more to go before Walt would have to travel back to Fargo. During that week he made travel arrangements and had time to be with his mother and admire her flower and vegetable garden. Over meals she exclaimed that this was the first home she ever owned and was happy with that and began to tell of her early life back in

Hey Gunther! Why Are You Here?

Germany and that she did not regret leaving that place. She was still sad the way her mother died. She also told Walt that uncle Hans recently went to Germany and bought an expensive car and drove all over the country. Aunt Trina in letters explained that Hans tried to show off but in the end, relatives even on his side felt sorry for Trina and thought of him as "that crazy American!" It was at this time his mother said with sadness in her voice that she always thought she would want to remarry and have more children but Hans spoiled those thoughts. In a little remark at one of these quiet talks she also mentioned Walter's father saying to her, "now don't get pregnant, " and saying in that same breath that she knew Walter was on his way. That was the only time he ever heard this from her. But now she was happy all this story, her story came out just right because she was now happy in a different way, a new experience. Walt did not know what questions to ask but as usual with others who talked about their lives he just listened. Later he did ask her about the kind of clients she had. She did tell that in two separate cases she was working for two clients who began to live together for a while before they married so then she would lose the income from one. But fortunately she was introduced to a friend and all was well. That too was a good time where she could ask for a raise in her wages, which was gladly given. And she mentioned one of her clients was Walter's former professor who suggested she insist that his mother was Mrs. Gunther not Emelie.

There were vague talks about what would happen to Walter after getting the Masters degree. Maybe he would go into teaching biology in high school because of fond memories of teachers he knew there, but he was not too sure. In all his letters home the future was not written about. Only the progress and some people he met. Nothing about a possible girlfriend, even now no girlfriend was mentioned. But the future, maybe do something in a laboratory because he loved lab work, but he would tell his mother as soon he was sure. He thought he was capable of settling down soon. She was happy to hear that.

In the next few days Walt decided to put the Chevy up on blocks and prepare it for winter. He filled his duffel bag with clothes he would need and was ready. In the meantime he got a formal letter from NDAC concerning the days of registration, his probable class

254

schedule, his dorm assignment, and other information to get him settled at the AC. He called Nick on the phone and said good-byes but Nick insisted he could take Walt to the airport on the appointed day no matter what time. His hours at the lumber company were flexible in this regard.

Hey Gunther! Why Are You Here?

Walt Fluegel

CHAPTER THIRTY-NINE: BACK TO THE NDAC

WHY ARE SCIENCES NOT PART OF THE HUMANITIES?

Somewhere as the plane was flying over the middle of America toward Fargo and Walt was tired of reading the usual stuff supplied by the airline he tried to get some sleep or relax or think of what his last year at the AC would bring. He wondered if he might become a scientist or a teacher because of his overall interest in biology and how life of all sorts works. In order to do this, one had to be careful of the differences between one critter from another or one plant from another. That brought Mrs. Carr of his first year of college into his thoughts about good observations, many observations and above all accurate observations. Without them one could not compare. That is one thing a scientist had to do and later tell this to students so they would understand the world of living things. If you were curious and wanted to know more, chances are someone wrote this information down somewhere. It would tell you something that was new to you, so either ask your teacher or professor or 'look it up' dictum from Dr. Dubbly and make it a habit. It seemed to be natural at this time but suppose you could not find what you were looking for? Strange as it may have seemed to him as he was being hummmmmd by the engine noise of the plane, professor Burns and his notes of 'expand here' and Dr. Sleeper who was doing research began to emerge as one concept. Research and 'expand here' were one and the same concept! Expand

257

here may help fill the pages with written material and research fills the page with new knowledge. This is how humans advance above other critters. It was easy to stretch the concept as to why were the sciences at colleges and even as far down as high school, why were sciences isolated from the humanities? Science is what people do and the humanities too are what people do. He didn't know exactly when or why these thoughts came and mulled around in his mind, but soon he was aware he was being asked by the stewardess to attach his seat belt. They were going to land soon in Fargo.

The final plane of several transfers from Fairbanks landed at the Fargo airport close to nine in the morning. Rather than fuss with trying to get a bus into town and then the AC, it was easier to hire a taxi and go directly to the AC. They stopped at the building housing the Bacteriology department and retrieved his duffel bag from the trunk of the cab. Walt was dropped off in front of Morrill Hall. The taxi driver said, 'Is that the building that has all the writing on the hallway wall?' Walt Gunther then said, 'Yeah, that's the building.'

After paying the driver he hauled his duffel through the doors and then up three flights of stairs and let it slide off his shoulder at the office door. It was wide open as usual but there was a new secretary at the desk pounding away at the typewriter. Walt knocked and she stopped typing and turned toward the door.

"Hello, I am Dr. Sleeper's student…my name is Walt Gunther…is he in? I just came from Alaska…can I leave my duffel here for a while?" He realized his speech seemed tired or was he distracted by the new person at the desk? He did notice the secretary did not look like Mrs. Baldwin who always wore a short white lab coat. She also had short but wavy hair.

She pointed toward Walt's right and said, "He is in his lab, go right in."

He opened the research lab and saw Dr. Sleeper and Annette at the Warburg manometers looking at a chart and discussing some result. They both looked up and showed surprise and a joy and so did Walt.

"How was your flight?"

258

Walt Fluegel

"I don't know how birds do it but I'm a bit weary of flying," everybody chuckled. But momentarily Dr. Sleeper turned to Annette and gave her a brief instruction and then gave Walt his full attention. Walt explained he left his duffel out in the hall but as soon as he can make dorm arrangements and go through enrollment red tape he would be back. Walt was asked to bring his duffel and put it on his desk and sure, by all means become a legal student, glad to have you back, we can talk more when you take care of things.

REACQUAINTING

By the time he was done registering and getting all the paper work done and getting a meal ticket, he decided to go to the cafeteria because he was famished. And it was noontime, breakfast time back in Fairbanks. He hadn't eaten a full meal for quite a while, just airplane food. The cafeteria in all ways was the same, the choices didn't change but he adjusted immediately. Some students were familiar by sight but this being Thursday perhaps more will show up by Monday when classes start.

Back at the Department the only ones he saw were Annette and her husband munching on the last bites of their lunch. "Dr. Sleeper had some business to do down town but Dr. Adams and I think Dr. Dubbly are in their offices," she said when Walt opened the lab door.

"Thanks," and soon all three met in the chairman's office. There was chit-chat about Alaska, Dr. Adams getting to know Fargo from being in Utah, and Dr. Dubbly's summer road kill project.

But Walt said he needed to retrieve his duffel bag and maybe take a nap because he wasn't sure he got much sleep on the plane. He would surely see them all tomorrow on Friday. He looked quickly into the prep room and said a quick, "Hello," to Mister Lemke. In the hall the department door was closed so he went directly to the research lab and saw Annette for a moment and got his duffel bag and went on to the men's dorm. He found the room, and as the lunch meal now began to take its slumbering effect he dropped his bag on the floor and lay on one of the two beds that were not made.

Hey Gunther! Why Are You Here?

"Hey sleeping beauty better wake up or you will miss supper, " he vaguely heard as he was stirring awake. Luck would have it that Norm and he both checked off the item in the official form last spring concerning possible roommates for the next year. All Walt could reply was a weak, 'hello,' and then a desperate question, "Where is the bathroom on this floor?" Norm gestured with his hands and Walt took off without his glasses but made it just in time he said when he came back. By this time he was fully awake and there followed the usual how have you been? What is going on? Good to see you! How did you do last year? That sort of stuff and what's new sort of back and forth questions and quick answers between them.

They went for supper and drifted toward the tables usually occupied by men dormers. More greetings and exchanging information on what's happening in their particular town. An occasional quiet, "That's a new one," and almost pointing toward the tables where girl dormers were setting down their food trays. A slight glance and a quick turn back to prevent staring seemed to be imitated by someone at the girls table too when a new guy joined the group. When Walt and Norm and a couple of other guys got up to leave there was commotion at the girls table as a bunch of guys entered the cafeteria. Maybe they were the football squad just returning from practice. Most of them were big and bulky and if anyone stayed long enough to watch them load up their food tray and hear the conversation they would be right.

This Friday was busy time for all secretaries on campus getting all handout material ready for the first day's classes. Many offices had their own Ditto machines usually used for pop quizzes, but the mimeograph machine used by the Bacteriology department was shared by other departments in that same building. The machine was busy cranking out all sorts of class material but someone had to do the typing ahead of time. Miss Maxine Lott did that for the Bacteriology department and on that Friday had no time for small talk. All Walt could do was say 'hello' as he passed by when the door was open.

THE NEW SECRETARY

Walt Fluegel

As the days progressed and routines developed Walt found that the mid afternoon staff coffee break conflicted with his Monday and Wednesday soils laboratory class. But the Tuesday and Thursday afternoon time was generally free to attend when he thought of it. Here he had a better chance to see Miss Lott doing other things than typing and filing and using the telephone. She, like Mrs. Baldwin stood at the doorway listening to the conversations with one ear ready for the office phone. Occasionally someone would use a technical or other word she was not familiar with. She found a way to ask to repeat the word and write it down in her note pad and then try to scratch it out in shorthand, and shortly later go to the big dictionary on its special table off the doorway and look it up. Walt also noticed the clothes she wore. They looked professional and expensive, but later Walt found that she sewed her own clothing. These clothes were different from what the girl students wore. Short jacket and skirt matched, different blouse colors went well with the suit jackets. Everything about Miss Lott was very feminine.

At times it seemed to be an understanding on campus that many Fridays were TGIF events. The women collectively on campus were "allowed" or insisted they could wear not so formal attire, meaning they should be allowed to wear slacks not skirts or dresses on that Friday. And blouses did not have to have fluff if they did not want that. Even the secretaries, young or old could go less formal on that Friday. There was no one to chastise them if all agreed. Somehow the "conspiracy" worked on these days. Miss Lott was no exception. When this happened it seemed that Miss Lott in her slacks could still be called very feminine. She kept wearing her button earrings, which went well with her naturally wavy hair.

A CORNUCOPIA

She seemed to have a flair for her office decor too. For example, anyone who ever went to a bacteriology lab class was familiar with the galvanized or stainless steel baskets used to prepare tubes of growth media for pure cultures of bacteria. She managed to sequester some baskets from Mister Lempke and make flower arrangements for her desk and file cabinets with them using artificial and straw flowers.

Hey Gunther! Why Are You Here?

At one time on the corner of her desk Walt noticed that one of the two baskets seemed to have fallen over and the flowers spilled over her desk. "Oops!" Walt said and wanted to pick up the basket and replace the flowers. Miss Lott stopped him and indicated that that tipped over basket was deliberate because it was on the far corner of her desk and it did not interfere with anything else there, and it looked very natural. "Oh now I see, it reminds me of a cornucopia," he said.

"What's a cornucopia?"

Walt tried to explain that some artist wanting to show food at harvest time painted pictures of baskets so full that when tipped back over you could not get all the food back in. It was a bountiful harvest time. That was a new concept for Miss Lott but it was the first real social contact they had with each other. Before he left her office Miss Lott said, "My mother grows these straw flowers, the rest I bought."

"They look very different, I never saw straw flowers before," he said as he left her office.

THE PHARMACY BOY FRIEND

Little by little either through talking at odd times with Annette or just asking, Walt found out the reason Miss Lott was secretary at the department. It seems that her boyfriend was attending the Pharmacy School on campus. Apparently it was the equal to a graduate program and had a good reputation and Miss Lott wanted to be near him. She was a secretary for the Welfare Department in Rush City, Minnesota. She had gained skills there so it was possible to make a transfer to the NDAC. Each weekend she and her boyfriend would travel home so she was not available for Friday or Saturday night dates, even though Walt asked often. Around the middle of November he wanted to do something a bit different. In the meantime he found out through Annette where Miss Lott lived. She lived about three blocks off campus in an apartment on the second floor.

SNOW ON A CHRISTMAS TREE

262

Walt Fluegel

Walt had gotten an idea of something special to do for Christmas from Mrs. H who used to prepare her Christmas trees in the following manner.

And so on one afternoon Walt bought a small box of Ivory Snow soap flakes, and a small Christmas tree being sold from an empty lot not too far from campus. He carried the tree to the house. He rang the door bell and asked if the lady was the landlord to Miss Lott. She was. Could she do a small favor for him? What was the favor? Walt explained and the lady giggled and said sure come into the kitchen with me.

She got out her mixing bowl and an electric mixer and experimented with how much water and flakes to add until the froth was consistent with very heavy cream. All the time the landlady asked innocent questions and sometimes said "how cute" as the both of them used ordinary dinner knives to slather the foam on branches to resemble snow. Walt told her that the snow would get stiff in time and be hard to take off but that is what was needed. Other little decorations could be added too but that would be Miss Lott's choice. Since the small tree no more than three feet tall was already on its own stand it didn't need any more support. When they felt they were finished, Walt told the landlady just to put the tree by Miss Lott's door, no note as to who sent it, let it be a surprise. When Miss Lott came home it was a surprise, an unexpected delightful surprise and when she could, she thanked her pharmacist boyfriend. No, he didn't do that. She wondered who? A few days later she asked the landlady who, and she said it was supposed to be a surprise so she can't tell. When Miss Lott asked to describe the guy, all the landlady said was "He wore glasses and was a bit taller than...." and did not finish her description when she saw a surprise on Maxine's face when she said, "I know who!"

THAT WOULD BE FINE

On that coming Monday or Tuesday morning when Maxine was asked if she wanted to see the play "Gaslight" on Friday night being presented by the NDAC Drama Department, she said, "Yes that would be fine, I am not going home this weekend." Walt was pleased

263

and made sure he would get the tickets to good seats. It was an entirely different play neither one of them saw before. It was a bit scary and one rooted for the woman and mentally booed the husband. After the play and at the Student Union they shared an apple and a pot of tea before walking back to Miss Maxine Lott's apartment. Another formal date on another Friday or Saturday night and one or two quick dates by walking into town during the Christmas rush on a Thursday night seemed a natural thing to do. On one of those Thursday nights in the commercial part of town they saw a Santa on a front entry to the store all lit up from inside. One could hear all sorts of Christmas music coming from inside the store. Walt spontaneously made a poem "Merry Christmas, Merry Christmas, Buy Stuff Here: Synthetic Santa Claus Spreading Good Cheer." They just giggled and walked rapidly down the street to keep warm. But close to Christmas, Maxine did go home to be with her parents but there seemed to be no one calling on her for any dates in Rush City.

I DON'T KISS AND TELL

Walt could not afford to fly to Fairbanks and back for the holidays but letters both ways kept him and his mother informed on how things were going. Except Walt did not tell his mother anything about Maxine, only that he now and then saw plays and heard choral music on campus with other classmates. He also told her he was doing well in some subjects and the harder ones he was working on and he was passing his exams. His research was going fine but it would be too complicated to tell her what it was all about. She understood and told her friends and they were happy for her.

In the dorm, each day transitioned into the next day with getting up, having breakfast, then classes, then lunch, then classes and so forth. Occasionally during the noon time there was the usual banter about girls or a particular professor, and social events or hometown happenings, then off to class again. Most often after supper Walt would be off to the lab doing preps for the next day. Norm—his roommate—was used to this but it was good because he too used this time for his own studies.

264

Walt Fluegel

At one night in the middle of January, Norm expected Walt to be at the lab but Walt was busy in his books. Walt said there was a slack time in his progress and had to think things through but maybe a good night's sleep would help. They got to talking about small things when Norm said he heard somewhere that there was cute gal in the Bacteriology department. Walt said yes he knows about her and that she was there because of her boyfriend in the college of Pharmacy. He went on further to say, "He may become a good pharmacist some day but concerning his girlfriend he didn't have the right prescription."

For a moment Norm was quiet then blurted out, "You mean you fancy her yourself?"

"Yes, I have been dating her for quite a while."

"You son of a gun, you never told me about her." He sputtered again, "I almost wanted to date her myself when I saw her the other day with some of the other secretaries. I'll be damned." Then some more hesitation before he asked, "Why didn't you tell me this sooner?"

All Walt could say with a big smile on his face, "I keep telling you guys, I don't kiss and tell." He kept smiling even when he went to bed knowing that a few days before he said to Maxine, "Who knows, maybe next year by this time we will be married."

AND THEY WERE

Their marriage lasted for 54 years until death did them part.

END

Hey Gunther! Why Are You Here?

Hey Gunther! Why Are You Here?
Walt Fluegel

EPILOG

Their marriage lasted for 54 years until death did them part. This book is largely about the life and adventures of Walt Gunther, which spans from an orphanage in New York to Alaska and then meeting Maxine in North Dakota.

FIRST OF ALL THEY LIKED EACH OTHER.

With marriage there became a circular Venn diagram with a good amount of overlap. How much? Enough to have a reasonably satisfactory life sharing experience. Some would say happy. Happy also means there were periods of joy, contentment and contrast so one knows that happy is there somewhere. If a problem arose "there is always an alternative." One aspect of their marriage their colleagues could not appreciate was the independence each admired in the other. The first major difference in conventional thinking was neither wore a wedding ring. "A ring represents a chain and I don't want to feel chained down," one of them said. A few years later when asked to have a ring, the offer was turned down again. There was no third attempt. When colleagues questioned whether they were married or not, one of the partners volunteered to show the certificate. No expressed doubts after that.

There were always two crescents outside the Venn overlap so the outside world knew only one part of one person at a time. After or during the child-rearing phase with its happy moments, the Venn diagram crescent on Maxine's side slid a bit while Maxine became a professional decorator in Duluth. During that time she was so good at sales and internal paperwork the company asked her to set up a training center for other decorators in the Twin Cities area. The numbers went into the hundreds. But before this while Maxine was still a regular decorator an incident proved her independence. One of her bosses from the Cities came for a visit to the mall store. He wanted Maxine to wear a dress rather than wear slacks and jacket. She

Hey Gunther! Why Are You Here?

looked him straight in the eye and said words to the effect, "You men just want women to wear dresses so you can see our legs. I would like to see your legs too so maybe you should wear shorts or knickers." He never made the request again. Did that mean Maxine wore the pants in the family? Certainly not! Walt wore the pants and Maxine wore the slacks even though her once her young alluring figure was "spoiled" because of having two babies. She was very alluring in her mature status. Some use the word "feminine." Walt liked this in her.

The two children went off to school and college too. Much earlier there was a strong interest in taking part in the Duluth School Board elections but Walt's academic interests held sway. However, one behind the scene event was attributed to Maxine's effort. It was the usual thing that elementary aged boys when they went to swim class had to be naked. It was not the right thing for young boys who wanted privacy. One member of the School Board was a woman. It took one phone call to that board member. "Suppose we insisted that girls be treated the same as boys?" The policy for boys was changed without any fanfare.

Walt also intensified his academic pursuits but could not acquire a PhD. However if acquiring a PhD was meant to train scholars to do research, several research papers were published in peer-reviewed journals. They added up to more than other colleagues in the Department of Biology combined. He was an assistant professor for many years until after the head of the department retired. Walt was then made an associated professor. Full professorship came to those with a PhD. Was Walt "One of the boys" in the department? That depends: he did not smoke or drink, did not go hunting or fishing, did not tell off color stories, did not discuss differences in religious faith, and perhaps other things most of "the boys" did. In their eyes he was independent but he was a member in the department for almost 30 years.

As time passed the Venn overlap outside crescents became smaller, meaning the overlap expanded, especially at retirement. There never were individual bank accounts or credit cards only one. Hobbies like photography and assembling puzzles were shared, walks and outings were shared, household chores were divided or shared, many meetings were shared, shopping was shared, even watching TV programs were shared. As their daughter once said, "You two seem to be joined at the hip." When Maxine came back from her women's club meetings she would tell Walt how lucky she felt knowing her women friends husbands might not treat their women folks as Walt treated her. Of course a smooch and hug always came with that announcement. On other occasions Maxine would say to Walt, "You know, sometimes you are very weird!" And always that was followed by a smooch or two and a healthy hug. A guy could not get a better compliment than that! He felt and said he was very lucky to be with her.

It was two brain tumors that caused the death that did them part.

Hey Gunther! Why Are You Here?

ACKNOWLEDGMENTS

Lori Gartzke of the Development Foundation // Alumni Association (NDSU) came to my rescue. After 60 some years to forget, I could not remember the name of one building on the North Dakota Agricultural College (NDAC.) Lori did some sleuthing and found that Morrill Hall did indeed have many inspirational inscriptions written on the hallway walls. The NDAC is now called the North Dakota State University. Thanks for your quick work, Lori.

Jeannie Phillips, Special Assistant at the Chancellor's Office at the University of Alaska helped me get my transcripts. What were my grades? That was not as important as some of the things I did at the U of A in the 1940s. She also sent me some of the (dormant) archives and some of my novice reporting were available. Thanks Jeannie for your help.

As a member of the Northwest Wisconsin Regional Writers I was gently persuaded with painless arm twisting by Russ Hanson and Donald Miller to write this book. Don in particular guided me in the process of getting the book in print. Thanks to both.

AND of course all the characters in the Book named for real and fictionalized, deserve a load of thanks for just being in the life of Walt (Gunther.) Many names were changed, as they say, to protect the "innocent and the guilty" alike. But all these characters helped in Walt's understanding of why he was "here."

Walt Fluegel

ABOUT THE AUTHOR

Walt retired as an associate professor of biology from the University of Minnesota, Duluth in 1986. He taught microbiology and general biology and the biological clock on the undergraduate level. He also did research on the aggregation in a certain bacterium and investigated the biological clock in the fruit fly. That research was published in peer-reviewed journals. Walt is now interested in doing computer graphic art and is easing away from photography, which was his primary hobby interest during his career. He was also a reporter of sorts for the camera club newsletter writing about the influence of the camera in our lives. This book, HEY GUNTHER! WHY ARE YOU HERE? is a sequel and partial overlap to the previous book HEY, GUNTHER! YOU DON'T BELONG HERE ANYMORE! Both books report on his life at the Wartburg Orphanage and life after that through high school, college in Alaska and the need to earn college money in the meantime. Part of that 26 - 27 year life adventure takes a predictable turn but then again he finally meets Maxine.

Hey Gunther! Why Are You Here?

WALT FLUEGEL

Walt Fluegel

Hey Gunther! Why Are You Here?

.